THE POLITICS
OF DISCRETION

THE POLITICS
OF DISCRETION

PUFENDORF AND THE
ACCEPTANCE OF
NATURAL LAW

Leonard Krieger

Chicago & London
THE UNIVERSITY OF CHICAGO PRESS

Library of Congress Catalog Card Number: 65-14428

THE UNIVERSITY OF CHICAGO PRESS, CHICAGO & LONDON
The University of Toronto Press, Toronto 5, Canada

TO ESTHER

PREFACE

History may be narrative, descriptive, interpretive, analytical, or significant. It usually exhibits these qualities in combination. No single quality or combination of qualities is inherently preferable to the others. The nature of the historical object and, even more, the kind of question asked of it determine the type of history to be written. This book deals in interpretation, analysis, and significance, not only because these dimensions seem particularly appropriate to the history of ideas, but also because each of them is a response to a reason for undertaking the work.

A historical interpretation tells where an event (in its broadest sense) came from. Since a chief purpose of this book is the inquiry into the process of intellectual diffusion through the examination of an intermediate stage in it, I have tried to establish for each category of thought the relevant ideas and circumstances available to the disseminator and interpretive of his assumptions.

A historical analysis tells what the event was composed of. Since a second purpose of the book is to gain an internal view of natural-law political thinking through the examination of a secondary interpreter whose mental processes are the more penetrable for their lack of either flawless logic or leaps of genius, I have presumed to take apart a complex of ideas in order to determine in detail how they were fitted together.

Historical significance tells where the event went to or toward. I have inquired along this line on two different levels. First, I have asked the obvious question about the converse effects of the ideas studied here upon the more general currents in which they were spawned. Second, the subject was chosen and its meaning plumbed—as the title indicates—for its contribution to the solution of a perennial problem, constant in Western history and relevant today. In its broadest terms, this problem involves the tension inherent in man's simultaneous commitment to logical coherence and to a reality that splinters logical coherence, and it involves further the adjustment which men make in their ideas to resolve the tension. Because the problem is a continuing one through various times and circumstances, the meaning for it of the historical events here under consideration connects history with fundamental human concerns that transcend history and by the same token connects the history that is to be understood with the historian who tries to do the understanding.

Seventeenth-century Europe is not a favored field of American study. My acknowledgments, consequently, are few, but all the more profoundly felt for that. I have dedicated this book to my wife because she understands better than anyone I know the inimitable truths that only the structure of a crystal can deliver about the world at large, and because she appreciates more than anyone I know the value of writing about them. Hajo Holborn, ever my friend and still my teacher, first indicated the figure of Pufendorf as a provocative historical problem and then, with infinite patience and wisdom, abetted my efforts to solve it. Carl Bridenbaugh, Bernard Bailyn, and Daniel J. Boorstin graciously entered into dialogues on the American dimension of Pufendorf's influence, establishing a desirable communication between the traditional divisions of history.

To Yale University, the Center for Advanced Study in the Behavioral Sciences, the Institute for Advanced Study, and the University of Chicago go my thanks for underwriting the release from academic duties which facilitated the preparation and completion of this work.

A note on the use of sources:

Pufendorf's three basic works on political theory—the *Elementorum jurisprudentiae universalis,* the *De jure naturae et gentium,* and the *De officio hominis et civis*—have all had competent English translations (Oxford, 1931, 1934, 1927, respectively). For the convenience of American readers, all references to these works are to these translations save in those particular cases where the translation does not convey the precise political connotation. For each of these cases I have specified the Latin edition used. Unless so specified, the reference is to the English translation.

CONTENTS

[xi]

Contents

INTRODUCTION

Samuel Pufendorf is known to American students—when he is known at all—as an obscure German with a funny name who followed Grotius in the early development of international law. He is better known to European students as a natural-law political theorist of the seventeenth century who contributed his mite to the secularization of politics and the growth of absolutism. He is, finally, best known to German students as a jurist and historian who blended political ideal and reality in the salutary principle of *raison d'état*.

None of these intellectual accomplishments is particularly remarkable.

Samuel Pufendorf was a university professor who held academic posts in Germany and Sweden and then left academic life for governmental research positions with a pair of high-handed princes, one in Sweden, one in Germany. This personal accomplishment was not particularly remarkable either.

Efforts have not been wanting to rehabilitate Pufendorf (or more precisely, because he has not been considered a primary historical figure since Leibniz' contemporary stricture upon him as "a poor jurist and a worse philosopher," [1] to habilitate him),[2] but this essay is not one of them. It may very well be that, as his admirers attest, Pufendorf's realism, liberalism, and patriotism make his combinations of ideas a pioneering achievement in the development of the modern mentality, but what will concern us here is a set of problems arising rather from his indubitably representative than from his putatively creative function in history. For Pufendorf raises questions at every turn, and when these questions are brought into conjunction they are all seen to revolve around a single issue of such general import as to make Pufendorf a symbol of a larger issue.

If we seek to assess the man's personality, we find that, although the scarcity of materials and Pufendorf's own scholarly preoccupations permit little more than an intellectual portrait, what little we do know is a puzzling mixture of courage and caution, arrogance and subservience, dignity and dependence.

If we seek to assess the man's work, we find it honeycombed with juxtaposed and unresolved combinations: the methods of induction and deduction; the principles of sociability and utility; the canons of rationality and authority; the endorsements of absolutism and constitutionalism; the concatenation of secularized natural law, Lutheranism, and history.

If we seek to assess the man's effect, we find it quantitatively divided between a contemporary influence that was immense and an ultimate impact that was minimal, and qualitatively divided between the liberal tradition it helped to nourish through Locke, John Wise, and Rousseau and the authoritarian strain it stimulated in Christian Thomasius and Christian Wolff, in Peter the Great, Frederick the Great, and Joseph II. With such figures as Frederick and Voltaire, the Pufendorf problem was epitomized in the undoubted influence he had over men who did not respect him and in the ambiguous political direction of that influence.

Pufendorf, in short, represents the fundamental human type of the mediator.[3] As a man he recalls to us the men of ✔ discretion whom we all know, the men who are bold and independent—at the right times, with the right people, and on the right issues. As a theorist he belongs to the domesticators of revolutionary ideas. He pounded, bent, and snipped the radical doctrine of the "new" natural law just as in our own age the doctrines of democracy, nationalism, and Marxism have in their turn been pounded, bent, and trimmed—until they became acceptable and respectable. As a historical figure he inhabits, along with a host of others, that second level in the structure of human society whence ideas are transmitted from the study to the forum, and experience is passed back from the forum to the study.

The Pufendorf problem is thus an integral one. From whatever angle it is viewed, it is the problem of the trimmer. To identify it, however, is not to solve it. To men of good conscience and particularly to intellectuals who pride themselves upon their rationality, compromise is neither final nor automatic. It is a process that we need to know more about, for it involves more than the mere juxtaposition of ideas with necessities, more than the separation of ideas from their effects, more than the simple limitation of ideas in terms of their applicability. In the process of mediation the basic and necessary disjunction between unitary ideas and multiform existence is bridged by various kinds of strands which substantially modify the ideas, reorder existence, and complicate their relations to each other. Only so could discreet men of tender conscience and sound reason live at one with themselves. Pufendorf was such a man, and it behooves us, in our own age of discretion, to see how he did it.

[1]

THE MAN

"Novelty," declared Samuel Pufendorf boldly, "in itself contains nothing false or wrong. . . . We should stop asking how new or old a doctrine is and investigate only how true or false it is." [1] At times, indeed, he went even further in praise of the pioneering spirit to hold that where reason was involved, "the more an author innovates, the more talent he shows and the more praise he earns." [2]

To defend intellectual progress on the continent of Europe in the seventeenth century was no mean feat, but despite the spectacular advances in the sciences upon which progressives like Pufendorf could and did call to buttress their general position, the persistence of tradition and authority in the cultural environment of the age took its toll. And so it was that this same Pufendorf blended prudence with his courage, sometimes justifying himself with a plea of irresponsibility, "since the writer who expresses the sentiments of the lord he serves sings the song of the one whose bread he eats," and advising a disciple that "the truth should not be told at all times by all people." [3]

There is, then, an inadequacy, a partiality, in the characterization that has been handed down of Pufendorf as a secure, fiercely independent, brash, and enterprising—albeit unselfconscious—representative of the rising bourgeoisie.[4] As a descendant of the Lutheran clerical estate who rose to high academic rank, Pufendorf was undoubtedly a bourgeois, but for the social classification to be mutually fruitful—that is, explanatory of both the man and the group—it is the *seventeenth-century* bourgeoisie that must serve as the measure, and in this period what it stood for differed in quality as well as in degree from the familiar self-assertive posture of the later middle class.

I. The Bourgeois in Seventeenth-Century Society

The seventeenth-century bourgeoisie was a corporation on the way to becoming a class. The very terms "bourgeois" and the equivalent German "Bürger" embodied, by this time, a multiplicity of meanings that reflected the group's plurality of roles.[5] As a corporation, it retained both its original medieval reference to the residents of towns and its subsequent variations upon this status in ascending degrees of exclusiveness: it could denote only those families that enjoyed the civil rights of the municipality, or even only the patrician oligarchy that came to monopolize the government and the mercantile power of the towns. In the words of a recent French commentator, to be a bourgeois meant to "belong to a very definite juridical category and a very fluid social class."[6] But the designation had also acquired another dimension of meaning which transcended the older generic connotation of a local corporation: it was applied to the generality of citizens who composed the states of western Europe. Even here there were variations. In France, where contemporaries preferred to confine "bourgeois" within its local reference and to denominate the same group the "third estate" in its national context, the class was distinguished from the nobility on one side and from artisans and peasants on the other. In Germany, the signification of "Bürger" itself was extended from citizenship in a town to citizenship in a state, following here the model set by the Roman *civis*. Unlike the French usage, the German defined, not a discrete social class of commoners, but what was common, in terms of civil rights and obligations, to all subjects, noble and commoner alike. If the variations betrayed the indefinite and undeveloped recognition of the bourgeoisie as an international or even a national class, both usages did coincide in the definite recognition of a literal class of rights and qualities generally applicable to the citizens of a state—however variable the incidence of application—regardless of local title.[7]

True to the semantics of its position, the urban propertied commons of the seventeenth century combined a well-defined status as a local corporation with an indefinite status as a broad and mobile social class. In England and the Netherlands the latter status found institutional definition in effective supralocal parliaments through which the commons claimed to represent a broader mass of burgesses than their actual constituents, but even here oligarchy and locality remained the juridical basis of representation, exhibiting a corporate persistence that was more intense in other countries where national parliaments were suspended or ineffective.[8] The mixture of the two social roles often enough led the seventeenth-century bourgeoisie into a kind of schizophrenia, attested politically by the alternation between revolution and restoration in England and economically by the gulf between the speculative adventurers and the timid *rentiers* in France.[9] And yet, divided as the status of the bourgeois may have been in itself, its divergent elements combined to produce a single coherent style of life which was a blend of the opposing categories. This style attained its most articulate and influential form in France, where the rise of classicism was the aesthetic counterpart of a bourgeois way of life.

The dominant values of this way of life were denoted in the striving for order, regularity, symmetry, and balance.[10] They were as manifest in the standards of the *honnête homme* and the *bourgeois gentilhomme* and in the proportions and layout of house and garden as in the approach to society and politics. In all these spheres a rational delimitation and differentiation of function served to integrate the mobility of the parts into the planned security of an equilibrated whole. Tradition and innovation equally contributed to such a redefinition of the well-ordered life. From tradition the bourgeois drew their persistent reverence for authority, their economic investment in landed property and customary techniques of production for the assurance of a stable income, and the orientation of their ambitions toward the acquisition of noble status within a social hierarchy which they accepted.[11] From their recent and contemporary increase of wealth, education, and self-esteem they derived an open-ended fluidity on both the upper and lower borders of their middling status. In this role they prized functional rather than prescriptive hierarchy and converted their old norm of local autonomy into the concentration of authority in a rational system for the performance of tangible services. The resultant of these two sets of tendencies was for the bourgeois to invest the operation of the new order in the authoritarian state. After a final series of revolutionary attempts, in conjunction with sections of the aristocracy, to impress their traditional prescriptive privileges upon the structure of the state around the middle of the seventeenth century, the bourgeoisies of the progressive nations in western Europe went over to loyal collaboration with and participation in the political institutions of *de facto* monarchical or oligarchic sovereigns.[12]

These were the most developed groups of the bourgeoisie, and they stimulated a literature which influenced scholars and writers from other parts of Europe. The international republic of letters remained a vital force in the seventeenth century, and the Western societies dominated it. A native German like Pufendorf, for example, not only found his mentors in the Dutch Grotius and the English Hobbes but was familiar with a myriad of lesser French and English publicists.[13] And yet, however potent such an indirect impact may have been, the immediate conditioning by a more retrograde social environment remained an independent and limiting factor. For Pufendorf, this factor is all the more considerable in view of the customary delineation of a decayed and stagnant German *Bürgertum*, crushed under the successive blows of the shift to the Atlantic economic axis, the restrictive triumph of political particularism, and the destructive effects of the Thirty Years' War.[14] In comparison with western Europe, the picture undoubtedly retains validity, and it still serves, as it long has served, to underline the utter dependence of the German society in general and the German bourgeoisie in particular upon the territorial state after 1648.[15] But as a matter of historical reasoning the traditional interpretation leaves the bourgeois participants in German state-building without a social base, and, as a matter of historical fact, its descriptive validity is now open to doubt. German trade and industry seem to have declined much less before the Thirty Years' War and to have been devastated much less during it than the simple thesis of retrogression postulated.[16] It would appear, rather, that the sporadic regional incidence of both depression and war left the German economic bourgeoisie with no integral and comprehensible character. Certainly the records of particular merchants reveal such anomolous combinations of economic traits as inertia in the market place with ready response to governmental stimuli, and the habitual striving for sufficiency with a sporadic spirit of capitalistic enterprise.[17] And so it may be

[9]

that the character of the bourgeoisie may be comprehended only from its more self-conscious and articulate intellectual branch.

If, then, the European bourgeoisie helps to explain a Pufendorf, a Pufendorf is needed to explain the German bourgeoisie. He mediated and translated the distilled experience of the one into forms recognizable in terms of the divergent experience of the other. He placed his primary emphasis upon the rational authority of the political sovereign who had become the object of bourgeois reverence all over the Continent, and thereby he made deliberate for central and northern Europe what in the west was a spontaneous growth. This mediation was possible because the west European bourgeoisie was, during the formative period of Pufendorf's thought, still in the final stages of the same process that the German bourgeoisie was just entering. Pufendorf needed only to intensify the directing and ordering role of the sovereign and to integrate the traditional social hierarchy more fully into the rational order of the new state to make west European ideas applicable to a more static society.

But if political authoritarianism provided a comfortable common denominator for the European and German dimensions of Pufendorf's thinking during the period of its systematic elaboration in the 1660's and 1670's, it became a problem for him when the societies of western Europe began to move into another way of life during the ninth decade of the century. The oppression and flight of the Huguenots, Louis XIV's rupture of the international equilibrium, the Glorious Revolution in England, and the growing resistance within France to Louis's exactions were political signs of the profound cultural change that was breaking up the order of an abstract and transcendent reason and turning the western bourgeoisie toward considerations of freedom with a looser organization around principles of a more empirically based reason.[18] Pufendorf was attentive to these signs of change, and they became stimuli to his later development as he strove to accommodate his system to the new European reality. It was, then, the overlay of the European upon the German bourgeois in Pufendorf, rather than any reforming tendency, that was reflected in the blending of liberal and conservative attitudes in his approach. He sought to rationalize the actual, and the actuality of his age which he perceived through the dual vision of a central European personal and a west European intellectual experience led him to account for a whole spectrum of authoritarian and liberating institutions.

II. PUFENDORF'S CAREER

Pufendorf's career ran along two different tracks, a curious separation that signalized the tension in his makeup. His external career conformed to the accepted pattern of his age. His intellectual career, on the other hand, was dominated by his struggle to assert the latest modes of seventeenth-century thought against the accepted pattern of his age. It is hardly surprising that the man at the center of these experiences cherished both traditional ends and radical means in his approach to life. But if the man—and his work—simply registered this duality, our story would soon be at an end. The fact is that he sought reconciliation, and to this too his career brings light. For despite their diverse tendencies, we find that the two facets of his career not only exhibited parallel stages of development but converged into a single set of professional and intellectual concerns toward the end of his life. Thus, his determined shift of intellectual attention from law to history paralleled his professional move from the academic post of university law professor to the official post of court historiographer, and ultimately his immediate pro-

fessional involvement with the state became an integral part
of his one final problem: the mediation between rational
freedom and positive authority. Pufendorf's life was not
simply a story but an evolution: never entirely untrue to the
essential nature of the man, only its unfolding revealed
progressively what that nature was.

The outer track of Pufendorf's career followed a well-
worn course. The external facts of his lineage, education, and
profession provided him with a framework of ineluctable
traditional requirements and values. What was dynamic and
liberal in his behavior lay within but not beyond the limits
set by the fundamental facts of his existence.

Pufendorf's origins were rural and strictly Lutheran, and
his early training was quite in keeping with the routine
passivity which was his birthright.[19] Scion of a long line of
Lutheran pastors, Pufendorf was born on January 8, 1632, in
the village of Dorfchemnitz bei Thalheim and was reared in
the mountain parish of Flöha, part of the Saxon Erzgebirge.
From the atmosphere of a Lutheran minister's household in
the backwoods of an Electoral Saxony which itself had stag-
nated into a backwoods of Protestant Europe with the development of a rigid confessional orthodoxy, Pufendorf received
a Lutheran impress that proved to be indelible. For all his
controversies with orthodox theologians and for all his reputation as a secularizer, his faith was unshakable, its principal
tenets held inviolate beyond the scope of these activities.[20]

Whether the Saxon influence as such was equally persistent is much more doubtful. Once he left Saxony he was
not attracted back to it. He thought of himself as German
rather than Saxon on those occasions when he considered
himself in more concrete terms than as a member of the international community of letters, and some of his favorite
targets were the devotees of Protestant scholasticism in
which his native state seemed to specialize.[21] But yet, even

without indulging in the encomiums of tribal characteristics like passion, independence, and wit which his fellow Saxon, Treitschke, was later to find mirrored in him, we may discern at least one vivid and durable trace of the early habitat. The fighting of the Thirty Years' War penetrated into the Erzgebirge during his childhood, and although neither his family nor he was touched directly by it, Pufendorf always retained the memory of the atrocity stories and the emotional response of horror—indeed, they stood out later as his earliest recollections—which were current in his neighborhood.[22] It is not too much, surely, to see in this secondhand experience a root both of his impulse to reorder political relations and of his reverence for powerful authority as the agent of such reordering.

The tradition-bound Saxon atmosphere played upon Pufendorf primarily through the state's institutions of learning, which he attended until the relatively advanced age of twenty-four. The substantive result of this Saxon education was to give Pufendorf a training *in extenso,* in a variety of fields unorganized by any general principle or dominant discipline—an appropriate preparation for the "eclectic" that Pufendorf was later to admit he had been.[23] The process began with his enrollment, in 1645, in the Prince's School at Grimma, an event which, dependent as it was upon the financial support of a local nobleman, afforded the poor minister's son an early lesson in the value of patronage. The course of study here was standard for such Lutheran establishments. Grammar, rhetoric, logic, and many hours of Bible study, sermons, and catechism in Lutheran dogma made up the curriculum. In one respect only did the school differ from others of its kind: it afforded more time for free reading than was the custom. Pufendorf used this time to immerse himself in the classics. Legend would have him a young rebel, rejecting the established courses for his extracurricular humanistic study,[24] but the facts were that Pufendorf conformed sufficiently to do well by official standards, that the school was indifferent rather than hostile to such study in the lower forms, and that he found support from sympathetic masters in the classics at the head of the upper forms.[25]

In 1650 Pufendorf moved to the University of Leipzig, sent under his father's orders to study theology in preparation for a career in the ministry. But, however pious he might be, for a young man with an inquiring mind, varied interests, and a lively feeling for the values of this world, Leipzig was no place to study theology. Never celebrated for its audacity, the university's traditional conservatism had degenerated during the intra-Lutheran disputes of the previous century into a mechanical and suspicious dogmatism. Pufendorf seems to have raised no initial objection to the plans for him, but it took only a brief contact with the Leipzig style of theology to convince him that this discipline could provide no organizing principle for an active mind or for all the knowledge it had to operate upon. Repelled by the sterility of this theology, Pufendorf reacted characteristically. He did not rebel against it; he did not lose his religion; he did not change his religion: he simply pushed theology into a corner of his mind and proceeded to ignore it. For the rest of his six years in Leipzig, Pufendorf did without an organized plan or unifying goal of education: with the signal exception of theology (and medicine) he spread himself into the study of every field offered by the university. Equipped with large stores of information and, what was more important, an appreciation for the most diverse forms of reality, Pufendorf left Leipzig in 1656 to continue his academic career at the University of Jena.

Pufendorf's two brief years at the Thuringian university were to prove decisive for his development, since he came away not only with his academic degree but with a chosen field for his endeavors and a central principle for organizing

[14]

knowledge around this field. The field was what Pufendorf called "ethics," [26] and the principle was the concept of natural law. What this crystallization of Pufendorf's ideas meant is discernible from the tendency of its inspirer, Erhard Weigel, the Jena mathematics professor to whom Pufendorf, like Leibniz after him, quickly attached himself. Weigel was a Cartesian who grasped the connection between the methodological rationalism of Descartes and the substantive rationalism of the elaboration of natural law by Grotius and Hobbes. He sought to construct, out of the new mathematical logic, a total system that would replace scholasticism as the channel to all knowledge.[27] Pufendorf was ever too much of an empiricist and too much the many-sided representative of what the seventeenth century called the "poly-historians" to become a complete Cartesian, but he did take from Weigel the faith in natural reason as the method and in natural law as its compatible substance which could be applied to the several forms of reality and supply strands of coherence to their comprehension.

Where Pufendorf's distinctive practical orientation did appear was in his conversion of his mentor's indiscriminate philosophizing into a concentration upon human "ethics" which he effectively redefined into the rules of social and political life. The influence of Pufendorf's older brother, Esaias, was undoubtedly at work in the determination of this focus. Esaias, like Samuel a refugee from theology, had already, as a lecturer at Leipzig, pushed his younger brother toward politics, and now the coincidence of his entry upon his long career in the Swedish diplomatic service with Samuel's experience at Jena helped the latter to see in law and politics the crossroads of his varied interests. "I think that which you do daily," he was to acknowledge to Esaias later, and he laid it to his brother's encouragement and example that he made his chief concern "the controllable

[15]

actions of men" in the sense of "civil life and public relations." [28] Again, what is important is not the source but the
tendency of the influence. Esaias' hard-bitten realism—he
was to achieve notoriety as a master of espionage as well as of
negotiation—was such as to make of politics the arena of
human actualities, and this influence, in conjunction with
Weigel's metaphysical investment in natural law, sufficed to
make the combination of law and politics Samuel Pufendorf's
matrix for solving the relationship between the rational and
the real which had, not for the first time and not for the last,
become the problem of the age.

When Pufendorf ended his student years in 1658 and left
Jena to seek his fortune—in his own words, "fame and
patronage" [29]—he departed with a characteristic gesture: he
refused the doctorate to signify his reprobation of the academic guild and its traditional scholastic ways, but he prudently allowed himself to be persuaded into the acceptance
of the master's degree which was essential for an academic
career.

An aggressive and ambitious young man with no money
and few connections, Pufendorf soon developed what might
best be called "selective conformity" as the pattern of his
career. Fortunately—although the relationship was more
causal than coincidental—his seventeenth-century world was
flexible enough to permit the development of such a pattern.
The growing insulation of the sovereign states had not yet
intruded too severely upon the international orientation and
opportunities of the humanist scholar, but it had already
loosened the domestic social structure, providing through the
princes' service new avenues of ascent for an educated commoner. Pufendorf could thus shuttle back and forth between
his loyalties to Germany and to Europe as a whole and he
could choose the political over the corporate way to prefer-
ment without violating unduly the canons of his age.

[16]

Pufendorf's Career

Finding no suitable post open to him in his native Saxony, Pufendorf accepted the position, which had been arranged for him by Esaias, of tutor to the family of Baron Peter Julius Coyet, the Swedish minister in Copenhagen. There followed the one truly eventful period in what was to be a placid life, and while we have no direct evidence of the impact made by these events, it is perhaps not too great a presumption to see in the brutal intervention of contemporary politics into Pufendorf's existence a further inspiration for him to view politics as a central human concern and the establishment of law for it as his central intellectual task. In August, 1658, shortly after Pufendorf had arrived in Copenhagen to assume his new pedagogical duties, Sweden suddenly reopened against Denmark the war which had been suspended during peace talks. Promptly redressing this violation of trust by the perpetration of another, the Danes proceeded to arrest the Swedish legation and retinue. As a fitting climax to this morality tale on the decline of chivalry, Baron Coyet, forewarned about the Swedish intentions, made a successful escape, leaving his staff and family to some eight months of Danish imprisonment. It is hardly surprising that Pufendorf, although bereft of books, felt impelled to spend his incarceration composing a treatise entitled *Elements of Universal Jurisprudence (Elementorum jurisprudentiae universalis)*, a kind of law of which he was himself in dire need. Pufendorf had not designed these notes for publication but rather, with his usual eye for the main chance, as a sample of his work to give his sponsors a basis for recommendation to a better post.[30] And yet, however occasional the motivation, it already contained, albeit in undeveloped form, the main points of his mature system. It was not until he arrived in the Netherlands, where he resumed his position with the Coyet family and circulated the manuscript to his brother and friends, that Pufendorf became convinced that its publication would serve

[17]

him well, and it was published at The Hague during 1660.

The timing of these events makes it clear that the free atmosphere of Holland could have had little influence upon his fundamental political ideas. What he did derive from his brief Dutch residence (1659–61) was the sophistication of his humanistic interests, for he undertook at the University of Leyden the study of that classical philology which was its specialty in the seventeenth century, and he published two studies in that field.[31] The philological emphasis in the Dutch universities was accompanied by a strong current of neo-Stoic ideas, but it is difficult to assess the strength of the stoicism which Pufendorf absorbed along with his literary education.[32] The larger explicit role which natural law was to play as the unifying scheme in Pufendorf's later juristic works may be considered a probable effect, and the copious citations from the Stoic classics a certain effect, of the Dutch period, but both these results were elaborations upon a previously prepared position rather than the marks of a turning point. Here, as in his entire adult career, Pufendorf's tendency was to develop the implications of his comprehensive principles in the light of a new influence rather than to alter them. For a mediator of the Pufendorf type, the canons of life and thought are too flexible to be convulsed by any new experience; they are simply bent by the weight of the experience which they undergo.

So we find the outcome of Pufendorf's stay in the Netherlands to be his choice of Karl Ludwig, Elector of the Palatinate, as the German prince he would serve. It was, for Pufendorf, a shrewd selection. Like his forebears, this Palatine Elector was a leader of German Calvinism, a relatively undogmatic species of the genus, but he stood, even more than they, for a policy of religious toleration in the tradition of the Politiques. Pufendorf's own latitudinarian Lutheranism was more compatible with this kind of Calvinism than

[18]

with any other confessional breed in Germany. Like his forebears, too, Karl Ludwig retained lively relations with his fellow Calvinists in the Netherlands, and as an alumnus of Leyden University he cherished particular connections with the group among whom Pufendorf was making his friends. And best of all, as an educated prince with absolutist tendencies the Elector was in the market for secularly minded scholars. Pufendorf announced his availability by dedicating his *Elementorum* to Karl Ludwig and faithfully expressing the combination of motives that attracted him to the Elector in the praise of the latter's "humanity" and his patronage.[33] The young jurist took care to have the dedication accompanied by a letter of recommendation to Karl Ludwig from Peter de Groot, son of Hugo Grotius and resident agent of Karl Ludwig in Holland, and to show his practical value by writing a defense of Karl Ludwig's position in his most pressing legal controversy.[34]

Karl Ludwig did indeed find these blandishments irresistible, and in 1660 he offered Pufendorf a professorship in Heidelberg University. The original offer was a chair in Roman law, but Pufendorf refused it, characteristically, because he felt that the plethora of commentaries left too small an arena for the display of his talents.[35] Pufendorf requested instead an appointment as professor of politics on the law faculty, but the Elector, on the advice of a reluctant university senate, then proposed an associate professorship (*Extraordinarius*) of international law and philology in the philosophical faculty.[36] Pufendorf was later to exalt the dignity and the novelty of the post by recollecting it erroneously as the first chair of natural and international law.[37] The actual position was obviously a contrivance by the university to meet the wishes of the Elector, but Pufendorf accepted it, since he needed the work and could justify his move with the consolation that this was indeed the first professorship if not

[19]

of natural law at least of international law in Germany. It was like Pufendorf to seek a strong sovereign with liberal leanings, and it was like him too to choose the more modern over the more traditional field of law. But despite the lesson of the benefits of princely over collegiate favor, it was also like him to yearn for a place in the establishment, which, for him as a jurist, meant membership in the law faculty. He was apparently even willing now to surrender possession of the international law in which he was later to vaunt his pioneering role, for the sake of academic respectability. The professorship which he coveted seems, from the appointment that was made at the time, to have been for German constitutional law in the juristic faculty,[38] and Pufendorf's essays on patriotism, published in 1663, and on Philip of Macedon, with its obviously appropriate discussion of irregular states, may well have been written to stake his claim to such a chair.[39] Whatever the identity of the professorship, it is clear from Pufendorf's own testimony that there was some such opening and that he was passed over in the selection of its beneficiary.

The disappointment strained Pufendorf's equilibrium to the breaking point. His initial response was to flare out with the most radical action he ever undertook—the composition (1664) and publication (1667) of his iconoclastic analysis of contemporary Germany, *On the Constitution of the German Empire* (*De statu imperii Germanici*), "inspired," as he frankly admitted just before his death, "by indignation" at the lost professorship.[40] He used the book as a vehicle to flay the whole species of German constitutional lawyers,[41] but he was not sufficiently indignant, it should be noted, either to publish it under his own name—he invented the Italian traveler Severinus de Monzambano for the occasion—or ever to avow his authorship publicly during his lifetime; nor did he fail to submit the manuscript to the Elector for his approval and amendments. His subsequent response to the prolongation of his exceptional position in Heidelberg was more authentically Pufendorfian: he sought to rationalize the given. He proceeded, in other words, to represent his professorship of international law as a chair in natural law—a representation that was easy for him, since he denied the substantive independence of the former in favor of the latter in any case [42]—and to be inspired by his university position to begin the writing of his magnum opus on the law of nature under which all other forms of law would be comprehended and explicated.[43]

But undeniably the hurt still rankled. When in 1667 Charles XI of Sweden offered him a full professorship in natural and international law on the law faculty of his new university at Lund, Pufendorf hastened to accept, despite what he later described as his halcyonic relations with the Palatine Elector, aristocracy, and Calvinist society in general.[44] He was later accused of having left under pressure, but while it is quite probable that the storm over his work on the German constitution—for his identity with Monzambano, though never admitted, was generally known—embroiled him with the Heidelberg jurists as with so many others, there are no real grounds to doubt Pufendorf's own story that the Swedes sought him and not he them or that he accepted the Lund chair simply to "improve my fortunes." [45] He was not driven by financial need, for he had an adequate enough income since his marriage in Heidelberg to a well-to-do widow, and the affectionate terms in which this man, usually so sensitive to affront, subsequently referred to the Elector, belies any official spur. The Swedish initiative, on the other hand, is plausible from the presence of young Swedish notables in his Heidelberg classes and the rise of his brother to prominence and influence in the Swedish foreign service. Pufendorf's motivation in the matter is important for two reasons.

[21]

In the first place, it points up his middling status during his adult life: he was sufficiently secure, both financially and professionally, to escape the radicalism of the uprooted, but not so secure that he did not continue to exercise an active option among given alternatives for the increase of his property and his prestige. In the second place, the moderation of his motives helps to remove the obfuscating feature of German patriotism from the traditional Pufendorf portrait, a feature which stems from observing the fact rather than the character of his essay on the subject. In truth, Pufendorf found in himself little sentimental resistance to leaving the nation of his birth. His transfer to Swedish employ, like that of Grotius before him, conformed to the supranational humanist tradition of seeking out the appreciative patron prince wherever he might be, and it conformed as well to Pufendorf's own hardheaded conception of a *patria* as "the seat of one's fortunes" and his consequent admission of natives and immigrants as equivalent patriots.[46]

In 1670 Pufendorf assumed the duties of his chair at the new university and began the eighteen years of Swedish domicile which were to be the most fruitful of his career. His craving for status assuaged by his ranking position and salary on the law faculty, he quickly completed and in 1672 published the magisterial work *On the Law of Nature and Nations* (*De jure naturae et gentium*), which was to be his chief claim to enduring fame. He capped it in the next year with an epitome under the title *On the Duty of Man and the Citizen According to Natural Law* (*De officio hominis et civis juxta legem naturalem*) which was designed and successfully functioned for more than a century as a textbook for law students. But just as his constitutional writings, with their insistence on the actual incompatibility of the German Empire with the traditional forms of the state, had embroiled him with the jurists, so now his political theory, with its

insistence on the independence of natural law from traditional religion, aroused the ire of the theologians. Once more
he was careful to cover himself with the approval of the
authorities that counted—King Charles XI, to whom he
dedicated the *On the Law of Nature,* and Count Gustave
Steenbock, chancellor of the university, to whom he dedicated *On the Duty of Man and the Citizen* and who directed
the university's official defense of Pufendorf.[47] Pufendorf was
quite candid about his policy of selective obedience. "I would
not fear to proclaim," he wrote openly in the preface to the
first edition of *On the Law of Nature,* "now that his Royal
Majesty has most graciously judged this work worthy of his
approval, that I tremble before the authority of no other
censor." [48] Nor did he neglect, in his dedication, to anticipate
accusations of sedition by identifying the king with the
progress of natural law and by spreading liberally through
the piece references to the Divinity and His close, albeit
undefined, relations with Charles's reign.[49]

The care was well taken, for the storms came. Led by the
open hostility of his Lund colleagues, notably the theologian
Joshua Schwartz and the jurist Nicholas Beckmann—sources
who gave Pufendorf's defenders the chance to blame the
opposition on jealousy of his large classes [50]—traditionalists
from Sweden and Germany waged a lively polemic against
the *On the Law of Nature.* No man to take lightly attacks
from his peers, Pufendorf struck back, as he had done in
defense of Monzambano, and his main writing between the
composition of *On the Duty of Man and the Citizen* and his
departure from Lund in 1677 took the form of rebuttals
against the detractors of his natural-law doctrines. These
defensive pieces, in which Pufendorf undertook to explicate
his assumptions in the direction of neutralizing the accusations of impiety and anarchy, were later (1686) collected and
republished as the *Scandinavian Polemics (Eris Scandica).*

[23]

The *Scandinavian Polemics,* however dissonant, turned out to be the swan song of Pufendorf's career as a political theorist. Its publication had been immediately preceded by the republication and rounding-out of his collected miscellaneous essays, stemming from his Heidelberg as well as his early Swedish years and focusing on the issues of constitutional form and practical politics which his venture as Monzambano had already revealed to be the second string of his juristic bow. With these *Select Scholarly Essays (Dissertationes academicae selectiores),* published at Lund in 1675 and republished at Upsala in 1677, this applied side of Pufendorf's writing career as a political philosopher came to an end just as his strictly theoretical work was to do shortly thereafter, and he entered into the second main phase of his life's work.[51]

It is characteristic of the way Pufendorf lived his life that his intellectual conversion from the philosophy of law to history was accompanied by a professional shift from academic jurist to official historian which was a product of only limited free choice. In 1676 the Danes captured Lund; it was this happenstance that led Charles XI to offer his displaced law professor the combined post of royal historiographer and secretary of state and thus channeled Pufendorf into a new career as professional historian. Charles's awareness of Pufendorf's potentialities for such a function may well have been aroused by the historical lectures which the jurist had delivered at Lund; but if they revealed a definite historical dimension in Pufendorf's thinking that enabled him to accept the king's proposal, still the theme of applied politics which was their dominant concern indicates that it was the post and not the lectures that spurred his development into a full-blown historian. Pufendorf published the lectures as the *Introduction to the History of the Great Empires and States of Contemporary Europe (Einleitung zur Historie der vor-*

nehmsten Reiche und Staaten so itziger Zeit in Europa sich befinden). Its composition in the German language (it was the only non-Latin work he ever published), the frank designation of it by the author as a textbook for "youth of high rank," and the derivative character of both its orientation toward and its techniques of history, all distinguish the book sharply from the historical writing he was to do as a professional. It may well be that only his new position persuaded Pufendorf to publish it at all, for its relatively late date of publication—1682–85—is otherwise surprising for a scholar who habitually hastened into print at the earliest opportunity. Pufendorf, in short, did not make his new career; he accepted a situation that was thrust upon him and proceeded to turn it to full account.

The new court historian settled in Stockholm during 1677 and remained for almost eleven years. Despite his imposing official titles, he concerned himself but little with the business of government.[52] His one extant memorandum, designed to show the continuing disadvantages reaped by Sweden from its long-standing policy of alliance with France, was itself largely historical in approach and substance.[53] Pufendorf interpreted his new duties primarily as an extension of his scholarly career, but his official position did leave its mark on the kind of scholarly enterprise which he now chose to pursue. He concerned himself, for the rest of his life, essentially with two fields of writing, and he entered upon both during his Stockholm period. The fields were history and religion, and in the one as in the other the official and the scholarly standards stemming from his hybrid profession were in conflict. He approached both fields from the angle of government, but within this approach he sought the independent validity of disciplined scholarship.

The history that he wrote—in Stockholm the *Commentaries on Swedish Affairs from the Expedition of King Gusta-*

*vus Adolphus into Germany to the Abdication of Queen
Christina* and the *Commentaries on the History of King
Charles Gustavus of Sweden* [54]—was the history of rulers and
their governments, but his available correspondence, the
bulk of which dates from his historical phase in Stockholm
and thereafter, shows clearly how definitely and how proudly
he identified his work with the autonomous calling of the
historian, with its emphasis on basic research, impartiality,
and "love of truth." [55] The same correspondence shows, too,
how painfully he struggled to match these obligations of the
historian with those to "the prince or state he writes about,"
particularly when he serves the prince "directly," is paid by
him, and is admitted to his archives as "an officer . . . to a
fortress." [56]

As a full-time historian who granted himself little occasion
for other writing,[57] Pufendorf's address to religion was merely
ancillary, but when he did find the time in Stockholm to
write and publish what he called "a little book" on the
subject, his approach to it through the problem of church
and state raised problems analogous to those of his political
history.[58] The occasion for the composition of *On the Relation of the Christian Religion to Civil Life* (*De habitu
religionis Christianae ad vitam civilem*) in 1686 was Louis
XIV's revocation of the Edict of Nantes, and Pufendorf's
preface set the book in the framework of a councilor's recommendation of policy on church affairs to Protestant princes.[59]
But he had, on the other hand, long cherished a philosophical
interest in positive religion,[60] and the theme of the analysis
was the objective extension of "civil science"—that is, the
principles of natural law—to the problem of religious institutions. Pufendorf's ambiguous position on church-state relations stems at least in part from the tension between the
policy-making and the scientific functions which he meant it
jointly to serve.[61] He could resolve the tension nominally by

positing a hierarchical organization of his audience—he declared his "certain maxims of civil science" appropriate
"above all" to princes and secondarily to "everybody . . .
with a middling knowledge of human affairs" [62]—but the flaw
ran through the substance of the book, obscuring the crystal-
line issue of toleration.[63]

This publication of his first work on Christianity did not
mark a fundamental turn in Pufendorf's career, for his
historical labors continued to have first priority, but it did
mark the juxtaposition of religion with history as the twin
concerns of his final years. It is hardly surprising, in view of
his past, to find that once more the development of an
intellectual interest was accompanied by a change in his
personal commitments. His dedication of *On the Relation of
the Christian Religion to Civil Life* to the Great Elector,
Frederick William of Prussia, was the first fruit of his recent
acceptance, in the same year (1686), of the historiographer's
post at the Brandenburg court, and his reference to the book
as "a proof of devotion" to his new patron has a familiar ring.
Frederick William had been wooing Pufendorf since 1684,
but it was only after the French revocation, when Frederick
William's emergence as a leader of the Protestant response
coincided with Pufendorf's literary entry into the fray, that
Pufendorf decided upon the change of masters. He could
now, with full assurance, claim "the gracious protection" of
his new lord for his book on the religious cause they shared,
and it can be surmised that the sympathy which this Calvinist
ruler of a Lutheran state could be presumed to have for
Pufendorf's latitudinarian approach to positive religion went
far to explain the latter's acceptance of the Berlin post a full
year and a half before he could leave Stockholm, despite all
the inconveniences of such a lame-duck interval.

But, as was usual with Pufendorf, circumstantial as well as
principled reasons lay behind his decision to move. He had

accumulated grievances in Stockholm that jogged his consciousness of intellectual and patriotic affinity with the Brandenburg Elector.[64] It was, moreover, the intensification of these grievances during the lame-duck period that rendered the move permanent. In the first place, since his interests lay exclusively in recent history, the approaching end of his account of King Charles X (1654–60) —the reason for his holdover in Stockholm—must have raised serious doubts about the obstacles he would meet in a sequel on the reigning Charles XI (1660–97), should he proceed in Sweden with his real passion for contemporary history.[65] Second, he had complaints about money because his emoluments in Stockholm did not enable him to live on the scale to which he felt entitled, and this discontent was now intensified by the distraint of the stipulated fee for the completion of the history.[66] But most important was his bitterness at the mistrust and hostility exhibited toward him by factions in the Swedish court, for he saw this hostility as tantamount to "dismissal" and was later to declare flatly that without it "I would never have left Stockholm." [67] After Pufendorf's agreement with the Great Elector the suspicion mounted to a point where Pufendorf was not permitted to take the manuscript of his Swedish history with him and this, in turn, pointed up an important scholarly handicap of the Swedish situation for Pufendorf: until the manuscript was permitted out of Sweden it could not be published, for no adequate printing facilities existed there for bringing out "any good book." [68] By January, 1688, when Pufendorf moved his family and himself to Berlin, the atmosphere had become decidedly unpleasant. His unpopularity, as he himself recognized, rested not simply on party intrigues and petty animosity toward a foreigner but more essentially on the critical judgments which his quest for professional objectivity led him to make about the Swedish past.[69] He was beginning now to pay

[28]

the price of making the best of two worlds: the yoking of official history with independent scholarship began, not for the last time in the history of history, to chafe.

In Berlin Pufendorf's working conditions were outwardly greatly improved. He accumulated, in addition to the posts of court historian and secretary with which he came, the benefices of judicial councilor and privy councilor and finally professed himself financially and socially content.[70] After a time even the squabbles that accompanied him wherever he went seem to have died down, despite the death of his patron, the Great Elector, shortly after Pufendorf's arrival in Berlin.[71] In the short span left to him he completed two major works and left the torso of a third. The change of scene had not appreciably affected his interests, but his Berlin productions did develop further the historical and religious concerns that had dominated him in Stockholm. His approach to history was now more self-conscious and his approach to religion, as his growing familiarity and sympathy with the Pietist movement attested, was more internal than it had been before. By 1692 he had completed drafts of his history of the Great Elector, an extension on the Prussian side and into the contemporary period, of the recent diplomatic history which he had already covered in his Swedish works, and of his *Divine Law of the Covenant* (*Jus feciale divinum*), an extension into theology proper of the preoccupation with positive religions already evinced institutionally in the *On the Relation of the Christian Religion to Civil Life.*[72] He then began but left unfinished at his death a history of Frederick III, the Great Elector's successor, which, with its long and uncharacteristic disquisition on the English Glorious Revolution, represented a final convergence of Pufendorf's historical and religious commitments.[73]

These final six years of his life in Berlin should have brought his career to a fulfilled and contented conclusion.

Instead, the opposed values and institutions which he had joined in theory broke loose to invade his existence. His wonted way out of an irksome situation, the choice of a more appreciative and appropriate prince, now backfired. Caught in his own network of conflicting obligations, he was unable to control the final sequence of events whose lethal result he foresaw and yet had to accept.[74] Belatedly, the insulation of his personal life broke down. Pufendorf's career was to become, at its close, a dramatic testimonial to his intellectual enterprise.

As long as Pufendorf encountered the hostility of subordinate or intermediate authorities, his obligations had afforded him no great problem. In such situations, whether in Berlin or Sweden, he followed one constant rule: "I go immediately to the Chief." [75] Nor would he be bound if a sovereign should turn suspicious, for he felt inviolable bonds of attachment to none. As he explained candidly: "I love whoever does me good and hate whoever does me ill. The state that does me good I esteem; where I am published there am I gladly." [76] He could, in short—and, as we have seen, sometimes did— find himself another Chief. In these respects his belief in the necessity of a supreme and indivisible sovereignty within the state and his acceptance of a pluralistic system of equal sovereigns among states were entirely appropriate to his personal predilections. But what Pufendorf therefore found difficult was to be subject simultaneously to two sovereigns who would equally do him good, and this was precisely what his position was from the time he moved to Berlin until it ultimately, albeit indirectly, killed him. When Pufendorf took the Berlin post he accepted not only the terms offered by the Great Elector but also the conditions imposed by Charles XI, and by them he acknowledged that he was only "loaned" or, more precisely and more tellingly, conferred "like a fief [*lehnweise*]" by Charles upon Frederick William for a period of two years.[77] Feudal arrangements were traditionally susceptible to conflicts of jurisdiction, and in this case the tradition was exacerbated by Pufendorf's function of writing for the Great Elector (and later Elector Frederick III) a history that covered much of the same ground and was in direct competition with the history written, but not yet published, by the same Pufendorf for the king of Sweden. Indeed, in view of Frederick William's sly attempt to apply his claims on Pufendorf toward the censoring of the Electoral role in the Swedish history and Charles's equally disingenuous suggestion that Pufendorf bring the unpublished manuscript of the Brandenburg history back to Sweden with him, the status of Pufendorf himself seems to have been reduced at times to that of an unwitting double agent.[78]

Given Pufendorf's attitude toward sovereignty, his divided loyalty was taxing enough in itself, but the pressure was intensified by the added burden which it placed upon his professional integrity as a historian. He was writing two histories on the same touchy subject—recent international relations—for two princes from their respective points of view. Neither book had yet been published, and each had to be approved by the respective princely authority before it could be published. The problem of official history was greatly complicated thereby, for the approval of each authority became geared not only to the submitted contents of its history but also to the presumed contents of the other, and Pufendorf, constantly harried and yet unable to cross-submit, had always to give reassurances on this score.[79] He had, moreover, actually to adjust his historiography to these expanded official standards, not only because the prior publication of the one history might cancel the publication of the other, but also because his integrity as their common historian required their compatibility.

Undoubtedly the political pluralism in Pufendorf's per-

sonal career entered strongly into the pluralistic historical
ethics with which he finally emerged. He perpetuated the
anomalous position which he so uncomfortably occupied
because the existence and the authority of many sovereigns,
each supreme in his own territory, seemed both necessary and
right to him. He was even tempted to cover the same period
for still a third time, in the Emperor's service and from his
point of view, religious and political differences notwithstanding, and desisted only because he was aging and comfortable in Berlin.[80] He made it clear in his various negotiations that when he could not be near the sovereign he loved
he would love the sovereign he was near, and he learned from
his own experience that it paid to love a multiplicity of
sovereigns, since they were the most effective check on one
another. When he was in Berlin he guarded himself by
letting it be known that he was still under the protection of
"a great king and queen" (of Sweden); when he was in
Stockholm he was guarded by the special recommendation of
the Elector; when he wanted to force the approval and
publication of his Swedish history he used, successfully, the
imminent publication of the Brandenburg side as his lever;
when he criticized the policies of Swedish royal officials he
indicated that it was to the king's advantage to have him do
this under Electoral protection, since otherwise it could not
be done at all.[81]

But despite Pufendorf's considerable skill in rationalizing
and exploiting the necessary, in the end he was drowned in a
surfeit of necessities. He could not dispense with either
Frederick, Charles, or Clio, and the service of two masters
and a mistress proved too much for him. He had clearly
decided against a permanent return to Sweden, but he could
not bring himself to give up his connection there. He wanted
to redeem and publish his manuscript history of Charles X
which the Swedes still held in pledge. Moreover, he con-

tinued to acknowledge his "humble obedience to His Majesty's wishes." Accordingly when King Charles issued a personal request and safe-conduct Pufendorf found himself unable to refuse. The aging and ailing scholar resignedly confirmed with the Elector the arrangements for his wife's pension and special grace for his daughters' families and set sail for Stockholm in the spring of 1694. The mission was a tactical success, for Pufendorf could return to Berlin and bring out with him a manuscript copy of his Swedish history and the royal approval of its publication, at the immediate cost only of depositing the collated original in the Swedish chancellery and signing an affidavit not to alter the officially amended text. If this arrangement seemed to liquidate his professional connection with Sweden, in reality he exchanged it for a silken bond. Charles shrewdly conferred a Swedish barony upon him and Pufendorf accepted it.

But the final accounting was exorbitant. The ennoblement which, as a symbol of status, the poor minister's son could not bring himself to refuse was followed by the fatal illness which he had long feared from his overcommitments. He suffered an embolism and, by a grim coincidence following for the last time the example set by his mentor Hugo Grotius almost a half-century before, died after the sea voyage from Stockholm on October 26, 1694.

III. INTELLECTUAL DEVELOPMENT

The personality that emerges from this outer career was closely related to the inner development that is to be our primary concern with Pufendorf. Nor is such a relationship between action and thought or personality and intellect the universal truism that it might first appear, for we have, as in Kant or Marx, enough examples of a decisive gap to make it a question rather than an assumption. In Pufendorf's case there can be little question. There was, to be sure, in him as in so many others a categorical disjunction, indeed almost a division of function, between a life that was devoted to security and ideas that were dedicated to originality, but in him, unlike so many others, an osmosis is traceable. If the pattern of his outer life can be labeled "flexible conformity" to signify his actual option of the most suitable patrons for his unorthodox ideas, then the pattern of his inner life could be analogously labeled "controlled innovation" to signify the circumscription of his ideas by his respect for the actualities. This is not a mere matter of imputation; it is a matter of Pufendorf's own acknowledgment. Some of his real opinions, he admitted once, "I have not had sufficient courage to publish, and they have been reduced to commonplaces." [82]

But the influence of the man upon the work went beyond the proscription of what he did not write: it infiltrated what he did write. From his Jena days on he recognized that the path of progress lay in the application of the new science to law and morals, and his intellectual tendency was always toward organizing all branches of these fields into a deductive, rational, unitary system which would simply satisfy the thirst of the mind for "principles . . . from which men could deduce everything" and "divisions to which men could refer everything." [83] But cutting across this tendency was a sense for the practical which had been nurtured by worldly experience. Because of this sense Pufendorf was ever mindful of the worldly aspects of intellectual concerns. He claimed that, in universities as in wars, "what comes first is money, what comes second is money, and what comes third is money," since "where one's subsistence is not properly provided for, one loses all desire to do anything." [84] But more than money was needed for the prosecution of intellectual activity. Pufendorf insisted that he would have been utterly

[34]

"destroyed" by his academic enemies if he had not acquired "faithful patrons" in high positions.

Money and patronage were thus for Pufendorf not only worldly goods in themselves but external conditions of intellectual production, and so it was that his production followed his profession. Moreover, external conditions did more than determine the form of his scholarly production; they were incorporated in his intellectual goals, where they formed an odd amalgam with his tendency toward abstract system. Particularly in his later years he stressed the necessity of *useful* knowledge, whether to characterize the purpose of his own work as "contributing something to the common good," or to define the educational ideal as "learning . . . what can be useful in the kind of life to which one intends to devote oneself," or to prescribe as the next intellectual task, once the idea of justice had been dispatched, the logical presentation of "those moral precepts which serve to enable one to pass in the world as a clever, prudent, and civilized man." [85] And even these he would have organized into a "science" in which "everything could be referred to its place" under "one intellectual intuition [*intuitu*]." [86]

Pufendorf's increasing absorption of a practical motif into his original tendency toward system endowed his intellectual career with a rare mixture of disjunction and continuity. Although his shifts from his initial dedication to the philosophy of law into the fields of constitutional jurisprudence, history, and lay theology were indeed touched off by the caprice of professional and political circumstance, the incorporation of circumstance into his philosophy meant in each case the expansion of his system by that dimension until what seemed arbitrary from an external view took on the character of a logical development internally. Because of Pufendorf's philosophical respect for facts and his capacity to make them

[35]

constituents of reason, his intellectual career exhibits a general coherence in which the categorical changes of his external career become the dynamic element in his thought, driving it continuously to the articulation of its implications.

The early Pufendorf made a radical distinction between "the disciplines which are subjects of reason" on the one hand and "true religion" and "political affairs" on the other; the rational disciplines were the arena for intellectuals, for they could make their name only by "innovating," while in positive religion and politics "nothing is to be innovated"—indeed, innovation is "a crime" (1674).[87] It was to "morality" and "the science of law and equity" as such rational disciplines that Pufendorf at this stage professed to devote himself, to the explicit exclusion of religion and politics as extra-rational fields.[88] But the changes in his professional fortunes which pushed him into closer connections with government and the concentration of the attacks against him upon the religious implications of his ethics combined to draw his attention increasingly to these alien areas of ultimate, reason-resistant fact. With this attention their status in his thinking changed and they became more and more relevant to his rational approach. Inexorably he moved his doctrine toward them.

The first step was to advance the line between reason and ultimate fact from between morality on the one side and politics and religion on the other to a position within politics and within religion, and this he did in his writings on constitutional law and the relations of Christian church and state, respectively.[89] But with Louis XIV's combined Protestant persecution and threat to the sovereign state system and with William and Mary's revolutionary defense of law and Protestantism (in Pufendorf's conception of the Glorious

Revolution), this advance seemed insufficient. In private his animus against Louis was such that it even evoked a dormant patriotism to spur the direct judgments he now made upon governmental policies, and at the same time he found himself drawn more and more into religious discussions until he finally confessed his heartfelt desire to "do something for the good of the Church and scholarship." [90] The shift in the intellectual cosmos which this direction of his later interests betokened emerged in his prescription that the "fact" of the Glorious Revolution could unleash a "great revolution in Europe" if it draws "principles" from those "who will defend it with the pen." [91] This willingness now to confront the facts of politics and religion directly with principles furnished the context for the last stage in Pufendorf's development: as political historian and as lay theologian he now sought to organize the realms of governmental action and positive religion with the categories of rational scholarship.

In the course of this development Pufendorf moved from the simple to the sophisticated mode of compromise. His problem was to validate a doctrine that was essentially universal, egalitarian, and anti-authoritarian in a real world that was primarily traditional, hierarchical, and monarchical and that, moreover, he had no intention of reforming. His first response—and this remained preponderant when his life as a whole is viewed from the outside—was to posit a division of function between the internal and external dimensions of reality and to assign to rational "science" the free reordering of internal relations within the immovable factual limits of the existing social and political structure. This kind of division is the classic simple mode of compromise, wherein opposites merely coexist. But Pufendorf's later response— and this becomes preponderant when his work as a whole is viewed from the inside—was to adapt his doctrine for the

[37]

accommodation of a contrapuntal kind of existence and to reorient his view of social and political reality for the purpose of rendering it rationally acceptable.

This most challenging mode of compromise—we may call it integral compromise—provides the chief thread of continuity through Pufendorf's writings, for he had built the potentiality of it into his doctrine even before his circumstances inspired him to articulate it. He shows us how to make a doctrine porous without sacrificing its essential virtue of rational necessity and how to make contingent existence reasonable without sacrificing its cherished inviolability, so that they may fit together. Given the substantive tendencies of the two realms, this meant the creation of an early model for the conjunction of a libertarian rationale with a conservative reality. The accomplishment of this integration fills the inner track of Pufendorf's career and remains his most relevant bequest to his twentieth-century posterity.

[2]

THE PHILOSOPHER

"It seemed worth making the effort," wrote Pufendorf in explanation of his preoccupation with law and morals, "to prove that what is handed down on this matter does by no means all rest upon vacillating opinions, but flows clearly enough from fixed and first principles." "Now, the knowledge which considers what is upright and what is base in human actions, the principal portion of which we have undertaken to present, rests entirely upon grounds so secure, that from it can be deduced genuine demonstrations which are capable of producing a solid science. *So certainly can its conclusions be derived from distinct principles, that no further ground is left for doubt."* [1]

The passion for certainty was the central inspiration of Pufendorf's whole corpus of writing. Through it he associated himself with the larger philosophical enterprise of his century, and since he saw his role rather in extending this enterprise than in creating his own total version of it, his starting point rested on the philosophical achievements of his age and is inexplicable without them. He was conversant with and drew upon such standard predecessors and contemporaries as Gassendi, Hobbes, Pascal, Spinoza, and, above all, Bacon and Descartes. But, as the combination of the latter

[39]

two influences would indicate, he belonged to no school; he explicitly dissociated himself from the "Cartesians," to whom, through his mentor, Weigel, he was closest.[2] His debt, then, to the century's pacesetters in the field of philosophy was not the adoption of a whole system but, over and above some discrete appropriations of specific concepts and arguments, the general orientation toward the function of philosophy which was by and large common to them.

I. Philosophy in the Seventeenth Century

Whatever their achievement may be considered to have been in the history of philosophy, from the point of view of intellectual history the uniform tendency of the seventeenth-century philosophers was the reconstruction of a cosmic order. Behind the keynote of "certainty" lay the widespread intellectual experience of revulsion against the traditional schools because of the confusion and the uncertainty which their divisions and conflicts had brought to primary principles and the equally widespread response of reprobating the traditional approaches and beginning anew with the simplest constituents of reality. We see it most clearly perhaps in the famous confession of Descartes that since in philosophy "no single thing is to be found . . . which is not the subject of dispute, and in consequence which is not dubious, . . . as regards all the opinions which up to this time I had embraced I thought I could not do better than endeavor once and for all to sweep them completely away, so that they might later on be replaced, either by others which were better, or by the same, when I had made them conform to the uniformity of a rational scheme."[3] Nor was Descartes an isolated example. The same drive had exposed Bacon's "idols" and was to be apparent in Hobbes's prescription that wisdom is acquired neither by the "reading of books" nor by the "reading . . .

of men," but only by following the injunction to "read thy self" and beginning with the consideration of thoughts "singly"—that is, with "sense." [4] Spinoza too "marked the fierce controversies of philosophers raging in Church and State, the source of bitter hatred and dissension," and therefore "determined to examine the Bible afresh in a careful, impartial, and unfettered spirit, making no assumptions concerning it." He set himself as his end the search for "some real good . . . which would affect the mind singly, to the exclusion of all else." [5]

For the protagonists of the seventeenth century's new wave the old systems had been strained to the breaking point by new facts, new ideas, and new beliefs and had forfeited their essential function of providing the human experience with the unity that gave it meaning. This unity the new philosophers were confident they could restore, first by beginning their chain of reasoning with the simplest and most indisputable perceptions—whether in the form of Bacon's "primary philosophy," Descartes' "clear and distinct ideas," Hobbes's "Sense," Spinoza's "true idea" of "Substance," or Leibniz' indivisible "monad"—and then by extending the area of truth through the employment of the method of mathematical science as a model for deducing propositions in a series of necessary demonstrations until "all those things which fall under the cognizance of man" would be "mutually related in the same fashion" as the "evident and certain" productions of the mathematicians.[6] The carry-over of the geometrical method to philosophy was enormously attractive; writer after writer espoused it because it seemed to ban "probable opinion," which they identified with disputation, and promised to cover all fields of knowledge with the growing consensus to be found in mathematics.

But there was another, more substantive kind of unity which the philosophers now demanded and to which their

[41]

new approach was an appropriate response. They rejected the age-old organization of reality into a hierarchy of being—a hierarchy which had been distorted beyond recovery by the multiplication of the essential concepts at the top and the proliferation of phenomenal knowledge in its lower echelons —and sought a new metaphysical conjunction of all reality. Here lay one of the main bases for the widespread abhorrence of scholasticism, an abhorrence which Pufendorf fully and explicitly reiterated. In part, to be sure, the hatred was aesthetic, a persistence of the humanist contempt for a graceless and repetitive jargon. In part it was practical, a disgust with the address of scholastic concepts and methods to the purposes of polemics. And in part it was intellectual, an impatience with the scholastics' quest for truth in terms of classifying particulars into known categories instead of continuously expanding the horizons of knowledge.

But above all, the rejection of traditional scholasticism by the seventeenth-century philosophers was epistemological and metaphysical, a dissatisfaction with its arbitrary bases of truth and with the complexities of the reality to which it attested. Against scholasticism as they understood it, the philosophers were convinced that both the knowing faculties and the knowable realities were universal and uniform, yielding coherent knowledge to all men equally from any part of nature. They held that certain truth derives from the dovetailing of intuition into particulars with deduction from universals, that essence and existence are parallel if not identical orders in nature as in God, that Being is distributed evenly throughout nature, and that it is knowable through the intellectual resources of the human mind as the only sure intermediary between God and nature.[7] The denial of such intermediary channels to knowledge as Intelligences, forms, and qualities and the resulting emphasis upon immediate apprehension as the highest kind of knowledge help to ex-

[42]

plain the prevalent indifference during the seventeenth century to the relationship between induction and deduction or
between empiricism and rationalism that was later read into
the age as a cardinal problem. Certainly for men like Descartes, Spinoza, Hobbes, and Newton the proportions of
sensory or experimental perception and of rational ideas in
the construction of knowledge differed, but what mattered
was not what divided but what united them: the belief in a
world so fashioned and minds so oriented that from their
interaction an integrated body of truths could be certainly
demonstrated. Descartes' casual ambiguity in applying the
term "experience" to both inductive and intuitive sources of
knowledge was a striking case of the common assumption that
the diversity of natural objects was a translucent veil over
their essential unity.[8]

But if the philosophers were dominated by the quest for a
new approach that would be attested by the common experience and common faculties of men in this world,[9] this revolution in point of view was qualified by the conservative
philosophical end to which they directed it. Their aim, to
reverse the familiar dictum of Marx, was not to change the
world but to reinterpret it. This characteristic of seventeenth-
century thought refers not only to its orientation toward
practice but also to its philosophical comprehension of the
main components and structure of traditional speculation.
The most literal and telling expression of this general attitude is that of the mature Descartes, for even after he had
elaborated his own metaphysics he confessed his decision "to
obey the laws and customs of my country, adhering constantly
to the religion in which by God's grace I had been instructed
since my childhood, and in all other things directing my
conduct by opinions the most moderate in nature, . . . and
to alter my desires rather than change the order of the
world." His enterprise, he wrote, was like that of people who

[43]

"cause their own houses to be knocked down in order to rebuild them, . . . when their foundations are not secure." [10] Proud as he was of his new physical foundations, he yet admitted that for the metaphysics of God and the soul "the greater part of the reasons that have been brought forward . . . by so many great men are, when they are rightly understood, equal to so many demonstrations" and characterized his own doctrine on these entities as aiming "to seek with care for the best of these reasons, and to set them forth in so clear and exact a manner, that it will henceforth be evident to everybody that they are veritable demonstrations." [11] Leibniz conceived his whole philosophical mission in terms of reconciling the new scientific approach with the traditional systems of logic and metaphysics, and even Spinoza, radical as his execution was, thought that he was but amending precedent philosophy and theology.[12]

For these philosophers the point of departure was new—the world instead of God—but the goal was as rigorous and comprehensive a system of accountability—short of final purpose—as their forebears had ever aimed at. Propositions deduced from axioms or "common notions"; things, souls, and attributes expressive of "essences" and grounded in the common matrix of "substance"; materiality and ideality joined by God: such components made up the shared cosmos of the philosophical tradition and its seventeenth-century critics. Despite the prominence of the analytic method in the latter, their characteristic approach combined analytic with synthetic procedures, the former to reduce the complexity of observed phenomena to simple constituents and the latter to deduce, from the constituents and their necessary relations, consequences that ultimately comprehended the totality of knowable reality in a single integrated system of truths. Much of what had been dismantled in the demolition reappeared in the reconstruction, not only for external reasons of philosophical respectability but because in view of the seventeenth-century purpose they continued to be internally needed. The seventeenth-century purpose was the re-establishment of a general order of things by creating a new consensus; to accomplish this the men of that era had to account for all the manifold reality that past orders had accounted for, but now by using as a base the putatively undeniable common experience of that reality itself; to accomplish this, in turn, they could build on such a base only by using all the unifying transcendent categories they found at hand, and indeed, in compensation for the original sub-stantive unity that they denied, by using them in an even more stringent way than heretofore. Inclusiveness and rigor, then, were correlatives in their philosophical enterprises; they sought to tighten the relations among things as they were.

A notable illustration was their treatment of the familiar Aristotelian metaphysical analysis of reality into "substance" and "accidents." For the scholastics, these terms represented the two fundamental categories into which reality was di-vided, and, whatever the relations between them, each re-tained an autonomous status, since they were united only in the higher Being which created both. The seventeenth-century metaphysicians retained "substance" but dropped "accidents" in favor of the term "modes," signifying thereby a crucial alteration in the relationship of the two categories. For by "modes" they meant the modifications or diversifica-tions of substance which are the variable ways for men to perceive substance in the realm of existence.[13] The modes thus become a recognition of natural diversity which enters into a tight logical dependence upon the unifying concept of substance as the part to the whole or as effect to cause.[14] Substance, in turn, moves from its former status as the unifying reality *in* nature to the unifying reality *of* nature.

This shift was registered most categorically in Spinoza, who replaced the traditional plurality of natural substances devolved from the unity of God with a single extended and thinking substance, at once natural and divine, but it was effective also in Descartes' notion of substance as a necessary inference from the experienced attributes of things and in the formal equivalence of Leibniz' substantial monads.[15] With these provisions the logical self-sufficiency of "substance" was achieved; the philosophers had naturalized the system of the Schools.

But even speculation on this level did not fully satisfy the requirements for the restoration of philosophical order. The seventeenth-century metaphysicians were driven beyond the coherence of nature to appropriate to themselves the unity traditionally dispensed by the Being of God. And once more their impulsion came not only from tactical considerations, from their bondage to the philosophical language of tradition, and from the incursions of their own religious faith, but also from the demands of their own systems. Their intellectual need of divinity reflected a tension between their starting point in heterogeneous nature and their goal of a fully integrated order that no natural unity, however fortified, could resolve. They could clarify the metaphysical connection of natural variations to substance but they could not go beyond the maintenance of plural substances, and so they called upon the idea of God to relate their substances. For Descartes He mediated between the intellectual and the extended substances; for Leibniz He governed the relations among the monads. Only Spinoza asserted the singularity of substance, but he did it by identifying substance with God to denote its transcendence—that is, its generality.[16]

Thus the philosophers of the seventeenth century recurred to a whole panoply of traditional integrative devices and categories to provide their world view with an immanent coherence. What made them usable was the conviction that they had been neutralized. The neutralization was thought to follow from the substitution of immediately intuited ideas and mathematically grounded axioms for the disputed authority of Aristotle and the theological Schools as the source of first principles, and from the substitution of an operative or mechanical for a purposive or final structure of knowable reality. But with the shift away from the arena of an objectively anchored transcendent reality in which the integrative devices and categories had been traditionally employed, the new philosophers met a formidable difficulty: they were continuing to seek a unified truth after they had amputated that ultimate level of reality in which it had been objectified. They overcame this difficulty and could retain the old categories in the new setting by altering the status of the unifying concepts from an objective to a functional validity, an alteration attested by their emphasis upon coherence over correspondence as the criterion of truth.[17] Syllogisms, essences, substances, and God were affirmed not as such but in the manner and degree of their contribution to certain—that is, coherent—knowledge.

To establish such functions within a system of nature the philosophers had to pay a price. In order to deny, as they did, the traditional primary assumption of a distinction between the One and the Many and to seek instead, as they did, the derivation of the One from the common experience of the Many, they had to relocate within the Many the distinction which they had originally denied. They could, in other words, utilize the testimony of nature only by selecting, within each of its phenomena, the dimension that was indisputably common to all and separating it out from the variable dimension within each phenomenon. Since, for them, only the certainly knowable was real and since they aimed at "a knowledge that takes in all things," [18] all natural phenomena were sliced into a real dimension that yielded necessary—that is, demonstrable—truths and a shadowy dimension that was not susceptible to this kind of knowledge. The former dimension consisted in the quantifiable factors —for example, extension, duration, order, number, motion —and the latter in the total impressions of phenomena in our perceptions—for example, heat, color, taste, sounds, sense. This is the familiar distinction between what Locke was to call primary and secondary qualities, and its role in the ultimate breakdown of rational metaphysics is well known. But for our purpose its importance lies rather in its contemporary effects. It led to the separation of what Hobbes called "Knowledge of Fact" from philosophy, which was essentially a knowledge of relations.[19] It led to an intensified pressure for synthetic methods and ideas to bridge the chasm cut by the original analytic: this was the pressure that created the monisms of Spinoza and Leibniz and the crisis of Pascal, for whom *l'esprit fin* and *l'esprit géométrique* must ever remain distinct. But it also led to the more representative crisis of ethics.

For the separation of the general from the individual, of law from purpose, however tolerable in physics and metaphysics, met its greatest challenge in ethics. Descartes came to ethics only in his last published work (*The Passions of the Soul*) and frankly saw it as "presupposing a complete knowledge of the other sciences," since it was a part of "philosophy . . . that we cannot learn until the end."[20] Hobbes admitted that "Moral Philosophy," as the "science of what is Good and Evil" has to do with "Appetites and Aversions, which in different tempers, customs, and doctrines of men are different . . . : From whence arise Disputes, Controversies, and at last War . . ." and he sought to convert it into the "true Moral Philosophy"—that is, the "true Doctrine of the Laws of Nature" from which general rules of peace could be deduced.[21] Spinoza approached ethics only in the third and concluding section of his work so entitled, after he had "laid a foundation" in metaphysics and psychology, and he found himself confronted with the problem of reconciling his admission that "the terms good and bad . . . indicate no positive quality in things regarded in themselves but are merely modes of thinking" which can render "one and the same thing . . . at the same time good, bad, and indifferent" with his "attempt to treat of human vice and folly geometrically," on the ground that "there should be one and the same method of understanding the nature of all things whatsoever, namely, through nature's universal laws and rules." [22] But despite their awareness of the problem, the ethics of the great metaphysicians remained, for their contemporaries and disciples, the weakest part of their systems, largely because of their persistent prosecution of a metaphysics not designed for it: Descartes deliberately rested his ethics on the mind-body union that was the most doubtful doctrine of his philosophy, while the mechanism of natural knowledge so determined morality in Hobbes, Spinoza, and—later—in Leibniz, as to render it quite unacceptable in their versions.

As a loyal son of his age, Pufendorf was both governed by its reigning conceptions and attracted to the repair of its deficiencies. The passion for certainty, the segregation of the natural arena as the forum for consensus, the methodological distinction between demonstrative and factual knowledge, the ultimate drive toward unity—all these qualities he shared, and to them he brought a crystallized recognition of their inadequate accountability for the variety of existing things in the field of morality, where the diversity of existence is most obtrusive.[23] "I waged hand-to-hand combat with Hobbes," he wrote, "while Descartes did not treat moral philosophy." [24] He had, to be sure, an original practical bent that led him to the concentration upon the applications of

[49]

morality in jurisprudence and history, but initially he considered himself a philosopher and he remained one sufficiently for the philosophical concepts of his era both to weave a main thread of continuity across the vagaries of his many-faceted writing and to receive themselves a further development from it.[25] Since this development was in the direction of accounting for precisely that multiform dimension of existence that his betters had found so difficult and that it took a Leibniz, a Hume, and a Kant to break into, the attempt would be hardly worth the recording did it not reveal an essential feature about the dissemination of ideas.

For Pufendorf possessed, as a secondary thinker, a great comparative advantage over his mentors. He was an occasional philosopher—that is, he worked up philosophical analyses only on those occasions in which his more mundane concerns required footing—and the scope of the analysis was defined by the occasion which it served. His occasional philosophy sufficed to keep the intellectual faith of his age continuously relevant, albeit at the cost of its logical integration. What had been rigorous system became with him a plastic set of assumptions, which were thereby rendered separable and susceptible to autonomous development subject to the more flexible limits of psychological rather than logical coherence. In this loosened form Pufendorf could apply seventeenth-century philosophy to the kaleidoscope of law and politics. By referring this kaleidoscope to a logic, a metaphysics, and a formal ethics as its ground, he endowed it with an apparent unity. By casting his logic, metaphysics, and formal ethics in the form of prefatory assertions and occasional arguments rather than a rigorously articulated system, he used them to cover notions that were only juxtaposed or externally related. He was thereby enabled to validate as fundamental truths divergent positive existences which jointly could not have composed a purely rational construction. In all its branches, then, Pufendorf's philosophy, in structure as in content, was designed to expound the varieties of reason that could account for a variegated existence.

II. Pufendorf's Method

With Pufendorf's logic, the owl of Minerva took flight in the morning. His one clear statement of it prefaced the early work that he himself later dismissed as "immature," but he never bothered to amend it, save by implication. The omission was not from sheer neglect. With the exception of Leibniz, his whole century tended to avoid the field, preferring instead the looser procedures of "method" to signify the expansion of the traditional logic by the dimension of the new metaphysics. The strain which his contemporaries placed upon the accepted logical canons was exacerbated in Pufendorf by his concern with the manifold of human society, and as his respect for this manifold grew during the course of his life the relevance of any formal logical position was correspondingly diminished. The seeds of its later disuse by him are visible in the early scheme, for even this one definite formulation contains the odd assortment of parts within an apparent whole which was Pufendorf's general way of making the best of two possible worlds.

Ostensibly Pufendorf took his logic, which he called simply "the art of reasoning appropriately and certainly," from "the new way of philosophizing" which he explicitly associated with Descartes and which consisted in "deducing everything from fixed principles and hypotheses through the mathematical mode of demonstration." [26] He applied this general description to his later as to his earlier work, although the explication of the mathematical logic and the radical execution of the geometric style characterized only the first major work, when the Cartesian influence upon him was strongest.

[51]

But even here the Pufendorfian amendments were in evidence. Unlike the substantive arrangement of his later writing Pufendorf organized his *Elements of Universal Jurisprudence* overtly on a scheme of mathematical logic, and this he carefully explained. He started, he wrote, with definitions, that is, with the identification of the subject matter through metaphysical classification (literally, through "primary philosophy"). From the definitions there followed what he called "the principles," from which "necessarily true declarations" about this subject matter "may be deduced." When applied to the discipline of law, these principles may be of three kinds: "common axioms" derived from metaphysics ("primary philosophy"); "rational" principles, or "axioms," whose truth, certainty, and necessity flow "from reason itself, . . . merely from the bare intuition of the mind"; and "experimental" principles, or "observations," whose truth, certainty, and necessity are "perceived from the comparison and perception of individual details uniformly corresponding to one another." The final regular step consists in the deduction of "propositions" from these principles, but it may be followed, "if it appear necessary," by an irregular fourth part "into which may be gathered those topics in which certainty does not clearly appear." [27] The *Elements* were correspondingly divided into two Books, the first on definitions and the second on rational and experimental principles—that is, axioms and observations. Each kind of principle was, in turn, equipped with its derivative propositions.

Now neither in its general format nor in its particular constituents does this logical process exhibit anything new or remarkable, but still the way in which the parts were placed together to form the ostensible process was revealing and characteristic, for it showed Pufendorf's predisposition, even in his most doctrinaire phase, toward the additive approach.

This was particularly striking in his equivalence of rational axioms with experimental observations as first principles, since he explicitly associated the former with Cartesian intuition and the latter with "common feeling and experience," a combination eschewed by the more rigorous philosophers of the seventeenth century.[28] Pufendorf, in fact, seems to have added Hobbes and Aristotle to Descartes in order to include as much of reality as he could under the order of reason. Where Descartes minimized the value of definitions, of syllogisms, and of sense perception, Pufendorf incorporated all three.[29] Where Hobbes ignored the metaphysical grounding of definitions and the intuitive source of rational truth in favor of linguistic consensus and a sensation-calculating reason, Pufendorf admitted all four.[30] And despite his explicit contempt for the Aristotelians because of ' their tortured Latin, their interminable polemics, and the fallibility of their demonstrations, Pufendorf's estimate of Aristotle himself was much more positive, as his copious citations attest, and his latitudinarian comprehension of definitions, intuition, induction, and deduction as equivalent paths of reason approached no contemporary as much as it did the Philosopher. But again, where Aristotle had denied demonstrable certainty to ethics and argued its autonomy as a field of probabilities, Pufendorf insisted that it was both demonstrable and autonomous.

In his mature work the structure of Pufendorf's logic was less explicit and less intrusive. In *On the Law of Nature* and the pieces which he wrote 'for its defense, Pufendorf continued to support logic as a fruitful discipline, retained his goal of propounding morals and law as a single demonstrable "science" wired by mathematical logic, and again prefaced his discussion with a brief sketch of this logic. But now the explicit logic remained a prolegomenon and no longer determined the organization of the material, a function that the substantive concepts and propositions of the argument now assumed. The earlier articulation of the 'logical process, moreover, now gave way to the more generic and casual simplification in which the logic of moral as of other science was depicted as a continuous series of true, axiomatic propositions, with "axioms" loosely defined to include both those propositions that "merit belief upon their own evidence" and those that are reducible to such.[31]

Now this formulation was misleading in itself, for Pufendorf's execution showed that he meant by "axioms" not only the kind of statements usually so categorized but also the kinds of statements that he had himself previously designated as definition, proposition, and observation, but the inconsistency becomes comprehensible and revealing in the context of Pufendorf's intellectual development. In the first flush of youth he had confidently expected no difficulties in placing law among "the sciences which are called demonstrative." Indeed, he had even felt that the application of the geometric method to law would be easier than in the natural sciences, since "it has come about, not without the special providence of the Creator, that the certainty of theoretical verities would have to be extracted from first principles for the most part laboriously, and, as it were, through a prolonged series of consequences; but the certainty of practical matters rests very easily upon an extremely small number of principles, and those most perspicuous, from which, for the most part, these practical matters can be deduced by a simple operation." [32] At this early stage, consequently, he had concentrated upon the classification of the first principles from which the deductions could be so simply made. In his riper phase, however, he found himself compelled to acknowledge complexities in the application of demonstrable logic to morals and law. While still asserting this applicability as strongly as ever, Pufendorf now found himself driven to make distinctions in the defensive effort to explain away its difficulty. He admitted that "moral entities . . . are not in an absolute sense necessary" and that "a degree of latitude" is to be found in moral and legal matters in contrast to the exactitude of mathematics. He could still maintain that "scientific knowledge about them" is not "utterly uncertain" only by excluding from morals all considerations that were not subject to measurement by law—including the whole realm of "facts"—and by distinguishing between "moral qualities" which were demonstrable and "moral quantities" which were not.[33] With this more critical attitude Pufendorf could no longer afford the luxury of open diversity in his first principles and consequently subsumed them in a generic description of the deductive process. He retained the primary level of definitions, which anchored the doctrine in the unified matrix of metaphysics, but he elided his former categorical distinction between rational and experimental principles.

Behind this changed orientation lay not merely the caution of age and a growing empiricism but a development in Pufendorf's purpose which made the shift of his logic a function of the different material which it was to organize. The two formulations are to be seen not as competitive but as successive; they represent different phases in Pufendorf's effort to extend the scope of indisputable reason to the varied phenomena of human reality, which had hitherto been the kind of reality most resistant to rationalization. From the beginning Pufendorf had declared, in contradistinction to Descartes, discussions "about the difference between the synthetic and the analytic method" to be "nonsense," a position which revealed the over-all consistency behind his variously oriented attempts to join unity of structure with extensiveness of scope.[34] In actual fact, however, the first stage of his development as a philosopher of law was addressed preponderantly to the analytic and the second stage to the synthetic phases of the joint method. In his analytical phase Pufendorf devoted himself primarily to the establishment of first principles as the basic constituents—like Descartes' simple natures—into which the welter of human actions was resolved, for at this stage his primary need was for a logical peg on which to hang the postulation of natural man and natural law as the simple, ultimate, and indisputable bases of political institutions. The procedure that was thus implicit in his *Elements* Pufendorf frankly described on another occasion as explicitly analogous to the analytical procedure of the natural scientist: just as the natural scientist goes behind the external appearance of entities, as they are presented in sensations, to "resolve them into their component parts" and reduce them ultimately to a "primal matter," so the moral scientist goes behind "the external variety" of political facts to resolve them into the component parts of the state and ultimately to the "conception of the condition and status of man beyond all society, arts, and institutions." [35]

But the analytical reduction was only part of the process, for from this beginning the scientist must then go on logically to develop the foundation, the power, the conventions, and the "peculiar conditions" of civil societies. This latter operation obviously called for the synthetic method, whereby visible effects were explained by deduction from the first principles considered as their causes, and it was precisely to this that Pufendorf turned in his later development as a legal thinker after his intervening attention to the German political and juristic scene had convinced him of the current gap between the enunciation of principles and the comprehension of political and legal reality. In his *On the Law of Nature*, consequently, the analysis was performed quickly, the exposition of natural man and natural law was achieved at the beginning, and the bulk of the work consisted in the explanation of particular doctrines, laws, institutions, and practices as deductions from them. Since synthesis was entirely a deductive process, Pufendorf could now emphasize a simple formulation of his method in terms of it.

There was nothing new for the seventeenth century, of course, in the combination of the analytic and synthetic methods. Even Descartes, who in general decried the latter in favor of the former, had to make his obeisance to both in conformity with the reigning temper of the age.[36] What was distinctive in Pufendorf was not simply his application of the combination to the field of morals and law—for that had already been tried—but his retention of its claims to an integrated logicality at the same time as he acknowledged the infinite variety of the objects in this field of its application. In the same field Grotius had ultimately surrendered logical coherence to the variety of his material, while Hobbes, on the other extreme, had used his logic as a Procrustean bed for the exclusion of incoordinate phenomena. Pufendorf would save both the inclusiveness of the one and the uniformity of the other.

To accomplish this feat, he conceived of moral and physical objects as formally analogous and substantively different. Hence the logic which furnished demonstrable certainty to the mathematical knowledge of nature was not distinctive to mathematics but furnished equally demonstrable certainty to the moral knowledge of man as well; at the same time, however, the incidence of this logic upon the substance of the two fields diverged significantly. By virtue of the inherent character of moral and natural entities, "moral *qualities*" (for instance, whether a given action be just or unjust) are the logical equivalents of "physical *quantities*," for in both cases the objects are commensurable (that is, measurable by a common law or rule) and consequently capable of necessary determination. "Moral quantities," on the other hand (that is, the greater or lesser degree of attributed esteem, virtue,

justice, or guilt), differ essentially from their physical coun-
terparts in being indivisible, incommensurable, arbitrary,
and "careless"—precisely unknowable in the Pufendorfian
sense of knowledge because they cannot be incorporated in a
relationship of logical necessity.[37] Thus for Pufendorf moral
and physical objects overlapped, but in such a way as to bring
their respective component parts into converse relations to
each other. This relationship implied a linear logic and a
dialectical metaphysics, a syndrome symptomatic of the tension between his drive toward rationality and his respect for
the vagaries of human existence.

Pufendorf chose moral qualities, which were not quantitatively abstractable, as his deductively certain ethical truths
because he recognized the circumstantial character of human
behavior, and he had to concoct special devices to make this
combination of certainty and circumstantiality viable. The
empirical motif which he had introduced into his early
analytic still informed his later axioms, but now as an uninte-
grated co-ordinate with deductive reason—"the dictates of
sound reason are true principles that are in accordance with
the properly observed and examined nature of things, and are
deduced by logical sequence from prime and true principles."[38] He labored under the corresponding necessity to
introduce the empirical motif into every stage of his deductive synthetic, but within the limits required to safeguard its
demonstrable character. Hence he adopted devices of both
inclusion and exclusion.

Pufendorf's inclusive devices were designed to rationalize
the broadest possible scope of existing moral and legal relations. Of these devices, four seem fundamental to the way
he thought.

First, Pufendorf habitually executed his deductive method
by dividing his propositions into two subpropositions of
equal validity, one categorical and the other comprehensive

and experiential. The function of the former was to lend conceptual rigor to its more empirical sibling, and, furnished with this rigor, the latter then became the principle from which further deductions covering ever wider sections of experience were made. According to a formal outline of *On the Law of Nature*, Pufendorf deduced two main parts from the discipline of natural law—its "plan [*architectonica*]," which asserted the moral foundation and fundamental principle of the natural law, and its "structure [*rectoria*]," which treated of its substantive "rules or principles." The remainder of the work consisted in deductions from this "code," organized in analogous fashion: the division of the natural-law code into absolute principles, asserting the universal duties of men, and hypothetical principles, applying the rules of natural law to the particular "conditions [*status*]" of men; from the latter, in turn, Pufendorf derived the balance of the work—the justiciable propositions pertaining to the natural, domestic, and civil circumstances of men.[39]

Pufendorf's second inclusive device was a kind of microcosm of his first: under each heading he divided and subdivided until he could claim to comprehend a large variety of legal circumstances under the rule of principle. Under the heading of hypothetical obligations, for example, he distinguished between congenital and adventitious hypothetical obligations: under the former he allowed, in turn, for obligations that were natural and civil, perpetual and temporary, non-mutual and mutual, perfectly and imperfectly mutual; under adventitious hypothetical obligations (that is, owing through promises or pacts) Pufendorf admitted both perfect (justiciable) and imperfect (non-justiciable) promises, express and tacit pacts, general and partial pacts, and he distinguished admissible from inadmissible error and fear in the obligation of pacts.[40]

Pufendorf's third inclusive device, and perhaps the most

revealing of all, was his bold and surprising reversal of method *in medias res*. The first part of his treatise was dominated by the deductive method in the direct logical form of demonstrating the implications of his axiomatic propositions, but when he had arrived at the level of specificity indicated by the "hypothetical" application of natural law to particular human conditions he reversed his approach and undertook to "examine . . . institutions" in order to "observe . . . what precepts of natural law, which we termed before hypothetical, *proceed from* them." [41] For Pufendorf, then, deduction in the sense of syllogistic subsumption under axioms gave way, at the level of concrete application, to deduction in the sense of necessary inference from particulars, however doubtful a logic this may have been. The axioms and their implications may be seen, in this procedure, as a kind of funnel, providing a mold of rational unity into which a congeries of existent legal relations was poured, ultimately to emerge as a connected set of concrete norms. Pufendorf felt unable to proceed directly from axioms to particulars, but the criteria which he used to establish the empirical consensus drawn from the testimony of custom, Roman law, and classical and modern commentators were indeed those axioms and their implications, with the consequence that this testimony converged into norms necessarily compatible with the pre-established axioms. Thus in his discussion of polygamy Pufendorf begins with the question whether the institution is or is not permitted by the law of nature; proceeds, not by direct deduction from the laws of nature, but by the examination of sundry polygamous practices and judgments upon them; and concludes, by using the natural law's prescription of social peace as his criterion, that prohibition of plurality of husbands is necessarily part of the natural law while the status of plurality of wives is inconclusive under the natural law. [42] The Pufendorfian method, exhibited in this instance, of building a logical structure toward the comprehension of actuality until the point of categorical choice within it, and then moving himself outside that structure to build an inclusive order of that actuality back up into the logical structure, is crucial, for ultimately it furnishes the pattern for his intellectual development in general.

A fourth and final device which revealed Pufendorf's concern with recognizing, relating, and rationalizing positive laws and institutions rather than discriminating among them consisted in his validation of a broad, flexible, "undefined" sphere within the natural law, into which a large variety of positive practices could be projected and by which they could be justified.[43] Thus Pufendorf was emphatic in declaring that the legal area of "permission," which he admitted as "a medium between what is enjoined and what is forbidden," was no "intermediate field" but rather belonged within the sphere of demonstrable natural law and was included in the certainty of its knowledge.[44] With the concept of "equity," similarly, Pufendorf asserted both the "latitude" which it permitted in the "gentler" bondage which it imposed upon men and the necessity which it retained as a part of law (*juris*).[45] Pufendorf's provision for such open concepts as well as for the large role of "adventitious" obligations (that is, contingent upon a previous act, such as a pact) within the demonstrable system of natural law furnished one of the seams joining his axioms to the empirical content of customs, laws, and commentaries. This device permitted the inferences from the latter to take the form of deduced propositions. Only so could he save the integrity of his system from the intellectual chaos of Hobbes's absorption of the natural into the civil law.[46]

So much for Pufendorf's inclusive devices. To guarantee the rationality and putative universality of his system he accompanied these devices with a set of exclusive devices which banned utterly refractory phenomena from this universe of discourse. For an intellectual temperament like Pufendorf's, which inclined toward the both-and or at most toward the weak either-or, such exclusion was not easy, and we find that the two devices which he employed toward the discrimination of what would later be called the non-logical from the logical were somewhat blunted in their operation and left tenuous connections between the two categories.

First, Pufendorf circumscribed the world of morals and law within its own particular field, rendering it independent of the newer connections with natural science as well as of the traditional association with theology.[47] The first of these segregations rested on his metaphysical distinction between the moral and physical realms, the second on his epistemological distinction between the truths of reason and of revelation.[48] But whatever other motives were involved, the importance of this procedure for his method lay in the opportunity which he thereby created for himself to seal off the sphere of legal relations from connections with a partial incidence and so with a disturbing effect upon his effort at comprehension. Thus Pufendorf strenuously rejected any approximation of the natural law, which he conceived as the law governing the actions of men, with the law governing the actions of all natural things, not only because the exact standards of physical laws would operate too selectively in the moral world but because association of men with other things would substitute extraneous criteria which divide men for the "sense of obligation" which rationally unites them.[49] The relevance of theology he repelled even more drastically, on the ground that any associated ethic would have not only sectarian reception but sectarian application.[50] He excluded thereby from natural law all activities and ideas oriented either beyond this life or in this life inwardly toward men's intentions.[51] And yet if Pufendorf liberated morality from these ties he did not isolate it. He held the methods of ethics and the sciences to be virtually the same, as we have seen, and if he held theology as such to lie beyond the pale he could not refrain from ultimate recourse to the action of God as the ground of his first principles, from the admission of "natural religion" into the law of nature as a buttress of social duty, or even from the admission into natural law of propositions drawn from the Christian revelation by "abstraction." [52] Thus the same passion for unity that led Pufendorf to delimit the field of morals for the sake of encompassing the bulk of what lay within it also directed him to look beyond that field for the secure bases upon which his 'floating principles could rest.[53]

By a second exclusive device Pufendorf dismissed the category of facts from the demonstrable science of natural law and assigned to this science only the category of relationships. He insisted that it was irrelevant "whether or not the subject of a demonstrable proposition necessarily exists," since necessary truth relates not to this subject—as distinct from the predicate—but to the "entire proposition" of which it is a part. What matters is not that the subject be "a necessarily existent entity" but rather that, if the existence of the subject is assumed, the connection of the subject with the predicate follows necessarily.[54] The existence of a thing falls outside the scope of moral as of physical science, for its truth, probabilistic or fideistic as it is, can enter into no necessarily true propositions.[55] Only relations among these hypothetical existents, logical in form through subsumption under a general law and knowable therefore by reason, can constitute such propositions, can enter into moral and legal science, and can claim not only logical but "actual" truth. Thus the process of bringing acts into existence is contingent, since it is subject to moral freedom, but, once determined, "the relation between

[63]

our acts and all the effects depending thereon, is necessary and quite natural, and therefore capable of demonstration" through its connection with "certain principles."[56]

The exclusion of particular facts as such permitted Pufendorf to make natural law and jurisprudence the forum of his ethics, since law was the real counterpart of the universal relations assumed by his logic.[57] At the same time, however, the separation of facts from their relations imparted a definite tendency to the system. For with his method Pufendorf could judge the effect of an action as it related to others but he could not judge it in itself. This meant that he could organize existence but he could not question it. Consequently, while he could criticize certain qualities of the existing institutions of his day and could try to reorient them toward conforming to a rational system, he explicitly refrained from applying his system of reason to the existence of those institutions themselves. It was not simply an *ad hoc* evasion, but an attitude consistent with his whole approach when Pufendorf excepted the two primary institutions of his time from his rational analysis. To "genuine philosophical liberty . . . divine revelation and the laws of the state are sacrosanct."[58]

Thus for Pufendorf the exclusion of facts tended to shade off into their acceptance. His equivocation here found expression in his ambiguous use of the concept "hypothetical." In its reference to the internal logic of his legal relations he simply denied that "hypotheses" applied, since in this sense it meant an imperfectly proved first principle whereas his own was "true, manifestly demonstrable, and as it were palpable."[59] But, as we have seen, he did admit of a large and crucial area covered by the "hypothetical precepts of natural law." The anomaly was only apparent, since the definition of hypothesis in this context—the presupposition of "some state or institution formed or accepted by men"—reveals its reference to a different forum: not to Pufendorf's system itself but to the interaction between the system and the fundamental facts of social existence. Once more, then, we find a tension in Pufendorf between the logic through which he tried to make universal sense of men's lives and the metaphysics in which he recognized the claims of a diversified reality to limit and to direct the application of this logic. Thus Pufendorf found it "necessary," for the fundamental precepts of natural law, "to presuppose that God exists," and he found it equally necessary to assume the existence of various state institutions whose relations were the objects of his natural-law discipline.[60] Kings, corporations, dicta of Roman law, prevailing customs, were all for him fixed points whose relationships he rationalized but whose right to existence he did not question. Religion and the state were the two unifying agencies in Pufendorf's system of natural law, and their very centrality led him eventually from the functional analysis of them within his system to the existential analysis of their source in positive religion and the established forms of the state outside his system, for on these its reality ultimately rested.

Pufendorf devised his method for application to his legal theory, but its difficulties not only contributed to his intellectual development out of that field but also adumbrated what there was of deliberate method in his subsequent positive studies.[61] Having reached, in *On the Law of Nature* and *On the Duty of Man and the Citizen,* the limits of concrete application which the synthetic facet of his deductive method could yield, and having through them established the legal indispensability of religion and the state for any kind of moral order, Pufendorf then left the confines of the law to come face to face with the facts of political and religious life which he had presumed in his rational system. His method left the way open for such a development, for he specifically joined history and theology as two "posterior" and "par-

ticular" disciplines which furnished useful factual knowledge, which could logically not furnish principles to the prior
and universal discipline of natural law, but which, by implication, might therefore be furnished principles by it.[62] Hence
when he moved into the fields of history and theology, he first
occupied, in each case, a transitional stage wherein the deductive method of his logical approach and the inductive method
of his existential approach seemed to dovetail. In *On the Law
of Nature* he had provided for the possibility of contemporary history by stressing the need for "a knowledge of civil
affairs" to approach the open problem of the lawful status
attributable to acts of government "which are commonly said
to be done 'for reasons of state,'" and in his first historical
work, on the contemporary history of the European states, he
began explicitly with the distinction between the "true" and
"imaginary" "interest of state."[63] With respect to theology,
similarly, in *On the Law of Nature* he had legitimized action
by the state for and against religious beliefs which support
and subvert the civil order, respectively, on the assumption
that "no true doctrine disturbs the peace, and whatever does
disturb the peace is not true."[64] In the subsequent *On the
Relation of the Christian Religion to Civil Life* he elaborated this position on the basis of natural-law principles
before proceeding with the particular study of Christian
doctrine and church history to give factual support to his
assumption.

But these bridges between the two main stages of his
development should not obscure Pufendorf's fundamental
recognition that each discipline has its own methods and its
own kind of proof; he provided for connections between his
general and his particular disciplines, but he specified that
there could be no continuity between them. One could not go
from the certainty of necessary general legal precepts to "the
faith reposed in historians . . . when they testify about some

[66]

fact"; nor could one go from external actions oriented toward general relations with things and men to internal actions oriented toward individual salvation.[65] To generalize about the two successive stages of his methodology (as Pufendorf himself did not) we may say that coherence gave way to correspondence as the criterion of truth when he replaced the demonstration of legal principle with the conformity of historical fact and theological doctrine to archival and scriptural documents as the test of validity in his final works. Thus in his Swedish and Brandenburg histories his overt intention was to relate what happened without making any general judgments, and he preferred to write on the history of foreign policy precisely because the subject matter in this field was "ephemeral and inconstant" and consequently, for him, most appropriate to the historical discipline.[66] In his *Divine Law of the Covenant,* similarly, he admitted that the concern for peace and order dictated by "right reason" must be subordinated to the saving truth of scripture, for "the rules of men cannot have precedence over the precepts of God." [67]

How shall we resolve this apparent paradox created by the manifestations of both a connection and a decisive break between the two stages of Pufendorf's method? The key to the solution lies in the reappearance, within the radically different approach of the later stage, of a systematic tendency reminiscent of the earlier. In his last work, on the history of the Prussian Elector Frederick III, an unprecedentedly long disquisition on the English revolution joined historical observation with political judgment. Even more obviously, in the *Divine Law of the Covenant,* he sought to build his scriptural exegesis into "a complete system of theology" through which the essential articles of faith could be distinguished from the inessential.[68] These tendencies reveal Pufendorf's attempt to describe existence in a way that would make the facts of this realm fit the presumptions that he had

[67]

made about them in his legal system. The system determined the relevant fields of facts to be investigated. These facts were then investigated independently, by methods "domestic" to them.[69] Finally, the results were organized into forms which made them usable in logical propositions.

Thus Pufendorf, in the course of his career, employed not one method but two, both of which cut across the familiar distinction between rationalism and empiricism. His deductive method included the observation of phenomena and his inductive method involved the rational reconstruction of unobservable facts, "for which there is no longer possible any actual testimony." [70] By virtue of his first method he conceived the dictates of reason in the light of existence; by virtue of his second method he perceived existence in the light of the requirements of reason. It is this complication in what started to be the method appropriate to a uniform science of man that lends insight into the basic pattern of Pufendorf's performance—the radical rational refounding of already established institutions.

III. THEORY OF KNOWLEDGE

Pufendorf propounded no general theory of knowledge. The different methods appropriate to morals, history, and religion required, for him, different kinds of knowledge, and he never doubted that reason, perception, and revelation could deliver, each in its own way, valid knowledge of its respective fundamental reality—laws, facts, and dogma. Since these acquisitions posed no fundamental problem for him, he needed no general epistemology to account for the knowledge of either generals or particulars.

What *was* a problem for him—indeed, the central philosophical problem of all his work—was the relationship of the particular to the general, and around this problem he did construct a delimited theory of knowledge. Since it was in the earlier stages of his intellectual career that he explicated the philosophical framework within which he was to work, he formulated this theory of knowledge in the context of the moral law which was then his chief concern. He undertook to explain our knowledge of the goodness or badness of moral actions, and in his view this question was distinct from the knowledge of good and evil in general and from the perception of an action in particular. Knowledge of the general principles of good and evil—that is, of the precepts of the natural law—is simply the product of the conjunction, established by God, of the rational faculty which inheres in every man with the order of nature; by this prearrangement, the law of nature, which is "imprinted upon us by the nature of things" through our reason, is necessarily true "since nature only puts forth what truly exists," and the logical operations of the rational faculty become identical with the "properly observed and examined nature of things [and men]." [71] For the moral universal, then, knowledge is an attribute of being, and its investigation is moved from the realm of epistemology to that of metaphysics. Not how we know but how God constituted the world so that we automatically know it was Pufendorf's problem on this level. The mere registration of existence is similarly unproblematical: truth, and the problems of truth, begin not with the perception that something exists, but only subsequently with "the congruence of the understanding [*intellectus*] with that thing." [72]

It was indeed the faculty of the understanding that was crucial for Pufendorf's theory of moral knowledge, for the kinds of knowledge derivative from the reason and from the senses, however valid, were morally ineffective without mediation between them. The knowledge of the moral law impressed by nature upon man's reason consisted certainly in the formal imperative to obey, the capacity to know its

[69]

primary principle, and the further capacity to demonstrate others from it. But what "reason alone" could know substantively of the moral law was, for Pufendorf, quite unclear. What it could not know, he was quite sure from the implications of human infancy, the hypothetical man from Mars, and the varying degrees of perspicuity which even mature men evince toward them, were the principles of the moral law in the form of "clear and distinct propositions," and he had to content himself with the probability that this original rational knowledge took the form of a "potency [*potentia*]" or an "immature disposition [*habitus imperfectus*]," for which "other experiences" were necessary before reason could apprehend it in the form of clear and distinct propositions.[73] But for these experiences, on the other hand, sensory knowledge was insufficient. Pufendorf did draw, from his metaphysical union of essence and existence, the epistemological implication that "we must always keep the existing thing before our eyes," and he affirmed the capacity of the mind, in the apprehension of "individual things," to abstract "general concepts" about "the universal and the perpetual" in these things from the mutable and the transitory. But his realm of existence included far more than these individual things. Whatever the status of the general concepts appropriate to individual things as such (Pufendorf did not expatiate on this), ideas on the relations *between* and *among* things—agreements, differences, causes, and consequences—make up a knowledge of existences which goes beyond sensory perceptions.[74] Between reason, which needs experience to make its universal concrete, and the senses, which need a generalizing agency to make their concrete data universal, Pufendorf forged no systematic chain, but the central position which he gave to the intermediate faculty of understanding makes it quite clear that his whole intellectual effort was mainly devoted precisely to connecting reason and the senses.

[70]

Through the understanding, for Pufendorf, sensory impressions are perceived and are adjudged so as to make them susceptible to the criterion of reason.[75] Thus the faculty of understanding is bipartite: on the one hand, it is the power of the "apprehension" of objects, that is, of displaying an object to the will "as if in a mirror" and of immediately perceiving its good or bad qualities; on the other hand, it is the power of judgment, that is, the examination of the relationship of the qualities of such objects to their norm—the general precepts of natural law. While Pufendorf never makes explicit the relations of the understanding either to the senses or to reason, it would seem from his usage of the term that his intent was to make the understanding the vehicle of organizing particular knowledge under the general or universal principles of reason. It is, consequently, to the second power of the understanding, whose function of adjudging moral actions—that is, objects—in the light of their conformity to general law Pufendorf calls conscience, that he devotes the bulk of his attention. Although in principle a "natural rectitude" belongs to this power of the understanding, in actuality a distinction is made between the knowledge of general precepts, which is certain, and the knowledge of particular facts, which is not. "Since true sensory perception gives only a rough idea of the real being of things and what may come from it," Pufendorf made provision for "doubtful conscience," ignorance, and error, all in reference to "particular matters."

On the side of the objects, similarly, "generic good and generic evil" are presented necessarily by the understanding to the will—the other faculty of man involved in moral actions—since the good "depends on the very nature of things," "is firm and uniform, and in no way dependent on the erroneous or changeable opinions of men." But because in particular objects "particular goods and evils . . . appear to a man . . . intermixed," on this level there "comes the

[71]

almost infinite variety in the wishes and desires of men, all seeking their own advantage, indeed, but each by a different road." Thus, for Pufendorf, the faculties of both the understanding and the will were composed of two powers, a power of apprehension and approbation that was not free and could grasp the necessary universal principles, and a power of judgment and choice that was free and that was dedicated to the examination of and choice between particulars.

The connection between these two sets of powers and these two orders of reality was contained in Pufendorf's conception of "the good," which he defined as "an aptitude whereby one thing is fitted to help, preserve, or complete another" and which he insisted was grounded in "the very nature of things." The good, therefore, for Pufendorf, consisted neither in an absolute which existed about and beyond particulars nor in "every entity actually existing," but in the general relationship among particulars. In Pufendorf's moral theory of knowledge, the true, in the sense of the general relations among things—that is, laws—is the good, knowable through reason and "in no way dependent upon the erroneous and changeable opinions of men." Therefore the fallible function of the understanding in locating the place of particulars in this lawful order becomes a moral as well as an intellectual duty. Thus it was that even after Pufendorf abandoned the field of ethics for his studies in history and theology his approach to the problem of knowledge retained a moral tinge: in each case the truth of the particulars which he sought to establish he measured on the scale of political or theological fundamentals considered as moral as well as existent truths.

It is obvious that, despite his systematic exposition of the understanding, serious flaws remained in Pufendorf's theory of knowledge, even within its moral limits. The most essential of these had to do with the *petitio principii* involved in the substance of natural laws which were not precisely knowable by reason and yet constituted the constant standard for the substantive action of the understanding. This epistemological flaw corresponded to the seam in Pufendorf's method: it was a calculated looseness in the structure of his thinking that enabled him to multiply the variety of actions supposably consonant with the moral law, to adopt the empirical approach of the impartial historian without sacrificing the claim to coherence, and to load a Lutheran content into seemingly bipartisan doctrines of theology.

IV. THE METAPHYSICS OF MORALS

"I have also," Pufendorf once admitted, "been in the [eclectic] sect." [76] Although he proceeded to argue that eclecticism in general, and implicitly his own in particular, ceased with the establishment of a science that could be "deduced demonstrably from right principles," in fact he never quite lost the eclectic tendency. His way was always to seek the both-and rather than the either-or. His metaphysics, limited in analogy with the other branches of his philosophy to a metaphysics of morals, was supposed to be a chain of necessary deductions, but its advance upon his former eclecticism consisted not so much in its choice among possibilities as in its more stringent organization of them.[77]

For the remarkable feature about Pufendorf's metaphysics of morals was the peculiar combination of doctrines which permitted sufficient identification of morality and actuality to enable morality to rationalize actuality and at the same time emphasized a sufficient dysfunction of morality and actuality to inhibit morality from changing actuality. The crucial concept which he ultimately hit upon to express this relationship was that of "mode," which connoted both a quality of substance and a condition of dependence. He deliberately

[73]

chose a term which combined both these meanings over the correlative terms "substance" and "accident," because the term "accident" connoted a relative independence. "For modes cohere inseparably to substance and can never exist by themselves, whereas accidents are in themselves true substances and can be conceived to exist independently of the Subject to which they are added." [78] As a mode, morality is distinguished from physical modes, which, unlike morals, "flow naturally from the thing itself, as it were." Moral entities, on the contrary, are "certain modes" "superadded" through the "imposition" of intelligent beings, to "things already existent and physically complete, and to their natural effects. . . . Hence the active force that lies in them does not consist in their ability directly to produce any physical motion or change in any thing . . ." but, as "concepts" which intelligent agency adds "to things and their natural motions," they produce "certain effects" through which "it is made clear to men along what line they should govern their liberty of action." Their cessation, like their commission, operates "without any accompanying change in the object to which they had been added," but, once committed, they "come into existence" through the free decision of their authors and make men "capable of directing certain actions toward other persons with a particular effect." [79] In all these respects Pufendorf seems intent on creating a realm of morality which would be independent enough of the material world to preserve the original freedom of its motions and yet conditioned enough by it to have a real existence of its own. What was characteristic here was Pufendorf's effort to have the best of both a dualistic and a monistic metaphysics, since he conceived the moral as a mode at once parallel to the physical and yet built upon it. It was characteristic too that in his unifying strand the stable physical realm conditioned the moral rather than the converse.

And yet not entirely. For if Pufendorf was to make moral reality palpable he had also to posit some kind of physical effect for it. He did indeed make such provision but briefly and embarrassedly, as if under duress. He conceded that moral entities might "furnish the occasion for augmenting or diminishing physical qualities," but otherwise he allowed for the extra-moral impact of moral modes not directly upon physical phenomena but only through "substances and their motions," which "they affect in a definite way [*certa ratione*]." [80] However loose his metaphysics here, the goal of Pufendorf's proportioning of moral autonomy and involvement is entirely clear. The purpose of moral entities "is not the perfection of this world of nature, as is the case with physical entities, but to bring order into the lives of men," for which reason "they are understood to be inherent primarily in *men*, but also in their actions, and even, to some extent, in things, as they are found in nature, acting either of herself or with the aid of human industry." [81] We have here a philosophical expression of Pufendorf's basic approach: to accept the realities of the world as he found them, to subordinate their traditional relations to a plurality of distinctions, and to reorder them along the rational lines "pleasing" to the minds of seventeenth-century men.

It might be inferred that Pufendorf's care to preserve the integrity of the physical modes in this discussion of morality's external relations was only a means of distinguishing the cultural from the natural realms of reality for the purpose of vouchsafing man full freedom within the former. But this was not Pufendorf's intention. His overriding category of "nature" comprehended both the moral and the physical modes, and consequently when he proceeded to analyze the internal relations of morality it was of a natural morality in which the conditioning of moral action by physical existence reappeared as a persistent qualification of human freedom. But

[75]

now the problem was hardly soluble by a general reference to substance as a common matrix, for physical and moral entities here refer no longer to two different kinds of reality but rather to two different categories for viewing the same reality.

Within every moral action there subsists a "material element" which is morally indifferent as well as the "formal element" which bestows morality. The material element of a moral action is "any physical motion of some physical force" in man—whether of locomotion, the appetites, the senses, the apprehensive intellect, or an act of will when considered "in its own natural being" and "as a product of a power implanted in it as such by nature"—provided that it is "capable of a direction that comes from my will." The formal element of a moral action consists in the "imputativity" of the action's effects upon social life to a voluntary agent who can be held responsible for them. And it is precisely in this imputativity of the effects of action upon social life that morality in general consists.[82]

But this transplantation of the material and the formal (that is, the "moral") into the moral action itself did not resolve the problem of their relationship. If, from one point of view, the material element could be considered simply as "the material of my moral actions," on the other hand it could comprehend all acts of will when considered in their "own natural being." As a result of this duality Pufendorf could concede that physically necessary things, the effects of man's "vegetative faculties," impossible things, compulsion, and ignorance rendered the material elements of actions predominant and worked against any imputation of morality. It meant, moreover, that the judgments of the specific balance of imputativity and non-imputativity were various in various circumstances and became a matter for particular judicial determination.[83]

When we follow Pufendorf to the third level of his treatment, that of the specifically moral (formal) element in moral actions, we find that although the physical mode is excluded by definition it reappears by "analogy" and once more, in this indirect form, blunts the categorical effects of his ethics. He introduces, in this context, the concept of moral "status" which, "by virtue of the analogy which it has with space" in the physical realm, operates as the circumstantial basis of moral affairs, "so that on it they rest such moral existence as they have, and erect their actions and their effects." [84] Status brought considerations of place and time into moral judgment, and it posited a varying assessment of obligations dependent upon such circumstances—or states—as the natural or civil condition, peace or war, liberty or servitude, private or public position, honorable or servicing rank in the social hierarchy. With such a concept of status, which forms rather than is formed, Pufendorf imported the pattern of a conditioning framework of existence into the moral life.

Pufendorf's distinction, in human affairs, between the physical and moral modes and his further distinction within the moral mode of sundry conditional states bearing upon moral action made it impossible for him to find the unitary standard of morality on the human level. He denied emphatically that moral actions were good or bad in themselves as embodiments of eternal principles, on the ground that, once embodied in nature, these principles were subject to the same confusion of the physical and the moral that characterized all human actions in the natural realm. They were consequently incapable of establishing an integral moral standard.[85] Nor does man's right reason furnish a moral law, since it is but "the medium through which that law is investigated" and requires a real object for its operation.[86] To establish a moral standard that would rationally relate for

[77]

nature the existent and ideal components that were irrationally mixed in nature, Pufendorf had to transcend the human level and have resort to God.

On the level of God Pufendorf joined all that, on the level of man, he had put asunder. His metaphysics of unity, as distinct from his metaphysics of duality, had reference not to human morality but to the divine *origins* of morality. It was in this context that he beamed his metaphysical discussion at demonstrating the unity of the moral imperative with the created nature of things. This was the function of his reiterated declarations on the indissoluble coherence of essence and existence. "We may abstract and conceive as much as we like as long as it is firmly established that everything created by divine will has as much existence as essence, as much matter as form. . . ." [87] He insisted, similarly, on the conjunction of God's understanding with His will, to signify the conjunction of the rational moral law with the actuality of a created nature appropriate to it.

The shape that this metaphysical unity took for men was the natural law, for in it the actual nature of things was given the form and force of a lawful norm for men by the explicit imposition of God's will, and it is only because natural creation and moral imposition are conjoint in God as they are not in man that the law of nature can remain an absolute unity for man and not fall subject to the diffraction characteristic of all his works. "Man's obligation to observe the law, the law itself, and the qualities which men's actions acquire from the observation of law can be derived from no other principle than the pleasure of God, together with His wisdom and beneficence." "This nature of actions [good or evil] is likewise by the determination of God, inasmuch as He formed the nature of man in such a manner that he is capable of understanding the law which is called natural and which exactly fits man's nature." [88] Time and again Pufendorf insisted that one must begin from, and not subject to further analysis, the integrity of God's act of simultaneous natural creation and moral imposition. The reason for Pufendorf's emphasis upon this point lay in his view that "good and evil is defined as agreement and disagreement with law, as the norm of actions" and that only the indissoluble unity of God's original act could make a moral law out of natural existence.

> Agreement or disagreement with rational nature is the quality of actions which are prescribed by natural law. Since it pleased the most good and wise Creator so to fashion man that his liberty would be circumscribed by fixed law, He simultaneously so shaped his nature that his actions that were prescribed by natural law could not fail to agree with his nature nor those that were proscribed by natural law to violate his nature. . . . Hence good actions certainly agree with the nature of man, but the formal reason of moral goodness does not consist in this agreement. . . . The ultimate reason why actions which are prescribed by natural law are to be done is the will and order of the Creator. . . . Since God determined by His free will to create an animal with a rational and social nature He could not fail to order and forbid in accordance with it, for otherwise God would deviate from the goal which He had set for Himself in creating man and would thereby contradict Himself. . . .[89]

Law, then, was for Pufendorf the form of the fundamental moral reality because only law combined an imperative with an actual object toward which men's obligations could be oriented, and the law of nature was that reality itself because its object was identical with the divine constitution of the natural world. By positing natural law as the fundamental reality and stipulating the morality of human actions to consist in their conformity or non-conformity to it Pufendorf adopted a relational metaphysics of morals—that is, the existence of particular moral persons and things consisted not in their natural being but in their relations to the general qualities of natural beings mediated through law. Thus he argued that "the nature of a thing" or "of an action" "could produce necessity but never obligation," for obligation required both the command of a superior and a general object which permitted a freedom of particular moral choice.[90] The metaphysical role of morality in Pufendorf may thus be seen as that which allowed particular natures to realize themselves by demonstrating their general coherence, and the path to such realization lay through the unity of God.

But if Pufendorf restored God as the capstone of a system devoted to the relations of rational men in this world, he thereby also left open a path out of this entire relational metaphysics. For the natural law that was imposed by God to relate the "ought" to the "is" was related to the nature of man "not by an absolute, but by a hypothetical necessity," and the relationship of men's actions to the natural law was similarly governed by "hypothetical necessity."[91] With this formulation Pufendorf intimated that the necessity pertaining to his moral system was logical rather than metaphysical: it indicated the certainty of the relationship between its rules rather than the absolute truth of its primary precept. The term "hypothetical" revealed the metaphysical limits of the rational moral doctrine, for it rested this doctrine upon a plausible assumption rather than upon an ultimate reality with necessary existence. However sure Pufendorf was of the "observations" from which "the nature of things and of man" was "constructed [*extructam*]," he had to admit that the latter "was not one of those propositions that are self-evident." [92] Consequently, if, on the level of human politics, all obligations which posited the existence of a positive institution must be termed hypothetical, on the metaphysical level his whole system of natural-law morality had a similar status. Ultimately, then, his attempt to account for political and religious institutions as necessary components of a general system of human relations led him beyond the system to an account of them in themselves as vital centers of men's actual existence.

[3]

THE MORALIST

When Pufendorf defined the keynote of his work as the overriding concern with "the controllable actions of man" he rightly acknowledged human morals to be the common denominator of his intellectual career.[1] His method, his theory of knowledge, and his metaphysics were assumptions elaborated only on occasion, under the pressure of opposition; his jurisprudence, his history, and his theology were consequents prepared by the particular kind of morality which he espoused: but the central core of his writing, the stuff on which his philosophical assumptions operated and the doctrine which underlay his empirical vocations, was his explicit theory of human conduct. This substantive ethics functioned as the decisive intermediary in the adjustment of the radical principles to the conservative practice of Pufendorf's age.

I. THE ETHICS

The main problem with which Pufendorf was to wrestle in his ethics was already implicit in his fundamental conception of it. Although he formally defined its object as "the rectitude of human actions in their order according to laws," this did not mean for him the simple analysis of the "ought" vis-à-vis the "is," since, as we have seen, the "ought" for him was itself the general form of the "is." [2] This meant that the discrimination between good and evil was subordinated, in Pufendorf's ethics, to the relationship between general unity and particular variety. Thus the will, which as the "internal director" impelling men to act "by an intrinsic principle apart from any physical necessity" is the prime moral faculty of man, "always chooses a generic good," but "still, as between individuals, we see a great diversity of desires and actions" "on particular goods and evils." [3] Now Pufendorf attempted to save his moral unity by making the heterogeneity of moral actions a problem of the understanding rather than of the will. Hence he posed the problem as the ambiguous comprehension of mixed goods and evils in particular things and the swaying of the understanding by "individual qualities of the mind," habit, passion, or external pressure. Yet he could not avoid building the problem of particular moral choice into the very structure of the will, for he underlined, as an essential quality, "freedom of the will," in the sense that, "touching a particular object before it (for in general it cannot help but turn to that which is good as such, or renounce evil as such) , it may choose whatever action it please. . . ."

Thus Pufendorf's analysis of man's basic moral capacity points simultaneously in two directions: toward "the general nature of the good," for which there is not only "the universal inclination of the will," but also "among all men . . . so wholehearted an agreement" that it does not depend on anyone's "state of liberty"; and toward the particular moral acts and objects, subject to the will as a "free faculty," without which "indifference . . . the morality of human actions is at once entirely destroyed." At one point, indeed, Pufendorf even balanced men's tendency to the good generically with "the common proclivity of human beings to the

bad" specifically. And, to emphasize the fundamental problem inherent in the relations of these two moral levels, he
held both that the obligation to pursue the good "does not
remove the intrinsic liberty of the will" and that the freedom
of choice cannot "bid the will to turn aside from the good as
such."

The obvious bridge between these two levels, for Pufendorf's substantive morals as for his metaphysics, lay in the
definition of moral action in terms of conformity to law,
since the law communicates a kind of moral necessity in that
the subject "recognizes he must bend himself to it" while at
the same time it requires, for its own moral operation, the
freedom of the subject to undertake or not to undertake the
actions prescribed by the law in order that the lawfulness—
that is, goodness—of his action be capable of being "imputed" to him.[4] Ostensibly, then, the relationship between
moral unity and existential diversity lay in the assignment of
the unifying role to law and the particularizing role to the
individual will. But Pufendorf argued emphatically against
such an alignment. In order to ensure the applicability of
morality to actuality, he made each level of the moral realm a
microcosm of the metaphysical relationship between the
moral and the physical worlds. The distinction between the
"moral" and the "natural" now became the ethical version of
the metaphysical relation between the "moral" and the
"physical." In terms of the individual, this meant the use of
the term "liberty" as both the "moral quality" which makes
moral imputation possible and the "natural liberty" which
simply exists and "is not destroyed by any moral bond." More
significantly, in terms of the law, it meant the use of the term
"obligation" to cover both the intrinsic bond of a rational
norm and the extrinsic bond imposed by "power," which in
turn combined the status of a "moral quality" with the
sanction of natural "force."

Thus, in his anxiety to adapt principle to practice, Pufendorf intruded the diverse requirements of the two levels into the very sanctity of the moral law itself. On the one hand, the authority of law comes exclusively from "the power of the superior [*potestate superioris*]," for only this power, and not any "sound reasons for its promulgation," suffices to remedy the "diversity of inclinations and tastes" of man and to "check his personal liberty," thereby fulfilling the function of law "to establish order and seemliness among the human race." A law, in this sense, is defined as "a decree by which a superior obligates a subject to adapt his actions to the former's command." But like most of Pufendorf's ostensibly categorical positions, this one also proved to possess an unheralded cleavage, for, on the other hand, "power" did not mean "strength alone"; a "superior" was not such from "superiority of nature"; and "obligation" required far more than coercion. Hidden in these concepts was the other qualification of law—the rational ground of the law and equally the consent of those who were subject to it. The power of the superior which founds the obligation of law includes "both the strength to threaten some evil against those who resist him and just reasons why he can demand that the liberty of our will be limited at his pleasure." These reasons, which include services already rendered, expectation of services to be rendered, and the subject's voluntary agreement to control by the superior, "should be sufficient, even without the fear" of physical sanctions, "to lead one to receive the command on the grounds of good judgment alone." It should be, but it actually is not. Thus Pufendorf reintroduced, in a subordinate guise, the duality which he had nominally excluded from his unitary concept of the law as power. Without a rational ground the power of the superior is short-lived; but without "a greater force than a feeling of shame and an appreciation of what is right"—without, that is, the fear of

[85]

the superior's strength—"among the vast majority of mortals the inconstancy or wickedness is so great that they prevail over these reasons for command." Power was a "moral quality" because it was grounded in reason and consent, but it could become operative in the actual world only insofar as it made moral provision for the natural "force" of physical punishment which could deal with the ineluctable fact of "natural liberty." Nature thus became the moral cognate of physical reality.

Pufendorf's ultimate purpose in his bifurcation of the grounds of law under the primary category of the superior's command was a fundamental one. His problem was to organize the diversity of free individual human wills under the moral necessity of a general rule, and for this function law seemed the apt instrument. But for law to fulfill this function its version of the general rule had to have independent existential status, else it would be drawn into the vortices of particular human existences and itself be fragmented. On the purely human plane that was Pufendorf's self-defined arena of consideration he saw only in the power of a constituted authority—in a particular existent with a general function—the means of lending actual existence to a universal and thereby rendering it concrete. But this view, which he expressed by choosing the prescriptive power of the superior rather than the rationale of the prescription as the primary basis of law and by devolving its inspiration of fear as the co-ordinate component of power, carried the danger of infecting the general quality of law with its particularized origin and thereby of destroying the delicate moral necessity that was bound up with its universality. The inclusion of the rationale of power thus articulated the universal dimension of law, but its accompaniment by the fear of power and its subordination to the superior's power as such revealed Pufendorf's reliance upon existing authorities as the organizing centers of his individualistic morals and his use of reason to clarify their relations. This proportion of reason to power in law had the effect of reconciling individual liberty with authoritarian decree by conferring upon the latter the moral validity of a general norm and thereby internalizing the command of the superior into a self-willed obligation. Through the participation of the subject in the reasons for obedience the law, which is essentially external, "restrains as by an inner bond the liberty of our will" and "fills its very being with such a particular sense, that it is forced of itself to weigh its own actions, and to judge itself worthy of some censure, unless it conforms to a prescribed rule." [5] Through this blend of monism and derivative duality Pufendorf furnished an ethical basis for authority and through the moral concept of law made freedom its internal dimension.

Now the authority to whom, in the first instance, Pufendorf applies this moral analysis is "the sovereign," "who has the highest authority in the state," and the law to which it is applied is "human," "positive," "voluntary" law, which "proceeds entirely from the pleasure of a legislator" and has its reasons in "the special, and sometimes temporary advantage of distinct social groups." [6] But the discussion on this level leaves unexplained some crucial moral categories, such as acts committed under the "permission" of civil laws (for instance, "the faults of kings"), "imperfect" rights (that is, when what is due us cannot be claimed in a human court), and both distributive and commutative justice (since both what is due from agreements between the individual and society and what is due from agreements among individuals have their basis not in the sanctity of the agreements themselves but in a pre-existing moral relationship which furnishes the sanctity) .[7] Not only these substantive concepts but the ultimate question about the moral status of law itself referred Pufendorf beyond the positive human level to the

[87]

"universal justice" and "natural law" which had their "reasons" in "the universal condition of mankind" and derived their authority from the next higher positive "superior" in Pufendorf's moral system—from God Himself.

II. THE NATURAL LAW

It was only in the context of the natural law that Pufendorf's ethics could become substantive, because it was only now that he could connect the formal, insulated moral relations of his previous analysis with reality. Where his previous criterion of moral analysis was what must be posited "if we do not wish to destroy all morality in actions," his criterion now was conformity to the actual nature of man, a consideration that was possible because the "superior" was at once the prescriber of the moral norm and the creator of the subject to whom it was prescribed.[8] Thus Pufendorf now repeated the gist of his ethics, recognizing the freedom of the will and counterposing to it the necessity of a law based upon the capacity of the understanding and the will to apprehend and obey it and upon man's need of it because of his "proneness to evil," his "nature . . . diverse and varied," his desires "manifold and confused," his "weakness." But Pufendorf now considered the description of man to be "such as in fact agrees with him, and not conceived simply as an abstract idea," for the simple and ultimate reason that "the most Good and Great Creator" so "endowed" him. The status of law, then, was no longer only that of a moral necessity if the good were to be realized but also that of an actual, created, operative, existent necessity, certainly knowable from "the condition of human nature" which required of man "that his actions should be made to conform to a definite rule."

Having established that the moral law was an existent restraint built into the nature of man, Pufendorf now identified the substance of the moral law with the law of nature. Its force derived from the will of God—the power of the superior—and its substance from the created condition of man, since the alternative access to God's decision through special revelation was excluded by the terms of Pufendorf's "universal" moral science. Obviously then, the identification of the moral law with the law of nature was a simple process of drawing the necessary consequence from the substantive character of mankind. But since all of men's visible works were refracted through their own divided, inconstant, and partial wills, the elucidation of the generic "nature of man" was not so simple, for "an induction or proof from experience is as yet imperfect" and hence it is impossible to achieve unity through consensus.[9] The nature of man, then, can only be known with certainty by conceiving him in his "natural state [*statu naturali*]"—the status characterized not by what "men choose and institute for themselves by their own will" but by what "God imposes upon them by the very fact of their birth," "abstracted from" all admixture with the "acquisitions and institutions of civilization . . . and civil societies." [10]

But Pufendorf's problem was hardly solved hereby, for he was committed to defining the state of nature "not as it can be conceived by abstraction but as it actually exists," and yet he had to admit that it "never actually existed" save in a "modified and partial" form.[11] Thus Pufendorf admittedly "conceived by abstraction" a state of nature which really exists prior to human invention but which should not be conceived by abstraction and has never really existed at all.

Pufendorf's ostensible solution, typically, was to deduce two subtypes from the state of nature. The first, which reformulated the generic concept of a natural state into a categorical proposition, was the "purely natural state" and it was this state of individual man, bereft of all human and divine assistance, that never really existed. The second, which Pufendorf called the "modified" or "mixed [*attempera-tum*]" natural state to signify men in social relations though without political association, did once really exist in the form of independent families and still exists in the form of the relations among independent political societies.[12]

And yet the problem was not thereby resolved, for it still left open the question of the status of the "purely natural" state, which, after all, reiterated his initial definition of the natural condition as such. Although man never existed in this state, it did have a definite reference to the existence of man. Pufendorf refused to equate it with the customary devices that referred the nature of man beyond his actual existence—that is, with the primitive condition which men and animals as creatures share, with the "ultimate," teleological nature of man (although this certainly exists in "nature's intention") , or with the paradisiacal purity of prelapsarian nature. Pufendorf's only direct explanation of the purely natural state was distorted by its function as a defense against theological objection: he not only denied that he had ever considered it among "those things that really exist" but even claimed that the purely natural state was for him "an assumption of the contrary, a deduction to the absurd" to prove infallibly the existence of its opposite—the sociability of man.[13] The argument does not hold up, for, as we shall soon see, the qualities of his natural state were not the opposite of the universal human qualities which he sought to prove, but it does point to the kind of existence which his state of nature implicitly did and did not have for him.

Pufendorf's problem was to frame a statement of fact that would also be a general proposition, so that it could serve as the logical basis for a natural law that would be both real and valid. To do this he approached the problem of devising a factual statement about the original constitution of man by "imagining," "positing," "conceiving" (*fingere, ponere, concipere*—Pufendorf used these terms interchangeably in this context) man "projected into this world and left wholly to himself alone" and then by applying to this hypothetical situation his knowledge of "man as he now is." [14] This process was a moral version of Cartesian doubt, through which seventeenth-century thinkers followed their penchant for making a cosmos comprehensible only by first breaking it down to its simplest interchangeable parts and then reconstructing it from them. Thus Pufendorf's isolated man in the state of nature was for morality a "simple truth," and as such this concept was the node marking both the end product of analysis and the origin of synthesis. It was a concept into which existence was fed at one end to come out a primary proposition at the other. The conversion of multiform existence into uniform truth was essential to Pufendorf's thought, and this was not the only occasion upon which he resorted to it, for, as we shall see, it was also crucial to the foundation which he laid for the formation of political society. His positing of natural man reveals the hidden assumption in this process: his attribution of existence to a universal. It was as a universal, that natural man "really exists"; it is as a particular existent that natural man does not exist and never really has existed. Thus Pufendorf's whole moral and political theory was predicated upon a circular approach: it validated the reality of human facts by a logic of general relations which depended upon those facts for its own reality.

The function of Pufendorf's circle was to enable him to start with the facts as he perceived them in the world about him and ultimately to return to them under the guise of logical necessity. Concretely, this meant that he started with the actual particular existences of men in institutionalized society, reduced them to the generic existence of universally

[91]

commensurable individuals, and from the universal moral qualities of these individuals framed propositions from which the institutions followed with both a moral and a logical necessity. In the terms of substantive ethics, it meant the conversion of men's social ties from a ubiquitous actuality to a universal necessity, and to work this conversion Pufendorf felt impelled to proceed with Hobbes beyond the unit of the family, which in Grotius and the traditional preceptors of natural law had served as the primary juncture of social existence and individual morality, to the individuals themselves. But where Hobbes radically separated the state of nature which he depicted as the moral basis of social existence from that existence itself by assigning the former exclusively to self-seeking individuals, Pufendorf dared not go so far in assigning a derivative status to the social matrix of established institutions. If society were no moral ultimate it had to be morally penultimate. Consequently, what began as a simple concept of the natural state was complicated in Pufendorf by its expansion to include pre-political society (in both its logical and temporal senses) as well as the individual person in its moral universe.

Pufendorf's earliest solution was, in effect, simply to juxtapose Hobbes and Grotius and to list self-love and the enjoyment of society as "two inclinations" "implanted . . . by nature" in man as his two fundamental qualities.[15] The moral law consistent with natural man so conceived—that is, the law of nature—was correspondingly dual: it stipulated both that "anyone whatsoever should protect his own life and limbs, as far as he can, and save himself, and what is his own" and that "he should not disturb human society." [16] But if this crude additive approach reveals the essential mediating tendency of Pufendorf's morals, it was, in the long run, intellectually unsatisfactory, and in his mature work he embodied the same tendency in an ostensibly monistic ethic. He changed simultaneity into logical succession and found in the consideration of the natural state first as "pure"—as it relates to the qualities of "isolated individuals"—and then as "modified" or "mixed"—"in relation to other men"—the means of deriving the moral necessity of society from the human individual while still allotting it a share of moral primacy. But to accommodate the respective moral qualities to a logical succession Pufendorf altered their contexts: the nature of man in its most universal aspect—that is, considered as an individual—was defined by his "weakness and natural helplessness [*imbecillitas atque naturalis indigentia*]" and "self-love" now became the moral quality appropriate to this condition; the qualified natural state of man—the level at which the universal qualities of individualized humanity crossed the particular actualities of social existence—was defined by his "sociability [*socialitas*]," a concept which now replaced the earlier "inclination to society." [17]

The change anchored Pufendorf's moral principles in a presumptive anthropological reality.[18] But it meant more than this. It was not only that Pufendorf affirmed an existential basis for his social morality but that he integrated both the generic existence and the values of the individual into it. "Sociability" followed from selfishness in the context of "weakness" far more rigorously than it could from a posited "self-love" alone. "For such an animal to be safe and to enjoy the good things which suit his condition it is necessary that he be sociable . . . ," since his condition would otherwise be "most miserable." [19]

As a logical consequence of weakness, sociability could, like weakness, incorporate self-love within itself. Sociability was therefore defined as "the kind of disposition of man" through which "he desires to associate with his fellows and so to conduct himself toward them that they take no occasion to do him harm but rather have reason to preserve and promote

[93]

his good." [20] Sociability thus took over as a synthetic *a priori* in man's approach to actual existence. "My fundamental proposition, into which nearly all the rest are resolved is this: man is a sociable animal [*animal sociabile*]." [21] The choice of "sociable" over "social" betokened the integrated role of the individualistic moral base in the concept of society.

The moral norms appropriate to man's fundamental moral qualities underwent a parallel development. The self-preservative and the social injunctions which Pufendorf had originally juxtaposed in the law of nature were now articulated in an implicitly logical sequence. Appropriate to the condition of individuals in the posited pure state of nature was the "natural liberty" expressed in the right to preserve themselves "by all means" and to act on their own authority and judgment subject to the power of no other man, since in the state of nature all are equal and there is no superior.[22] Appropriate to the qualified natural state of social relations was the law of nature, whose fundamental proposition now consisted in the one prescription conformable to man's sociability: "Every man, so far as in him lies, should cultivate and preserve toward others peaceful sociability, which is suitable to the nature and the goal of universal humanity." [23] And just as sociability was the existential form of self-love, so did the natural law become the moral form of natural liberty. Through it natural rights were transformed into natural duties, taking their place as "duties toward oneself" alongside the duties to God and to other men among the "corollaries" of the fundamental natural law.[24]

It was at the stage of the sociable state of nature and its attendant natural law that Pufendorf brought man's faculty of reason into play. The first function of reason was to identify the natural law by recognizing its rationale—its conformity to the fundamental actuality of universal humanity—and to accept its validity as an imposition by God prior to and binding upon any social or political action of men. Only on this level of human nature did the "should" meet the "is," and only on this level was the natural law not only knowable but actually known by all normal men. The secondary function of reason was the specification, through deduction, of duties under the natural law, and it was in this process, through the increasing intrusion of variety, that the different degrees of the use of reason among men appeared. In the initial stage of this function—the definition of the universal, co-natal duties immediately implied in the natural law for men considered in their social state of nature—the unity was still marked but yet sufficiently attenuated to open the possibility of the more flagrant variegation that lies behind the difficulties of ethics both as a science and as a way of life.

The first group of generic obligations immediately deriva-tive from the law of nature were the duties of natural reli-gion, for "religion . . . is in truth the ultimate and strong-est bond of human society"; "man would not be sociable . . ." without it. The duties of natural religion, then, have nothing to do with salvation but have to do only with the rational precepts of religion "insofar as the latter subserves the promotion of peace and sociability in this life." [25] From this social function of religion practical prescripts followed logically enough: the honoring of God in mind and act as a resultant of loving Him for benefits conferred and hoped for, fearing Him for His penal power, and obeying Him for His creation and governance of the world. Even the moral neces-sity of holding "right views of God," upon which Pufendorf insisted, could be sustained insofar as they are postulates of the practical reverence—the recognition of God's existence, creation of the world, and continuous governorship over it and the affairs of men. But in a fourth theoretical principle the limits of a necessarily deduced natural religion were

[95]

strained, for here Pufendorf affirmed that "no attribute involving any imperfection applies to God." Although this is a restatement of the familiar proposition that God is infinite and cannot be measured by any finite and therefore human category, its inclusion by Pufendorf here opened a gap in his moral logic which reached beyond the sphere of his morality to the realm of positive religion.

The function of this fourth principle in Pufendorf's scheme was to serve as a postulate to his grounding of the authority of the natural law as such in the will of God to the exclusion of any intermediate categories, but if this principle served peace and sociability by emphasizing the authoritarian over the rational ground of the natural law, by the same token it opened the rational ground to doubt. When, on another occasion, Pufendorf explicated the principle, he held the proposition that the essential justice of God was the archetype of the natural law to be "unknown to human reason alone," since divine attributes cannot be derived from finite human reason, and yet he admitted, to save the rationality of the natural law: "That God is essentially just, that he inflicts injury upon no one, that He keeps His promises, that He is truthful, that He exercised judgments upon His creatures by laws suitable to them, are propositions known to natural reason alone." [26] This question of divine justice was to tantalize Pufendorf until toward the end of his life he resolved it theologically. The necessity which he felt to find a higher ground for the rational judgment that "God is essentially just" when reason could not know what that justice was, like his necessity to find backing for his putatively rational judgment that "not merely Atheism and Epicureanism, but not a few other beliefs as well, which are destructive to *true religion,* good morals, and human society" should be excluded from men's minds, drove him beyond the realm of unaided reason.[27] Because the apex of his ethics was divine authority he had ultimately to support it with positive faith.

The natural law prescribes, secondly, the universal duties of each man to himself, but in the social format of the natural law these acquire a different context from the rights which are the natural endowment of men considered purely as individuals. Now, man "should properly give his first attention to himself" so that he may "glorify" his Creator and "become a fit member of human society," "since he will fulfill his duties towards others more satisfactorily as he exercises himself with greater care for his own perfecting." [28] Thus self-interest changed from an individual right to a social duty, and it was the addition of self-perfection to self-preservation as a proper norm of individual activity that was intermediary to the change. For self-perfection meant primarily the education of man's mind to "matters which concern his duty"— "that the impulses of the mind be regulated and governed by the rule of right reason" "to endure the social life." The social context of individual self-perfection meant, moreover, its qualification not only by the ideal but by the existent circumstances of the social order. The choice of a life calling, for example, should be determined not only by "bodily and mental ability," but also by "birth, fortune, parental authority, command of the civil authorities, opportunity, or necessity."

But despite his general formula for the integration of individual rights into social duties Pufendorf recognized a continuing fissure where the basic right of self-preservation "seems to conflict with the precept of sociability," for "where both parties live in a state of natural liberty, even though they could presume, and ought to presume, that others would observe toward them the duties of natural law, still, on account of the wickedness of human nature, they are bound never to be so free from concern as not to surround themselves with timely and legitimate defenses." In his elabora-

[97]

tion of the problem Pufendorf uncovered a moral antinomy that led him first to the development from general morals to specific law within his system and secondly to the recognition of the existential realm outside it.

First, because the law of sociability "must be so interpreted as not to destroy the safety of individuals" and yet legislates against the "disturbance" of social peace, which individuals cause when they prefer "violent defense" to flight or submission, the moral status of the right of forceful self-defense against unprovoked aggression in the state of nature is in doubt. For while Pufendorf affirmed, explicitly against Grotius, "an unlimited freedom" of forcible self-defense against undeserved attack upon one's safety, honor (chastity), and property, he specified that the moral status of the right—whether obligatory or merely permissible—depended upon the importance of each party to other men, that the fact and the degree of the self-defense depended upon the fact and degree of the danger—a particularly touchy problem for the case of preventive defense and of the amount of property warranting violent defense—and that its duration depended upon the judgment of the sincerity of the attacker's "repentance." In all these cases, Pufendorf stipulated, the uncertainty and therefore the right of self-defense would be far more narrowly restricted in the state of political society than in the state of nature.

But secondly, not even with the adumbration of the political state could Pufendorf satisfy himself that he wholly captured the genie of individualism which he had released. He recognized in self-preservation an ultimate "right and privilege of necessity," which derived from no law but simply from the recognition of the ineluctable "fact that a man cannot avoid straining every nerve for his own preservation." This individual right, moreover, holds both in the social state of nature and in the political state, for self-preservation *in extremis* is so ingrained in "the condition . . . of human nature" that for both the natural and the positive law "a case of necessity is not included under a law which has been conceived with a general scope." Since morality consists in conformity to law, the right of necessitous self-preservation obviously has no moral status for Pufendorf: it marks the limit of his system. But although it plays no overt role in the further development of his theory, the silent influence of this undigested individualistic nugget is discernible in two different directions. It worked as a continuing external challenge to his political system, compelling Pufendorf to various devices for making an attractive civic ethos out of social utility in competition with self-preservation, and it worked ultimately to divert Pufendorf's attention beyond his political system to contemporary international history, where the right of necessity exercised by the individual sovereigns in the state of nature was most in evidence.

The final set of duties binding upon all men by their original constitution are their absolute duties to one another, as prescribed by the natural law. First, no one should injure another; should injury occur, compensation for loss should be rendered.[29] Secondly, every man should recognize the "natural equality of men" by treating every other as his "equal by nature." By natural equality Pufendorf did not mean equality in capacity (he admitted parenthetically with Hobbes that men were approximately equal in body but denied that they were so in mind), but "equality of law [*aequalitas juris*]," based upon men's equal subjection to the natural law and consequently their equal obligations to one another. Thirdly, every man should positively "promote the advantage of another, as far as he conveniently can," and every recipient in turn should show gratitude. In general, this is a straightforward enough social ethic, and Pufendorf considered the natural law and its derivative social duties

[99]

effective enough to hold against Hobbes that the social relations of the state of nature—men's fundamental disposition
toward one another—made for a condition of general peace
among men.[30]

But even more than in the case of the other categories of
natural duties, upon closer examination the simple social
ethic opens out toward the recognition of variety and the use
of jurisprudence to regulate it. For the three duties of men
toward one another do not in themselves suffice to produce
the condition of general peace that characterizes the state of
nature. There is needed a fourth duty, considered not quite
on a level with the absolute duties but yet necessary to redress
a crucial weakness in the circle of the absolute duties. The
weakness refers to the third of man's mutual duties, that of
positive humanity: this duty confers obligations and rights
that are only "imperfect"—that is, valid but lawfully unenforceable in the states both of nature and political society.[31]
This leaves only gratuitous performance, but because "not all
have such natural goodness" and because the obligation is too
general to permit appropriate benefits to appropriate individuals, "it is . . . impossible to deduce from that one
source all that men were entitled to receive to advantage from
one another." To complement the positive duty of humanity,
therefore, Pufendorf adduced the "general duty which we
owe under natural law . . . that a man . . . fulfill his
promises and agreements." Not only this, but the natural law
commands, "in a general way and indefinitely, that men enter
into agreements of some kind or other since without them
social relations and peace between men cannot be preserved."
Thus, unlike the absolute duties, the force of the obligation
to make agreements and keep them is not authoritative but
pragmatic. It serves to convey the moral obligation of natural
law to particular actions undertaken "by my own consent"
and for "my own advantage."

The sanctity of the promise is thus crucial for Pufendorf not as an original but as a transitional duty. Pufendorf himself called it "a transition" from duties that were absolute—that is, *a priori*—to those that were "conditional" or "hypothetical"—that is, contingent upon an antecedent act of man—but this formal terminology does not adequately express the function of the promissory obligation. The promise or the pact (a bilateral promise) which constitutes the posited antecedent act of man funnels the obligations of the moral law which is consonant with the universal will of man into the realm of particular actions which depend upon particular men's consent, since both the generic natural law and particularized consent meet in the promise. Thus, whereas in the pure state of nature Pufendorf associated the concept of "right" with man's natural liberty to do what made for his self-preservation, in the context of the promise he defined "right" as the "natural faculty to do something . . . which concerns some moral effect in the case of those who have the same nature as I." Both the acquisition and the transfer of a right, in other words, now assume a promissory agreement on the part of other men recognizing the individual's power of disposition over men or things under the conditions of the natural law.[32]

Since, for Pufendorf, most of men's social and political relations are actual products of their particular wills, the validity of these relations follows from the sanctity of promises and pacts—in a word, from contracts—in which the moral law is henceforward embodied. Through the alchemy of the contract the moral discrimination among human actions passes over into their legal organization.

[101]

[4]

THE POLITICAL
THEORIST

I. The Role of Natural Law in Seventeenth-Century Political Theory

In politics as in natural science and philosophy the characteristic intellectual of the seventeenth century sought a new axis of explanation. The emergence of insistent new realities had so overburdened, complicated, and riven the traditional framework of rationalization that it no longer provided theoretical satisfaction. The heightened powers and functions of the monarch, the altered status of religion, the subjection of historic corporations, the increasing economic and social mobility of the enterprising commoner, and the intensification of sporadic dynastic rivalry into a regular competition among states—these facts and their concomitant ideas were now realities with which the traditional system of an organically integrated hierarchy joining people to ruler in a religiously articulated community could no longer cope. The scholastic distinction between real and personal or public and individual "subjects" of sovereignty; the legists' vacillation between the principle of the ruler's superiority to the law and the practices of his restriction by it; and above all the confusing disruption of the community into two opposed religio-political systems, with their double standard which recognized the political claims of superior or subordinate magistrates depending upon their respective clerical affiliation: such tergiversations of sixteenth-century theorists were challenges to their successors.

The common focus of the response was the renovation of natural law. The direction of the renovation is familiar enough—the reversal of its structure so as to base it in individuals, work it through the natural community of men, and complete it in God instead of its former basis in God, mediation by a religiously cemented community, and devolution to individuals. Nor is it difficult to see why the idea of natural law, with its pre-Christian origins, with its obvious analogy to the laws of physical nature which were undergoing displacement from the cosmic scheme of Creation to the uniformities of specific equal phenomena, and with its appeal to the universal rational faculty in man, should be chosen as the new axis.

But the obverse side of the choice, while not so familiar, is equally important. The political theorists of the seventeenth century were modernists rather than revolutionaries, explicators rather than reformers. They organized their political systems around the doctrine of natural law not only because it was susceptible to the new and secure origins of politics in the undeniable facts of individual human existence but also because they were vitally interested in reconstituting a viable political order and they could retain the traditional function of natural law as the immanent principle of coherence among men for this purpose. In their reformulation, moreover, natural law as normative coherence was so intertwined with natural law as actual coherence that it served less as an ideal for action than as an explanation of existing institutions and a designation of their mutual relations.

But however authoritarian the intent, the very process of clarification brought with it a necessity of theoretical choice and decision on issues which had not previously called for them. Theorists had long since, to be sure, inquired into the fundamental questions—the source and location of political authority, its powers, the forms and organs of its exercise, the grounds of obedience and resistance—but so integral was the traditional approach to the human community that it tended rather to aggregate than to discriminate in its answers. The tendency was appropriate to periods in which social stability and religious uniformity made possible and desirable the co-operation of all kinds of authorities toward a common orderly end. In these circumstances divine ordination, election, and custom had all been deemed to converge in the sources of political authority whose goal was the external facet of a generally shared and vaguely defined edificatory end, with the share of each governing organ often an addition of locally prescribed customary rights. Certain of these aggregates were to persist through the seventeenth century and beyond: notably, the conflict over the forms of government, an issue that was subsequently to become crucial, was not yet a vital issue for the seventeenth-century natural-law theorists, except for the passing episode of mid-century English revolutionary writing. What did become crucial for the seventeenth century were the theoretical issues arising from the actual disruption of consensus on the proper field of collective action and from the conflict of the authorities who were the collective agents: the issues, that is, of defining a specifically political sphere of indisputable order, of locating an equally indisputable source of authority within it, and of reordering relations among the existing authorities in the light of it.

[104]

Pufendorf's politics belonged to the common enterprise of the natural-law school, but they played a special role in it. This role consisted essentially in his contribution to the main problem faced by the theorists of natural law in the seventeenth century—the problem of squaring the individual rights which constituted for them the only certain basis of politics with the authoritarian political order which had to be the consequence of these rights if they were to explain the world in which they lived. For Pufendorf as for posterity the great mentors of the seventeenth-century enterprise were Grotius and Hobbes, but just as he found them on opposite sides of a necessary common ground in moral philosophy so did he place himself between their answers to the crucial political problem.

Aside from his aspersions upon the intrusion of religion into their political works (upon Grotius for his "new doctrine in religion" and upon Hobbes for his "abominable" religious theories, "peculiar to himself") the one general critique that Pufendorf delivered upon them was the misleading one-sided observation that the "incomparable" Grotius suffered only from the limitation of the subject natural in a pioneer work but that Hobbes's "Epicurean" reduction of statecraft to "utility and preservation" was radically opposed to Pufendorf's own "Stoic" conviction.[1] But the operative position which Pufendorf adopted toward the two masters in the running commentary on their specific tenets interspersed throughout his own work indicates a more genuinely mediatory attitude on the key issue. With Grotius he maintained the social emphasis that organized individuals into institutions under an effective law of nature even prior to the formation of political communities. With Hobbes, he always retained the touchstone of individual self-interest as the foundation to which reference must be constantly made: "It is the common nature of man that I love who does me good and hate who does me ill. In the state that does me good, I esteem it. . . ." [2] He rejected in Grotius the intentional logical laxity through which the latter sacrificed both the individualistic derivation and the categorical definition of political authority in favor of accommodating the traditional porosity of the political function and the traditional plurality of its agents.[3] He rejected in Hobbes the overly rigorous logic through which the unmediated individualistic basis of political authority persists as the only bond of political society, for it did not make enough accommodation to the actual force and variety of political institutions.[4] Pufendorf's special contribution to natural-law politics stemmed from his balance of rational and empirical qualities: he supplied an individualistic rationale to the realities of a monarchical and corporate political society. Thereby he endowed the natural-law doctrine with the progressive tendency that was missing in Grotius and he muted its revolutionary possibilities that were implied in Hobbes.

The task was difficult, and Pufendorf accomplished it by applying to politics the devices that had already served his ethics: from the categorical assertions which saved the logic of his individualism he deduced the variety of applications that incorporated it and converted it into an internal qualifying dimension of social and political institutions.

II. NATURAL INSTITUTIONS

The "qualified" or "mixed" state of nature was a crucial concept in the logic of Pufendorf's politics. He developed it to show that the individual, while still sovereign in the sense of being "his own master, . . . subject to the authority of no man . . . , living in natural liberty" with the power "in accordance with his own judgment and will . . . of doing everything that agrees with sound reason . . . by every

[106]

means to preserve his body and life, and to banish what seems to destroy life," yet involves himself in social institutions.[5] Property, marriage, family, slavery, are all such institutions which logically precede the formation of political society and indicate, despite the individual's original liberty, his natural subjectivity to authority, however partial. Pufendorf's primary concern was to show that all these institutions, without exception, have their effective ground in contract,[6] and thus in the mutual consent of individuals who voluntarily abridge their own liberty for cause. So far, so simple. Nor did Pufendorf have difficulty in demonstrating, according to his premises, that the rules for the conduct of these institutions are derived, even without civil states, from the natural law. And yet there are two complications in the logic, complications which are important to us not for the evaluation of Pufendorf's theory but for their illumination of the unconscious concerns which underlay the overt goal of his valid logic.

The first of these difficulties was the variation in the respective ultimate foundation and consequently in the status of institutions ostensibly parallel by virtue of their common immediate basis in voluntary contract and their common derivation from the natural state of man. Property or dominion (Pufendorf equates the two terms) is the institution that reveals the strain most clearly, for Pufendorf based it upon two different levels of origins. On an elemental level, the right of men to "dispose all things and animals to their own use or advantage or pleasure" redounds to the will of God, as revealed in the needy constitution of man.[7] But what the will of God thus validates is the antecedent condition of property, not property itself, since His will also authorizes possession in common, which was the actual arrangement of primitive man. Nor does the law of nature prescribe the institution of property, although it indirectly "advises" it when circumstances make it fitting to the social peace which the law does prescribe, and the natural law does regulate its use after its institution. On the actual level, then, property— "the right by which the substance . . . of a thing belongs to a man, so that it does not belong by the same way to an- other"—has its immediate ground in the voluntary conven- tion, "at least tacit," among men stipulating mutual recogni- tion of present and future exclusive possession, and its ultimate ground simply in utility—"to avoid quarrels and to introduce good order" for things that had become relatively scarce or had someone's labor invested in them.

Natural too—that is, based immediately on human conven- tion and utility independent of civil law—are the institutions that have developed around the acquisition and exchange of property: occupancy, prescription, money, prices, testaments, commercial contracts, rents, loans, partnerships. In his long disquisition on this branch of private law, the constant thread is Pufendorf's repeated effort to show that these institutions, like property itself, stem from neither the civil nor the natural law but from the mutual agreement and convenience of men. The relationship to civil law was no problem for him, since its function was simply to protect and specify the already established institution and the rules for its conduct—in prescription, for example, to designate the time- span for possession to become ownership. Pufendorf's fre- quent recourse to the Roman civil law was no violation of this position, since his discriminating use of it was entirely consistent with his position that the Roman law was valid only for the natural law that was mixed into it.[8] But the re- lationship of property to natural law was troublesome to him, since he required this law to regulate property relations but at the same time denied its responsibility for their exist- ence even in the state of nature.[9] The underlying reason for this apparently gratuitous difficulty which Pufendorf made

[108]

for himself will become apparent from its reappearance, *mutatis mutandis,* among the other institutions of his natural state.

Although marriage, like all natural institutions, derives immediately from contract between equal individuals specifying mutual services and obligations, its ultimate ground is the direct prescription of it by the law of nature as the embodiment of the will of God.[10] Pufendorf deduced this from the propagating faculty in the original constitution of the human creature and the necessary requirement of marriage to regulate it. The basic rights and duties attendant upon marriage follow as a kind of mixture from its status as a contract between equals and its function under the natural law: from the first come the exclusive mutual access to the parties' bodies and the mutual promise of continuous cohabitation; from the second, manifested in "the natural condition of both sexes," come the husband's direction of the household and the wife's obligation of obedience; from both together come the limitation of the husband's dominance to the purposes of the marriage, its exclusion from the power of life and death, and its restrictions in disposing over the wife's property. But despite the certainty of Pufendorf's main deductions from the convergence of convention and natural law in the case of marriage, a gap did remain. This time the law of nature could not regulate relations of the institution for whose existence it was responsible. Pufendorf confessed his uncertainty about the status under natural law of two important actual marital relationships founded on the contractual character of marriage—notably, polygamy involving plurality of wives and the whole question of divorce.[11]

Necessarily associated with marriage was the institution of the family, since the production of offspring was included in the prescription of the natural law. Like the institution of property, however, the family could be properly explained

[109]

only by the attribution of a more specific grounding in succession to this elemental cause, since, for Pufendorf, our knowledge of God through the human constitution suffices to explain the constituents of a family but not its characteristic structure—not, that is, the relations of its members, particularly those of parents and children. These relations consist in the combination of equality, since "our offspring . . . is our equal, so far as the rights naturally belonging to men are concerned," with inequality—"that is, subject to our government [*imperium*]." [12] Pufendorf derived this combination from two equivalent grounds: the natural law, which "has laid upon parents the care of children" and "enjoins upon parents that they exercise sufficient sovereignty over their children" "to direct the actions of their children to their good," since immaturity would otherwise make the social life "inconceivable"; and "the presumed consent of the children themselves" to their obligation of obedience under the parents' government, based on the presumed agreement of the child "to a rearing so advantageous to him" and expressed in a "tacit pact." It follows logically that the parents' authority does not extend to the power of life and death, that it may be transferred for the good of the child, that the mature offspring may for good reason join another family, since "they are not obligated to give up looking out for their own interests," or each may establish his own wherein he becomes "in all things free and possessed of his own right."

But what does not follow logically, in Pufendorf, from his blend of natural law and individual consent, are any conclusions on such problems as the issue of maternal versus paternal government, the relations of parents to mature offspring remaining within the family, and the obligations entailed by the undefined filial reverence of mature offspring outside the original family but subject to the duty of gratitude for past services. It is revealing that Pufendorf could resolve these problems only by going beyond the state of nature to adumbrate a political relationship or to call in the actual arbitration of the civil authorities. By virtue of the first alternative Pufendorf could account for the persistent parental authority over grown children still within the family only by adding to the "tacit pact" a concept of the family as a proto-political society to replace the natural law which no longer applies to the case. "For just as distinct families have somewhat of the form of states, so their heads bear some analogy to royal government." [13] But for the specification of these powers as for the validation of patriarchy over matriarchy and of the rights of the separated offspring Pufendorf proceeded from the shadow to the substance of the political magistrate, invoking typical civil laws for his definitions.

At the other extreme from the intimacy of marriage and family with the natural law was the status of slavery. Pufendorf was articulate enough about its "disadvantages"—that free men have more opportunity "to look after their own welfare" and that free men are subject only to general laws while slaves are also subject to the special orders of a fellow subject—but he nonetheless vindicated it as a natural institution.[14] Indeed, he even broadened its usual scope by going beyond the familiar conqueror-captive relationship to include master and servant who trade permanent maintenance for permanent labor service. Pufendorf's purpose in thus expanding the disadvantaged institution was evidently to emphasize its origin in contract, an origin obviously obscured in the martial forms of the institution. Consequently, he made these forms a later development patterned on the master-servant relation. "Therefore, the origin of slavery was due to willing consent and not to war, although war was the occasion for a great increase in the number of slaves and made their lot a harder one." [15] Pufendorf needed to stress the contractual basis of slavery because for him this was its exclusive ground. He rejected its ordination by God and its establishment by nature: its status as a natural institution was purely and simply a voluntary contractual act exchanging material necessities for material conveniences. So abashed was Pufendorf's discussion that he refrained from the explicit mention of natural law in connection with it, although this law was implied in the rules he laid down for the institution's operation. It is hardly surprising to find, with the natural norm so tenuously represented, that Pufendorf's discussion was filled with uncertainties on the crucial issue of the limits upon the master's powers. Where he did not try weakly to distinguish between the implied terms of pacific and martial contracts he attributed the protection of slaves to "the law of humanity," which we know from another context imposed only "imperfect" or unenforceable obligations.

Now clearly, apart from the common denominator of their immediate origin in contract, these institutions—property, family, slavery—occupied vacillating and varying positions in the state of nature. Certainly it would be difficult—and Pufendorf never attempted it—to give a uniform characterization of the state of nature in terms of them. But Pufendorf's inability to achieve logical finality on the principles underlying natural institutions exposed a vital fundamental belief—between the rights and interests of the individual on the one side and the needs and laws of human society on the other a natural gap and imbalance would persist that could be filled and redressed only by the institution of a political sovereign.

But a second difficulty, more serious albeit also unacknowledged, beset Pufendorf's notion of natural institutions: in view of the valid authorities established and recognized in marriage, the family, and slavery, what distinguishes the mixed state of nature from the civil state? Although he usually wrote as if the prime attribute of the natural state were the "natural liberty" which gave each individual the right to "conduct his own affairs at his own discretion and decide by his own judgment on the means that concern his own preservation" under his own execution of the natural law, Pufendorf himself recognized the limited scope of this natural liberty by qualifying the general statement to except whoever has, by "some previous act," "a superior by whom he is controlled." [16] Nor was this exception a trivial matter, for included under it were all females and all unmarried adult children of both sexes as well as the more academic category of slaves. Effectively, it reduced the agents of natural liberty to household heads or, as Pufendorf once indicated parenthetically, to "patriarchs." [17] And yet, he never drew from this qualification any conclusion about what then defined the mixed state of nature for the whole universe of individuals, which was his starting point. But this gap in Pufendorf's logic had an important function for his theory: through this ambiguity he could—and did—write generically of individuals when he was actually referring to household heads and, by thus attributing original rights to large groups of already organized individuals, ease the passage from the variety of individual freedom to the uniformity of political subjection.

But Pufendorf's problem of deducing bound subjects from free individuals was not wholly resolved thereby. In his effort to show man's natural preparation for voluntary subjection to political society he created another ambiguity: he attenuated the substance of the difference between natural and civil society which remained the one constant formal assumption behind his state of nature. Since political society was itself regional and therefore necessarily plural, how did the plurality of civil states essentially differ from the plurality of independent households? What did the categorical distinction of which Pufendorf made so much between the absence and presence of a political sovereign mean beyond the lesser or greater numbers of individuals made subject to human authority? Pufendorf beclouded the distinction particularly in his attribution to natural institutions of the same term— "government [*imperium*]"—that he used for the supreme authority of the body politic. Nor did he apply the term loosely, since he denied it to the authority of the husband over the wife while investing it in the father, the family head, and the master. The rationale behind this usage lay in Pufendorf's implicit assumption that government was determined by the degree of control, this degree to be measured by its scope—the kinds of activities for which it was competent. Thus government was denied the husband because his authority was acknowledged for "matters peculiar to marriage" but not necessarily for "other acts as well," and this did not suffice to constitute government. And just as the degree of control determined whether there was government, so were there distinctions of degree, as measured by scope, within government: Pufendorf attributed "some government [*aliquod imperium*]" to family heads, asked "how much government [*quantum imperium*]" is appropriate to masters, and characterized the authority in the civil state literally as "the supreme government [*summum imperium*]," although the ordinary translation of this into "sovereignty" obscures the comparative element which distinguishes it from the state of nature.[18] Behind this graduation we may again note Pufendorf's effort both to adumbrate political obedience in the nature of man and yet to retain its derivation from the autonomous rights of the individual. We may also begin to see, in the canon of scope, the difference of kind behind the differences of degree in Pufendorf's distinction between natural and civil society.

Pufendorf did start to make an overt logical distinction between the two states, but interestingly enough he did not carry it through. From the generic concept of society he

[114]

deduced the two types of simple and composite societies, a deduction which he seemed to equate with the formal relationship between natural and civil societies. He denominated the "marital, paternal, and lordly society"—epitomized in the "family"—as "simple and primary" constituents of the "great" or "most complete [*perfectissimae*] society" which was the body politic. "For just as the human body is composed of various members which themselves exhibit the form of bodies, so do political states [*civitates*] consist of lesser societies, of which some are simple and primary and the others a little more composite, usually going under the name of corporations [*collegiorum*]." [19] Pufendorf then carried this theme on into his narrative of how "the household heads [*patresfamilias*] left behind their natural liberty and decided to constitute political societies."

But this existential relation found no echo in the moral and legal basis which Pufendorf recognized for political society. Here, where the issue was theoretically crucial, he identified the constituent units of civil society simply as "human beings," "physical persons," and "individuals," used in apposition. He acknowledged that "human beings [*homines*]" lived "previously" in scattered families, but they and not the families or family heads legally "instituted" the political state.[20] The treatment of ethical and legal relations as an order of reality distinct from the discrete facts of past and present existence underlay Pufendorf's whole political theory. Without this distinction, not only the basis of civil society but the family household itself would become inexplicably inconsistent in his presentation, for he recounted, in his anthropological history of the state of nature, an actual paternal dominance which according to his legal analysis is generally established only by the law of the civil society.[21]

So Pufendorf could not go the way of traditional natural-law doctrine and use the relationship between simple and composite to make families the prime components of civil society. He bothered neither to identify nor explain his reference to corporation as "a little more composite" ingredient of the political state, but since it obviously muddied the categorical distinction between the simple and the composite it also showed how little store he set in these logical concepts. He asserted them because they indicated the continuous development from man's natural to his political propensity for social organization, but he could not execute them because they were vitiated by his equally strong insistence that individuals and their rights persisted through natural into political institutions as a common basis of both. The political state was for Pufendorf, to be sure, a "composite moral person," but like all such "composite moral persons or societies" it was formed by the union of "several human individuals." And to complete the paralyzing antinomy, in this fundamental moral context Pufendorf designated the family not as the "simple" unit of his social context but among the "composite moral persons or societies" to show its analogy to the political state as a parallel association of individuals.[22]

Pufendorf's actual differentiation between natural and political institutions lay primarily in their respective ends. His explicit treatment of this issue was negative and scattered. He measured the deviation of each natural society from the goal of political society and epitomized the generic difference between the two human levels only in terms of the inadequacy of the former to fulfill the end for which the latter was created. The implications of his argument, however, were more positive and more revealing. His explicit standard of comparison for the two human conditions was the goal of "mutual defense" which, given a considerable multiplication of the species, made men "not content" with their natural institutions and became the end of civil society.[23] Marriage, the family, lordship, could not make mutual defense their end, first because they were all too "small" to accomplish it but secondly also because each had its own end that was something other than mutual defense. But if Pufendorf's references to these natural ends are taken out of his tendentious context and viewed positively, then they turn out to be not only impressive as norms but, by Pufendorf's own assertion, attainable through man's natural institutions alone. They include both the provision of "the necessities of life" and the satisfaction of man's "desire for society"—that is, his sociability.[24] Clearly, then, it was not that the ends of natural institutions were absorbed into political society as a lesser within a greater entity, but rather that the distinctive character of political society derived from the distinctive end which it was designed to serve. All that related to mutual defense lay within the sphere of political society; all else remained with nature.

If Pufendorf thus shared, with the bulk of later liberal natural-law theorists, the notion of a state of nature which articulated a level of fundamental rights in man underlying civil society, authorizing the individual's role in it, and securing immunities from it, he differed from them in that these rights were for him only of instrumental and not primary interest. He was primarily interested in defining the distinctive sphere and function of politics as the only certain guarantor of order in contrast to natural activities which were, from this point of view, only subordinately the loci of rights, but principally the loci of variation. He designed his treatment of natural rights to show that the difference in their limitation by natural and political social relations was only a matter of degree and that the political function was as fundamentally grounded in man as any other.

III. The Foundation of Political Society

The basis of political society was, for Pufendorf, ostensibly simple. Its ground was neither nature nor sociability nor

[117]

necessity but a voluntary action by man "for some utility which he will derive from it for himself." [25] The action is embodied in a linked set of contracts through which men consent to the establishment of a political association and a sovereign whereby this utility is procured. The simple and familiar general formula, however, covers a problem which was of vital concern to Pufendorf, and its solution worked distinctive features into the particular terms of the formula. The effective cause of the state was not natural necessity; it was not natural law or social morality; it was not even utility as a general moral principle, since it was only a particular expression of utility—the utility of mutual defense—that was involved. His problem, then, was this: How can man, "who does not incline to be subject to anyone but to do everything at his own pleasure and to favor his own interest in all things," through an act impelled by a specific utility create a political society in which he "suffers a loss of natural liberty and subjects himself to an authority which includes the right of life and death—an authority at whose command one must do many things from which one would otherwise shrink and leave undone many things which one greatly desired to do." [26] How, in other words, does man go from particular free acts of self-preservation to permanent involvement in the "composite moral person" that actualizes the prescriptions of general moral law? Pufendorf's answer was an epitome of his approach: he analyzed the facts of self-interest into a set of conceptual relations which he gradually led, by a process of political logic, into conjunction with the set of conceptual relations which he derived from the facts of authority.

To show how this process worked, a preliminary question must be asked of Pufendorf which he did not ask of himself. Why did he choose to reduce the effective cause of the state to the utility of mutual defense? [27] Even if we grant his desire to find a distinctive function for the state in self-defense, the reason for his grounding it in individual self-interest rather than in the moral obligation of the natural law to which it apparently conformed so well remains unclear. Certainly his balanced view of human nature did not require this position. He chose, obviously, to emphasize in support of his option the "wickedness," the "insatiable desire and ambition," the "malice," "ferocity," "harshness," and "other vices" of man, such that to "a great multitude every right is worthless whenever the hope of gain has enticed them" and "if there were no courts, one man would devour another." [28] But the Hobbesian motif that Pufendorf approves here he had explicitly rejected in another context when he had argued that the natural relations of men to one another were so basically amicable as to constitute their essential condition one of peace rather than war.[29] The most authentic expression of his position on the issue was characteristically an intermediate one—his summary statement that the typical relationship of one man to another was that of "an inconstant friend" and that the prudent man "keeps the peace with all, as something which can presently change into war." [30] Pufendorf's shift from this graduated existential judgment to a categorical misanthropy in the context of political origins is reminiscent of the pure state of nature which Pufendorf "posited" from the "existing" mixed natural state for the purpose of deriving a primary logical proposition about individual rights out of a mixed actuality.[31] Now, too, his purpose was to underline beyond cavil the constituent role of consent and contract in the formation of institutions.

But we must carry the argument one step further. Pufendorf could conceivably have argued again—for he had so argued for the state of nature and he certainly believed it—that the operation of natural law leaves the individual morally free and that individual consent and mutual contract

[119]

are consequently voluntary means of fulfilling the prescriptions of the natural law. But he did not so argue now, in reference to the origin of the state. Apparently—for the explanation must be inferential—Pufendorf based the state upon the self-seeking utilitarian motive not so much because he meant to start from ultimate individual liberty per se as because he meant to start from the ultimate variability inherent in natural liberty and self-interest. "With men there are as many ideas as there are individuals." [32] For Pufendorf human liberty persisted, albeit diminished and transformed, from the natural into the civil state; the definitive development, upon which his process focused, was from diversity to unity. The state of nature was actually mixed because the good came from the general law, the evil from free individual acts, and no certain relationship subsisted between the two. Men decided to come out of the state of nature because it was "inconstant" and "untrustworthy." Pufendorf initiated the origin of political society from natural evil not because it represented his judgment of the whole nature of man but because it did represent his judgment of man's individualized aspect, whose constant, trustworthy, and necessary relationship to the unity of general law within the state he intended to demonstrate.

Thus while Pufendorf developed the *function* of political society out of the second or mixed stage of man's natural state, for the *foundation* of political society he returned to the posited pure state of isolated individuals and built it parallel to the institutions of modified nature. This foundation is relevant to the distinctive feature of Pufendorf's contractual theory of the state. His is probably the most elaborate system of political contracts in the long history of the doctrine, since he started from Hobbesian individuals but had to integrate them into not only a political but a moral totality. From ancient Rome until the end of the sixteenth century theorists were explicit only about the ruler-ship contract—that is, the pact between the ruler and the community. From the Monarchomachi, and particularly Johannes Althusius, philosophers, publicists, and jurists articulated the social contract—that is, the constitutive pact among the members of the community—and, as is well known, thenceforward for the best-known of the natural-law school—Hobbes, Locke, and Rousseau—this was the only valid founding contract. But most disciples of the school during the seventeenth and eighteenth centuries, less rigorous than the masters, subscribed to both contracts. Pufendorf required not only the two contracts but a constitutional "decree" as the three indispensable instruments for the foundation of all states.[33]

In Pufendorf's case as in so many others of the natural-law persuasion, the theoretical function of the contractual device was conditioned by its epistemological status. He admitted that no written records existed for the origins of most states and that these origins are therefore "unknown, or at least . . . not entirely certain." And yet not only did he insist that his two pacts and a decree were not "imagined" but he claimed that they were "necessary" for the understanding of contemporary political association and subjection. The pacts, then, were necessary truths known "by reasoning [*ratiocinando*]" about the origin of states from the existing fact of them.[34] They were realities cast in the form of logical propositions, political facts cast in the form of the necessary relations between them.

The succession of contracts and decree was thus a logical succession demonstrating the gradual organization of heterogeneous self-seeking individuals, the simplest units of humanity, into a single body under a unitary authority that was still ultimately grounded in the rights of those constituent individuals. In Pufendorf's summary statement:

. . . The diversity of inclinations and of judgments in discerning what is of most advantage to a common end . . . may be cured by uniting the wills of all in a perpetual bond, or by so constituting affairs that there will be for the future but one will for all in those matters which serve the end of society. . . . But the only final way in which many wills are understood to be united is for every individual to subordinate his will to that of one man, or of a single council, so that whatever that man or council shall decree on matters necessary to the common security, must be regarded as the will of each and every person. For whoever voluntarily grants his power to another is held to agree with his will. . . . When such a union of wills and strength has been made, then there finally arises a state, the most powerful of moral societies and persons.[35]

By virtue of the initial contract, which creates the "rudiments of the state," "a multitude of humans, enjoying natural liberty and equality" but joined by universal desire for the "safety and security" which is their lowest common denominator, agree, each with the other, on their "intention to unite in a single permanent association [*coetum*]" for the purpose of administering these concerns in common. Pufendorf rooted this contract in individual rights, since it is entirely voluntary and limits its scope to the coincidence of individual self-preservation, and he underlined this ground by recognizing the "usual reservation" of the right to emigrate and the possibility of "conditional adherence" to the contract whereby the individual stipulates his right of secession if the association's decision on the form of government should not meet with his approval.[36]

There follows, necessarily, a "decree," enacted by a majority of the initial contractants and binding upon all but the conditional adherents, which determines the "form of government" to be introduced into the state. "For until they have settled this point, nothing that makes for the common safety can be steadily carried out." [37]

The third and final stage, from which "the completed state results," becomes necessary "when the ruler or rulers on whom the government of the association is conferred are appointed" and takes the form of a second contract between the ruler (s) and "the rest [*reliquos*]" by which the former binds himself to "care for the common safety and security" and the latter pledge him their "obedience." This voluntary subjection of their wills to his will assigns to the ruler the use of the subjects' powers for the common defense, thereby making the state "one person." [38]

Now, in this schematic form the analysis looks like a simple utilitarian account of the progressive convergence of many wills to individual security into one will to common security. But three important difficulties with the scheme indicate a whole dimension of assumptions behind it of which Pufendorf was not himself aware and in terms of which it must be reconstructed.

First, the scheme has obvious ambiguities inexplicable in a thinker who prided himself on his precision, save on the supposition that they had reference to an implicit level of his thought. Thus: How did the particular rulers get appointed? Who were "the rest" that entered into the second contract with the rulers—the association established by the first contract or, once more, the individual contractants? Surprising as it is that Pufendorf gave no direct answers to such urgent questions raised by his own scheme, even more confusing were the double answers which he dropped parenthetically in the different contexts of later special discussions. On the first question, he argued in the special context of aristocracies that the rulers are chosen "by their names or other distinctive signs" in the group which enacts the constitutional decree, but when he also argued, in the special context of rejecting the divine-right doctrine, that "a certain person may be designated and his sovereignty conferred in one and the same act," it was clearly to the second contract that he was attributing the designation.[39] On the second question, he argued in a special anti-Hobbesian context that the other party to the contract with the ruler is "the free people [*populus*]," who neither start nor end as a mere "multitude" but "remain one association [*coetum*]," held together not only by the new sovereignty "but also by the first contract." [40] But he also argued, on the same issue in another context, that this other party consisted of "individuals [*singuli*]." [41] With this answer the first contract seems to become superfluous, a conclusion which is reinforced by Pufendorf's refusal to decide whether the "decree" on the form of government is an "opinion of many wills joining into one or a pact of individuals with individuals," since the latter option assumes individuals not essentially more integrated than at the start of the contractual process.[42] The evident reason for the ambiguities was Pufendorf's need to show both the increasing organization of individuals and the persistence of their rights. Consequently, he made his logical mesh so broad that so specific an act as the appointment of governors fell through it and came to rest upon an underlying network of presuppositions.

Pufendorf's second revealing difficulty appeared in his belated provision of a place for the natural law and God as its author in the process of state-making. After he had traced the process as a rational whole on the basis of contractual consent inspired by individual rational utility, he announced that "another principle must be added, if government is to acquire special efficacy and sanctity," and for this reason he announced his agreement with the prevailing opinion "that states and their supreme government arise from God as author of the natural law." [43] The problem which this moral ground raised for Pufendorf was evident not only from its retroactive position in the argument but also from the peculiar mixture of roles which he attributed to it. On the one hand he emphasized the distinctive moral necessity of the state as the only "human institution," of all those recommended by "sound reason," without which "the dignity and security of the human race cannot be preserved." [44] On the other hand, however, he was careful to avoid the direct assertion that the natural law prescribes the institution of the state, arguing rather that under the condition of expanded population the establishment of civil society was a dictate of human reason recognizing its necessity for "the order and peace which is the purpose of natural law"; and he was just as careful to stress that even thus indirectly God and the natural law have authorized neither the forms of government nor particular governors but only "civil government" in the sense of a general "order of commanding and obeying in which . . . there is something supreme and independent." [45] Thus the function of the natural law in the foundation of the state is at once necessary and indirect. The clue to the meaning of this intermediate function may be found in Pufendorf's strenuous denial that sovereignty is "a physical quality" and his insistence that it is indeed "a moral quality." [46] It indicates that the level which underlies Pufendorf's contractual process and to which its difficulties should be referred is a level of moral meaning.

Pufendorf's third and final difficulty with his series of contracts points in the same direction. Since his announced goals—peace and security—were similar to Hobbes's he felt the need to defend the necessity of his three-stage process against the simplicity of Hobbes's single social contract and he could do this only by intimating that state-making involves the construction of a moral relationship behind and between the new facts of politics.[47] Thus the apparent contradiction in Pufendorf's criticism of Hobbes's scheme as conferring both too much and too little power upon the sovereign can be resolved, like his political ambiguities in general, by reference to the moral substratum of his political position. Pufendorf objected on the one hand that Hobbes's one pact, which simultaneously associates the constituent individuals and institutes the sovereign, invalidates the rights of the individual subject against the sovereign and fails to recognize the gradual organization of individuals, through contract, into a "group" that is itself capable of concluding a mutually binding contract with the sovereign. But he also objected to the same single pact of Hobbes, on the other hand, because in the absence of a separate rulership contract the disobedience of one subject entails the anarchy of all and in an aristocracy and democracy the nobles and people, respectively, are released from all obligations. What reconciles Pufendorf's divergent points of view here is his fundamental notion that the "natural liberty" of individuals is joined to the "natural strength" of the sovereign authority by way of a moral detour.

> These matters will be understood more clearly, if we consider that subjects by the submission of their wills do not destroy their natural liberty of will, by which they are able in actual deed to withdraw what they once gave, and refuse the obedience which they promised; nor are the strength and faculties of subjects actually turned over to the sovereign in such a way, that, for instance, the strength which lay in the shoulders of all subjects passes to the shoulders of the sovereign.[48]

[126]

The passage from liberty to authority works rather through a "moral quality" in which liberty takes the moral form of contractual consent, develops into "voluntary submission," and emerges on the other side of the moral relation as coercion by the "natural strength" of the ruler—that is, compulsion "to obey the commands of their rulers by . . . fear of punishment and extrinsic coercion." [49] Behind Pufendorf's conviction that a moral process must operate a continuous connection between the individual and the sovereign was his assumption that a state required not only passive obedience but the active transmission of positive support from the subjects to the ruler. But save by "moral qualities," which "come about by pacts from a mutual agreement of wills," "there is no other transfer of strength possible between men." [50] Thus individual rights furnish to authority a force which it can get from no other source, but they can furnish this force only by being unified through contractual consent into a moral submission whose terms are freely accepted by the governor.

We are now in a position to reconstruct Pufendorf's process of state-making into the form it would have taken had he been able to make explicit the assumptions which actually explain it. The function of the first contract is to convert the multitude of natural individuals, with the orientation of their natural liberties toward their own discrete securities, into an association of moral individuals, defined by the voluntary convergence of their wills upon the common security, since a moral person, for Pufendorf, is simply one with a function in a "common life," which, in turn, is established by the voluntary direction of the free will "to bring order into the lives of men." [51] It is at this intermediate point, with the group formed by the first contract, that the natural law becomes effective as the moral norm for the subsequent activity of the moralized individuals of the group. Thus it is that Pufendorf could insist on the role of natural law in the formation of the state while he could deny both that it prescribed the initiation of the process and that it took effect only after the state had been established.[52] The entry of natural law into effect between these two terminals, at the conclusion of the social contract, had an important implication: it added a moral bond to the state-making process only in respect to the function of security which was the purpose of the contract; in all other respects both man's natural liberty and provisions of the natural law remained unaffected.

Within the moral sector of security the natural law now exercised a moral compulsion on men to unify further their convergent wills toward mutual safety, and the result was the decree on the general form of government which determined the manner in which the constituent individuals would voluntarily submit their wills to definition and execution by a single authority. At this stage, then, the members of the incipient civil society existed on two levels: a group of natural individuals, who, as individuals, continued to feed their consent into the moral corpus; and an association, which, as a composite moral person, was articulating the submission of its joint will to the general laws of security through the moral differentiation of itself into subjects and rulers. "A moral quality, such as sovereignty, may be produced in another by the united action of those who individually do not possess it formally before that time, so that they are rightly regarded as the productive cause of that quality. . . . In the same way the voices of many men, when modulated to each other, produce a harmony which did not before exist in the individuals." [53]

With the nomination of the sovereign, two levels of rulership appear to balance the two levels on which the constituent people exist. The rulers too have both a moral and a natural quality, the former as the contractually established unifying moral will and the latter in their capacity of men with "natural strength." It is this duality that gives rise to the final stage in the state-making process—the second, or rulership, contract—which consists in starting from the moral conversion of natural liberty into moral sovereignty and leading it back out to the natural world which is now qualified by the existence of authority. The rulership contract thus operates on both levels: it at once articulates the reciprocal moral relationship between the associated people and its appointed sovereign and binds each subject, considered as a natural individual, and each ruler, also considered as a natural individual, to the exercise of their rights and force in accordance with the moral relationship—that is, each individual's contribution to the ruler's administration of the common security.

This intertwining of natural and moral processes is crucial for Pufendorf, since he was enabled thereby to interpolate a moral consent of subjects to justify powers of the sovereign for which he could show no actual consent. Thus he denied that "what a superior takes from subjects by way of penalty is taken away with their consent," since this would leave the power of the superior "over the life of the subject . . . in the control of the subject himself." [54] For the same reason he denied that the punitive power was rooted in natural right, holding that there was no right of punishment—only of defense and compensation—in the state of nature. The punitive power of the sovereign, then, comes from consent only through the moral alchemy of the state-founding process:

> Just as in the case of natural substances there may result, from the mixing and balancing off of several simple substances, a compound in which are to be found qualities not observable in any of the ingre-

dients of the mixture, so moral bodies as well, composed of several men, can possess some right, consequent upon their union, which was not formally
inherent in any of the individual members, which
right also, arising from such a banding together, is
exercised by the governors of those bodies. . . .
In the same manner there can exist in the head of
a moral body the faculty of restraining each member by punishments, which faculty, however, was
not before that time in the individuals.[55]

A second function of Pufendorf's complicated state-making
process was that it enabled him to recognize the actual variety
of political institutions and practices and yet to refer them for
their unity to the other—moral—level of their existence,
since it was a process that left people and rulers alike with a
politically relevant natural as well as moral existence. Not
only does a natural level of individual life persist, since "it be
beyond the power of man to take away the intrinsic liberty of
the will and at the same time by some intrinsic means to
compose men's judgments about things into a lasting harmony" but even the "people," as a group, does not, after its
conferment of sovereignty, "cease by natural death": it "does
not indeed thereafter exist as a perfect person," but it "still
exists as a physical person" bearing moral obligations.[56]

The persistence of natural persons and groups within the
state made it possible for Pufendorf to return, once he had
completed the foundation of the state, to his historical distinction between family heads and other persons, opposing
Hobbes's literal attribution of citizenship to all individuals
alike, and describing a hierarchy of "principal" and "derivative" citizens.[57] On the side of the sovereigns, Pufendorf
could recognize several actual ways of acquiring sovereignty
on the principle that while the consent of the people is

needed for legitimate sovereignty, "still this consent is secured in different ways." [58] On this basis he justified political
obligation to rulers who had seized their sovereignty by force
if they then strengthened it by a subsequent pact—even if the
popular consent to it was actually fear-ridden—and to hereditary rulers on the grounds of an original pact. Through its
contractual foundation the state thus conferred a moral
organization upon the variety of customary and utilitarian
practices. Typical was his juxtaposition of natural and moral
grounds for accepting a usurper:

> Here our decision must be that the matter may
> come to pass that it is not only lawful but also oblig-
> atory to obey as one's sovereign him who has posses-
> sion, no matter how secured of the kingdom, it be-
> ing understood that the lawful lord . . . can no
> longer fulfil any of his duties as a prince toward
> his subjects. For although the other's commands
> lack the force to obligate, because they lack lawful
> power, it is still the part of the prudent man to
> take counsel for himself and his affairs, . . . lest
> he rashly imperil his life and fortune. And this is
> what would happen should he by his vain refusal
> draw down the wrath of the possessor upon his
> head. . . . Moreover, since one's country cannot
> do without some sort of sovereignty, and the pos-
> sessor is after a manner guarding the public safety,
> a good citizen, and one who loves his country,
> should not furnish the cause of still further tur-
> moil by useless stubbornness. . . .[59]

Pufendorf saw in the state essentially a service institution that catered to mutual security as the most negotiable
sector of men's interests, and he consequently attributed its

reason for being to men's voluntary negotiation of their natural rights to this service. In this respect he carried on the revolution in political theory which had been initiated by Hobbes when he delimited the function of the state to the provision of a legal order and based the state on its beneficiaries. But the complex of supports which Pufendorf added to this main pillar of its foundation indicated that the reduction of politics to the ordering of commensurable units of security, however responsive to the new military, diplomatic, and legislative activism of the territorial state, did not account for the whole of contemporary political relationships. There remained in the new states an ethical motif, still rooted more or less directly in religion, that instigated a direction of political authority and a degree of political obedience far beyond what so basic a self-interest as safety against aggression could require. Even in terms of its distinctive service function, the modern state requires an autonomous moral factor to stabilize the relationship between individual and mutual security; it was this recognition that went into the foundation of Pufendorf's state and is its contribution to the history of politics.

[5]

THE JURIST

Jurisprudence retained, in the seventeenth century, the practical tendency that had presided over its Roman origins. Both as a profession and as a field of knowledge it continued to supply rules of law for application to judicial cases and statutory decrees, and this function prevailed equally whether the source of the legal rules was precedent, custom, or the Roman law. But seventeenth-century jurisprudence also retained the secondary characteristic of its Roman origins: it perpetuated the tendency, which had been initiated in Stoicism, to connect positive laws with philosophical principles by seeing in the law not only a social but an ethical and even a metaphysical reality. By Pufendorf's time it was precisely this connection that had become an urgent problem.

The problem was an old one, but recent developments in jurisprudence, associated with the names of Jean Bodin in the sixteenth century and Hermann Conring in the earlier seventeenth, now made it urgent. Whereas both Roman and customary law had nestled more or less comfortably in the shadow of a traditional natural law whose protective role was generally accepted without question, the sixteenth- and early seventeenth-century emphasis upon the independent derivation of legal rules from local history and human will made the relationship of these rules to the logic of natural law questionable. Particularly in the realm of public law, where the new juristic positivism took the form of a revived constitutional law, did the problem of the relationship to the natural law, with its rational doctrine of exclusive sovereignty, become both substantive and acute. The parallel, unreconciled course of these two tendencies in both Bodin and Grotius is a prominent indication of the fundamental difficulty.

The response of subsequent jurists was to participate in the recasting of the natural-law doctrine with the goal of articulating the connection of fundamental truths with the variety of positive laws and institutions. The issue at stake was not merely the academic one of restoring coherence to the legal order but the political one of attributing an ideal value to one or another of the actual constitutional forms of the state and thereby of discriminating among them. Formerly, the logic of political theology had performed the service of constitutional preference, and it would take until the revolutionary end of the eighteenth century before an alternative system could be worked out which would subsume the constitutional distribution of power under the laws of politics with the same necessity that subsumed the laws of politics under the moral law. The outstanding juristic fact of this long period was the divergence between political morality and constitutional actuality, and the outstanding juristic activity was the effort to reconcile them. Pufendorf stands at the beginning of this effort: he reveals both the resistance of the new realism to a linear system of politics and the urgent need for unity that would eventually overcome it.

Pufendorf's whole purpose was to represent existing institutions as logical deductions from the moral and political theory that validated political life in general. It was, however, precisely at this level, where the principles met the practices of states, that Pufendorf shifted his approach from the specification of political consequences to the inference from legal actuality. In the course of his elaboration upon the operative relationships in the conduct of states the theorist gave way to the jurist.

I. FROM POLITICS TO JURISPRUDENCE

On the level of political logic the internal relations of Pufendorf's state descended necessarily from the rules of its inception and formed a closed circle. "We maintain that the legitimate power of a king and the duty of citizens exactly correspond, and we emphatically deny that a king can lawfully command anything which a subject can lawfully refuse." [1] The lawfulness (*ius*) which is thus the criterion of both authority and obedience is determined by the function of the political relationship—the mutual security that is "the end of instituted civil society." This function is made into fundamental law by the contractual obligations among the citizens and between ruler and subjects, which have it as their exclusive object. Within the sphere defined by "the common safety and security," the ruling authority is entitled to operate "according to its own judgment and discretion," in respect both to what it can itself perform and to what it can compel its subjects to perform.[2] It follows, then, that for Pufendorf the ruler of every "regular" state is a "sovereign," with all the qualities that Bodin and Hobbes discovered in this concept of authority—supremacy, unaccountability, monopoly (in one organ), and indivisibility (of function). For the subject of every state, the sovereign is "sacrosanct and inviolable," since there is "necessarily joined" to the very nature of sovereignty "the obligation . . . of immediate obedience in doing or not doing what it commands"—so long as the rulers "stay within the limits of their power." [3]

The decisive question then becomes the specification of the functions that validate the monopoly of power by the sovereign. Pufendorf here cut a swath for his sovereign through all the fields of human activity and opinion which had traditionally been the concern of the authorities, but he now delimited the political sector by segregating in each field the area relevant to the maintenance of "peace" and establishing only the sovereign in charge of it, but of it only. To use a spatial analogy, if the varied functions of man are represented as vertical divisions, the political function, as Pufendorf conceived it, was a horizontal division cutting across and through them.

Thus the legitimate powers of the sovereign include not only the military and diplomatic functions obviously necessary to repel foreign aggression and the legislative, punitive, judicial, and appointive functions obviously necessary to protect "the security of citizens . . . against fellow citizens" but a whole panoply of less obvious functions insofar as they serve the same ends. Sovereigns possess the power not only to tax and regulate the use of property for "the welfare of the state" but also to increase "the private fortunes of their citizens," since "the vigor of a state lies in the strength and resources of the same." [4] The rights and powers of "subordinate bodies"—corporations or lesser societies—over their members "are all defined and limited" by the sovereign in order to exclude any conflict of authorities; the sovereign has, moreover, the power to create such subordinate bodies, and only the sovereign has the power to create, in particular, a noble class, since legal inequality must devolve exclusively from the right to command other men. [5]

Beyond these economic and social capacities, finally, the sovereign also has a legitimate wedge into not only the activities but even the opinions relating to the ethical and religious disposition of men. "Since the actions of men are controlled by their several opinions, and most men are in the habit of judging things in accordance with their habit, or as they see the matter is commonly judged; and since very few can by their own ability distinguish truth and honor, it is expedient for the state that it resound with such teachings, publicly taught, as are in harmony with the proper end and need of states, and, at the same time, that the citizens' minds be imbued with them from boyhood." [6] What "the end and need of states" in this field requires, moreover, is not only "an interest in right conduct" so as to engender the disposition to obey the laws but also "an external means" to make men's varying "individual opinions . . . and judgments, so far as possible agree, or to prevent at least their differences from disturbing the state." The civil sovereign, therefore, has the power not only to examine and "to drive . . . out of the state" such beliefs "which, thrusting themselves forward under the guise of religion, or in some other way, overturn the law of nature, and the principles of sound politics, and so are of a nature to infect the state with mortal diseases," but even himself to "openly profess, as it were, such beliefs as agree with the end and use of states." [7]

The circulation of command and obedience between supreme sovereign and constituent subject runs smoothly within these lawful channels defined by the orderly purpose of the state. The normative political relationship which Pufendorf set up in this model embodied his commitment to rational order and has secured to him his historical place among the theorists of absolutism. [8] But the unmediated relationship between a citizenry with an original monopoly of rights and a sovereign with an ultimate monopoly of power was an inherently unstable one. It could work logically for a political model but was subject to modification when the

[137]

model was applied to the manifold of existence, and with Pufendorf's temperament this was an application from which he could not refrain. The crucial political function which marked the transition and opened the self-enclosed legal process to intrusion and complication by the other levels of reality from which he had initially suspended it was the jurisdiction over jurisdictions—that is, the right to determine the extent of a power. He began by attributing it, in consonance with his political logic, to the sovereign, but then proceeded to recognize the limitations of this prerogative by the actualities outside the model.

Pufendorf's point of departure was the demonstrable general principle, in terms of his system, that the jurisdiction over jurisdictions had to lie in the exclusive purview of the sovereign. In view of "the greatest diversity of judgments and desires . . . to be observed among men, because of which an infinite number of disputes can arise," it is the rightful function of the sovereign to define "what a man still retains of his natural liberty," "what natural obligation gives rise to an action in a civil court, and what action does not do so but depends solely upon the honor and probity of men." [9] The sovereign, in other words, has not only exclusive authority over all rights and activities that fall within the function of the state but also the exclusive authority to determine what rights and activities do fall within the function of the state. Now, as we have seen, the realm that exists outside the purview of the state is the realm of nature, but for Pufendorf this realm is not integral but consists itself of two levels. There is the pure natural condition, dominated by the variously expressed natural rights of individual men to their own preservation, and the mixed natural condition, dominated by the non-political social organization of men under the natural law. The state is founded upon impulses from both these natural levels but is co-extensive with neither. It is initiated by the individual's right and interest in security, but it absorbs only that part of the right and interest which is conjoint with his fellows' and leaves the residue of the original right and interest in being. The state becomes similarly a means to realize natural law, but it covers only the security requirements of a moral law that prescribes a broader norm of sociability.

Despite his attribution to the sovereign of the right to fix both frontiers between nature and politics, Pufendorf did acknowledge the ultimate functional integrity of the two natural levels apart from politics. On the level of natural liberty, he recognized the right of the individual, "by denial, hiding, or flight," to "avoid" any civil punishment legitimately decreed upon him.[10] On the level of natural law, despite his assertions that a chief object of states is "the ability to secure the safe exercise of natural laws," that through civil laws the sovereign enforces the laws of nature, that through equity "what is wanting in civil laws is supplied by the law of nature," and that without the natural law "the civil law would be condensed into a fairly small compass," he also insisted both in practice and principle upon the discrimination between the law of the state and the law of nature. Not only does the sovereign have a discrete field of legitimate civil activity in which he imposes justice on security matters that are left "indifferent" by the natural law; not only do all men possess a discrete field of activity subject only to natural law in such exemptions from politics as "purely internal acts," "faults of the mind . . . resulting from the common corruption of men," and "the means to merit high praise which comes from having lived a life of rectitude out of mere reverence for God": but "a civil law could . . . be passed which is opposed to natural law," since "justice . . . , truth and rectitude depend upon . . . the nature of things," which cannot "be fashioned by supreme sovereigns

[139]

at their pleasure," and the fundamentals of institutions like property, marriage, and the family, resting outside the state, may not be violated by the laws of the "civil power." [11]

Thus if, from the moral point of view, Pufendorf stipulated the unquestioning acceptance of the sovereign's authority as the will of the state which provided the only necessary connection between the self-interested liberty of individuals and the other-interested obligation of natural law, he had also to acknowledge that the total actuality in which this moral relationship was embedded intruded disturbances into the automatic workings of the legal mechanism.[12] These disturbances were manifest in the actual variety and complexity of existing political practices and institutions which testified to the additional arrangements devised by men to guide the exercise of their natural liberty toward their legal duties and their legal duties toward the ultimate purpose of the natural law. Pufendorf had, in short, to go beyond the normative will of the sovereign to account for the actually winding frontiers between natural rights and the state on one side and natural law and the state on the other. From this generic point of view he now admitted that in fact "turbulent or querulous citizens" commonly represent legitimate civil laws as injustices to themselves and that "a state and its head" actually do inflict upon citizens injuries which are unjust by dint of a violated contractual right or the "community of natural law" subsisting between the sovereign and the citizen.[13]

In his earliest essay Pufendorf contented himself with asserting the doctrinaire legal authority of the sovereign over subjects' actual claims in behalf of natural right and law by advancing the concept of the sovereign's "imperfect [that is, unenforceable] obligation" to signify that these claims lacked the legal status to be enforceable.[14] In his mature formulation Pufendorf still espoused the authoritarian side, but now he dropped the moralistic doctrine of the imperfect obligation in favor of more directly prudential considerations:

> Since such is the condition of human life that it cannot do without some inconveniences, and since there can hardly be found a man on earth whose manners are so regulated that he can satisfy everyone to a nicety, it would be foolish as well as impudent to wish to rise in revolt against a prince for merely any kind of grievance, especially since we ourselves are not always so exact in meeting our full duty toward him, and since the laws commonly overlook the lesser shortcomings of private citizens.[15]

With this shift in standpoint from rigorous political logic to the balance of law and practice Pufendorf opened the way to a more flexible and realistic relating of sovereign to individual.

II. The Structure of the State

In order to show how men were actually directed into their role as lawful subjects and how rulers were actually channeled into exercising their sovereignty within the proper sphere of the state, Pufendorf implicitly revamped his simple scheme of a closed circuit bearing the direct and reciprocating forces between individuals and sovereign by acknowledging the validity of four intervening factors in what now became an architectonic structure of the state. He introduced patriotism and revolution as clamps holding subjects and rulers respectively in place, limited sovereignty and a hierarchical society as conduits for the relations between them.

Pufendorf developed a doctrine of patriotism during the

period of maturation from the earliest essay to the definitive formulation of his political theory, and the special interpretation that he gave to it clearly reveals its use for him as an existential support of the subjects' obedience.[16] Starting from its actual rank "almost in first place" among the things to which men are tied by "tender affection," he proceeded to argue that the valid basis of the emotion, and of the obligation which it sentimentally buttressed, was the due "reverence" for the services rendered to the individual by the state. He denied that the mere attachment to one's native soil was the effective element in patriotism, for only "reason and the hope of utility" could create a lasting bond, and he applied the semantic derivation of *patria* from *pater* to show both the psychological roots of the concept in the benefits of the care appropriate to the functions of the father and its anthropological roots in the transfer of the security function from the patriarch to the sovereign.[17] Patriotism is thus "adjectival": it bestows an added increment to men's obligation for benefits received and expected, and the special relationship to which it applies is the political relationship between sovereign and subject—it is *"patria civitas"* rather than *"patria terra."* "Through states, maximum security . . . is conferred upon our fortunes. Since the term *patria* borrows much reverence and love from its origins, any state [*civitas*] in which one fixes the seat of his fortunes, whether through birth or immigration, begins to be called by that name." [18] Pufendorf thereupon pinpointed the function of patriotism as a reinforcement of lawful political obligation by recapitulating his political doctrine to demonstrate the parallel scope of patriotism and citizenship. "As much as the fatherland [*patria*] can demand from its citizens by law, so much are they understood to owe it. . . . Fatherlands are owed from that common obligation by which we are citizens." [19] Patriotism, like citizenship, does not authorize transgressions of conscience, but

[142]

it does reinforce the rule that "the presumption of justice always accompanies the orders of a superior." [20]

Secondly, Pufendorf recognized the valid possibility of resistance to the ruler as an actual sanction to help direct the will of the sovereign toward the proper definition of his sphere. Since Pufendorf asserted the legal monopoly of force by the sovereign within the political process, his doctrine of resistance can be understood only in terms of its application outside the political process.

> These two statements are by no means the same: A people has the power to use force against its kings and bring them to terms if they have not ruled in accordance with its desires; and, there belongs to a people or to individuals, in the face of danger, and when the prince has become an enemy, the right to defend their safety against him. [21]

Leaving aside the license to emigrate and to avoid punishment which Pufendorf recognized as the persistent reserved natural right of individuals at any time, he admitted the validity of active resistance, with due cautionary admonitions, for two general transgressions, one for each of the frontiers separating the political from the natural sectors of man.

The first general cause of legitimate resistance consisted in the failure of the ruler to assume the legal position of sovereign by governing not at all or not enough. [22] To this extent the ruler can be held "to have resigned his sovereignty," implicitly to have re-entered the state of nature in relation to the citizens, and to wrong them by claiming the "emoluments" of the ruler's post when natural relationships actually prevail. What is violated here is the subjects' natural right to the security for which they had contracted.

The second valid occasion for resistance is furnished by an excess of authority, when the ruler intrudes his political power into matters covered by the law of nature with an "extreme and unjust violence" so palpable and so lacking in any pretext of state security or necessity that the political relationship becomes irrelevant and the ruler becomes "an enemy" in the state of nature.[23] This right of resistance on the authorization of natural law applies both to individuals and to whole peoples. It applies to individuals when the ruler visits a dangerous injustice upon a subject and again when he commands the subject to undertake in defiance of the natural law an action for which the latter is held responsible before God. On the former issue flight is recommended but fight is permitted; on the latter issue passive disobedience is a moral necessity: neither issue warrants support by fellow citizens. The "people" as such are entitled to resist only when the ruler's authority to command both what the natural law dictates concerning security and what makes for security apart from natural law is actually overborne by his "hostile intent directly to subvert the safety of the whole state." Since this safety, once constituted, is necessary to the ends of natural law, the people are empowered by the sector of natural law lying beyond the political society to enforce it against the ruler who has divested himself of his political authority. In Pufendorf's view, then, resistance is valid against actual rulers rather than legal sovereigns. He designed his doctrine of revolution not as a guarantee of rights but as an exhortation to rulers that they maintain for the sake of good order the integrity of the political realm.

Thirdly, Pufendorf qualified his univocal doctrine of sovereignty by admitting the validity of institutional limitations upon it. He had asserted emphatically in his legal context that the man or the council in whom sovereignty was vested exercised a power that was supreme, exclusive, and indivisible. The sovereign was indeed subject to divine and natural law but he was accountable for his conduct under them to none but God, and he "is free from civil laws, or rather is superior to them." [24] And yet, just as he acknowledged an extrapolitical human accountability to the natural law in the form of a circumscribed right of resistance, he also acknowledged an extrapolitical restriction of the sovereign's power over civil law in the possibility of "limited sovereignties [*imperiorum limitatorum*]." A limited sovereignty was one in which the ruler bound himself at the time of his accession, either through a promise or a special contract with the citizens, to "a definite manner of holding . . . and administering sovereignty, . . . in accordance with certain basic laws" and in conjunction with a popular or aristocratic council without whose consent no civil law is valid. [25] In the initial formulation of his political theory Pufendorf had registered the existence of such institutions but had denied them a special status: all political sovereignty was "absolute" and in such a situation either the king or the council was the absolute sovereign, depending on who dominated whom. [26] Now, however, Pufendorf rejected this very point, in the form of Hobbes's espousal of it, and maintained that, while every sovereign must be "supreme," both absolute and limited sovereignties are valid forms, comporting equally well with supremacy. [27] It is easy to see in this turn of Pufendorf's his susceptibility to the fundamental laws and the corporate representative estates that still bulked large in the political reality of his day. [28] His specific discussion of the councils that limited the sovereignty of the prince was in fact focused on "the estates [*ordines*]." [29] But what was important here was not his notice of them but the rational meaning which he could attribute to them in view of his rigorous doctrine of sovereignty.

Pufendorf's formal rationale for a sovereignty that was

[145]

limited and yet both supreme and undivided was that it was "restricted to a certain manner of procedure" in comparison with the regime of the absolute sovereign, who pursues the same political ends but entirely in accordance with his own judgment.[30] Although the restriction means that the laws and other acts of the limited sovereign deviating from the stipulated fundamental laws and consent of estates are void, yet "all the acts of sovereignty can be exercised as well in such a monarchy as in an absolute one." "Whatever the state desires it desires through the will of the king" still; the effect of the restriction by fundamental laws and representative consent is simply to pose a "necessary condition" under which the sovereign will has effect. Examples of such restrictive laws would be the provision that an established religion could be changed, extraordinary taxes raised, offensive wars declared, or part of the realm alienated by the sovereign only with the consent of the people or its representatives. The sovereign's relationship with a council of the estates which was established by contract between king and people and effectively limits the king "in certain spheres of action" by the necessary condition of its consent requires, if he is sovereign, that he retain the powers of convocation, dissolution, and legislative initiation. Finally, all such contracts between limited sovereign and people are to be interpreted as having a reserve clause to the effect that "those conditions and agreements never lead to the commission of anything which would prejudice the common safety of all, and the public welfare, and lead to the overthrow or dissolution of the state." Should there be no opportunity to amend such conditions by consent, "the king will be empowered carefully to correct pacts which are destined to lead to the destruction of the state." [31]

This is tortuous reasoning about popular laws and assemblies which "condition" and "limit" but do not share or even diminish the ruler's sovereignty, and the one assumption on the basis of which it makes sense is that the function of the restrictions is to keep the ruler a sovereign—to keep him within the political sphere in which he remains supreme. Thus Pufendorf's grounding of limited sovereignty:

> But since the judgment of a single man may be easily misled in seeking out what is for the welfare of the state, and not all are gifted with such soundness of mind that they know in such great liberty how to control their lusts when they battle with reason . . . , it has appeared advisable to many peoples not to commit in so absolute a fashion such power as this to a single man, whose judgment is not immune to errors, and whose choice easily turns to base desires. . . .[32]

This motive is obviously similar to that of an absolute sovereign who appoints his own council and declares its approval necessary for the validity of his own laws, in order "to avoid making any decisions through imprudence, or on the urge of flatterers, that would be prejudicial to the state." [33] Since the ruler can in this instance make his will prevail against the council, such an institution obviously works no restriction upon his absolute sovereignty. The similarity of its motive and function to the authentic limitation of sovereignty by contractually based councils indicates the theoretical role which Pufendorf provided for corporate political institutions: they helped to fix against nature the boundaries of the state within which the ruler exercised supreme, exclusive, and undivided sovereignty.

The fourth and final conditioning institution assigned to confine subjects and sovereigns within their proper channels was the social hierarchy, which may be viewed as the underpinning of the representative estates where they existed and their substitute where they did not. Here again Pufendorf's provision makes sense only as an attempt to account for an actual institution of his time in such a way as not to disturb the direct and reciprocal political relations between individual and sovereign which he found to be the fundamental element in the state. Since the logic of his politics brooked no intermediary between the individual and the sovereign, intermediary institutions must be reduced to either terminus or they must be located outside the political relationship. In actual fact the social hierarchy did have political ramifications, and in Pufendorf's theory it did have a political relevance as one of the institutions confining individuals and sovereigns within their proper political spheres. Consequently, Pufendorf did both: he located its basis outside the state and made its political sector a function of individuals and sovereigns. He did not, of course, do this explicitly, but it can be safely inferred from his treatment of specific problems associated with the issue.

A social hierarchy is made up of two components: distinctions among men according to differential value, and the organization of men into discrete corporations. Pufendorf's analyses of these factors were separate but parallel, and from the combination of them his doctrine of social hierarchy emerges.[34] He attributed the roots of both factors to men's nature, independent of the state. Not only is "status," as the location of men within society, a fundamental element in human relations, but "esteem," as that kind of status "in accordance with which they can be equated or compared with other persons, and ranked either before or after them," also exists "outside a state even in natural liberty."[35] Both "simple esteem" (distinction among men according to their general tendency to observe the requirements of natural law) and "intensive esteem" (distinction among men equal in simple esteem according to the degrees of "honor" shown

[148]

particular excellence of mind and performance in fulfilling the end of natural law) are fundamentally "natural." Analogously, there are also special bodies, such as the family, which characterize the natural condition of men. But natural distinctions confer only the capacity to receive differential honors; the "right" to such honors, which involves not only a legal ranking of men but their enjoyment of unequal rights in conjunction with it, comes only from imposition by the sovereign for special performance relevant to the ends of the state. Similarly, natural corporations and special corporations formed by the agreement of private individuals within the state, albeit for extrapolitical ends, receive legal recognition and protection as well as regulation from the sovereign to align them with the ends of the state.

Because distinctions among men and their capacity to form special corporations have their foundations in human nature and their legal effectiveness in the state, the political role of both institutions, for Pufendorf, entered into the standard relations between individuals, with their residual natural rights, and the sovereign, with his monopoly of authority. For the ranking of citizens, this meant that only the sovereign can assign enforceable privileges but that he should look to individual worthiness as his canon of selection:

> Although one man or another may appear to have been unworthily raised above his betters, yet the man who undertakes to request another station for such, or to be restive in his own, can be punished as no better than a rebel to the supreme power of the land. . . . Yet, . . . they [the princes] will be the more careful in this matter by reason of the fact that, unless the dignity and prerogative of eminent citizens are measured by the benefits and

aid which they do or can render the more needy, they are to be regarded as silly and idle. But since if princes were always to assign every citizen a place in keeping with his intrinsic dignity, it would be a nuisance for them to go so often over the lists of their citizens and give them a new order, . . . the most convenient course seems to be that of according distinction, at least to the outstanding citizens, by the offices which they perform in connection with the commonwealth.[36]

It follows that after a sovereign has conferred "badges of honor" upon a citizen "as his own personal possession" the citizen may indeed be divested of their associated legal "immunities and privileges, . . . as the condition of the state requires," but he "cannot regularly be deprived" of the honors themselves, any more than of any right or possession rooted in the state of nature.[37] As for corporations, analogously, Pufendorf reduced them all to a source either in the wills of the individual citizens or the will of a sovereign, and he stipulated that the members of such corporations were bound by corporate action only when it conformed to charters approved by the sovereign. Thus, by virtue of their natural origins, Pufendorf could make the benefits of class distinctions and corporate organization to sovereigns and subjects alike dependent upon the proper discrimination of the political from the natural realms of activity.

The outstanding juncture of class and corporation in contemporary European society was the nobility, and it was explicitly upon this institution that Pufendorf tested his principles in the climax of his discussion. Nowhere is Pufendorf's caution and the comprehensiveness with which he adapted his theory to all existing institutions more apparent, and nowhere is more clearly manifested his singular contri-

[150]

bution in commending the acceptance of the natural-law doctrine to the corporate society as well as the sovereign authorities of his age. On this issue he shifted the mode of his treatment from the deduction of principles to the description of contemporary practice, and he allowed his own principles to come through only in his implicit predilection for some practices over others, in his equally implicit endorsement of what "some who argue" have argued, and in his rationalization of the nobiliary institution.

In the course of his description Pufendorf allowed the issue raised by the discrepancy between the requirements of his political theory and the actualities of nobiliary privilege to emerge in the form of the divergent practices of various "nations [*gentium*]," and he resolved this issue, as so many others, by converting it from a question of rights against sovereign *authority* to a matter of conditions operative upon sovereign *policy*. Thus he noted approvingly that "in some states little heed is given to birth, and every man's nobility is derived from his own virtue" and that in ancient Rome hereditary nobility, possessing almost no privileges, "did not establish a peculiar order in the state," but he had to account for the fact not only that "many states have seen fit" to establish nobility by birth but that "the character of the Roman nobility was different from that which now obtains in most of the kingdoms of Europe. For with us the nobles form a special order, distinguished from the rest of the citizens in dignity and peculiar rights." [38] It is, moreover, hereditary in title and military in function.

The problem raised by the nobility for Pufendorf's juristic theory stemmed from the contrariety of his two equally cherished convictions about it. On the one hand, the nobility as a hereditary class has no roots in nature, since nature does not "vary her process in the creation of nobles and commons," "a man builds his nobility upon his own virtue," and consequently "there appears no necessity in nature itself why a son should succeed to the offices of his father." On the other hand, the sovereigns of states have a perfect right to impose and endow a hereditary nobility by commanding that a man "be put in a class distinct from the commons, which together with its rights he can in the future hand down to his posterity," even though the prince thereby "works no change in the man's nature and origin, nor does he endow his mind with any new vigor." [39] Certainly Pufendorf hereby achieved his aim of reducing the rights, privileges, and immunities of the noble class to revocable political products of the sovereign will, but the price of thus justifying the existing nobility by its subordination to the ruler was the danger of excluding the natural aristocracy of talent and consequently of cutting the sovereign off from the common mass of natural individuals whose respect constituted this aristocracy and whose support constituted the state.

Pufendorf's solution was to advance the argument that even if natural distinction authorized no legal privilege the sovereign should be guided by natural distinction in determining on whom the endowment of honors and its associate special rights would conform with the ends of the state. Where the military function of the contemporary nobility has closed accession to the caste by honorable civilian commoners, the sovereign must simply create a set of appropriate honors and privileges for this new mobile aristocracy of merit:

> There are some who argue . . . that a state suffers from no light disease, if the supreme civil power is so drawn and bound to a certain social class, in assigning its affairs of state, that it cannot avail itself of the service of other citizens in matters for which they are recognized to be particu-

larly suited; especially when that power is not allowed to choose able men for this social class. For if any prince finds himself forced to favor the nobles only in order that by their aid he may be better able to restrain the rest of his subjects, this is evidence that his power is tottering and has almost completely lost control, since he is forced to join a conspiracy, as it were, with a part of his citizens, and depends no longer on open authority. . . .[40]

Pufendorf clearly aligned himself with this position (he even slipped from the subjunctive to the declarative mode during the course of representing it).[41] He accepted the political rationale for heredity in the nobility—its incentive to service in the ennobled and its tradition of service for the descendants—and he did not dispute the institution itself, but, with the additive inclinations of the trimmer, he also adduced the natural talents of the enterprising commoner to urge the continual expansion of the privileged class by governmental fiat.

III. CONSTITUTIONAL FORMS

From the beginning to the end of his intellectual career Pufendorf exhibited a supreme indifference to the constitutional location of political power within the state, an issue that was subsequently to dominate the politics of the Western world. In his earliest treatise he laconically noted only that "as the special forms of a commonwealth vary, it [the supreme power] inheres now in one person, now in a certain few, now in the whole people," and he implicitly validated all three traditional varieties of constitutions.[42] Some thirty years later he was not only holding the same position but making his constitutional relativism even more positive:

[153]

Scripture says that we should obey the sovereign
that has authority over us, whether it is monarchical, aristocratic, or democratic, absolute or limited. A Lutheran citizen who is monarchical is a
rogue in a democracy. . . . The kind of state in
which one is raised and to which one is accustomed
usually pleases him the best. It is no wonder, consequently, that the Swiss and Dutch are good re-
publicans; were they otherwise it would be a fault
in them.[43]

In his discussions of sovereignty, to be sure, he sometimes
slipped into the use of the term "prince" as a synonym for
"sovereign" and he did once note a "conspicuous advantage"
of monarchy over democracy and aristocracy in the practical
benefit of having the performance of sovereign acts possible
at any time and place rather than only at fixed times and
places of convocation, but he neither emphasized the point
nor made a principle of it.[44] In fact he balanced it by
noting the precedence of democracy over monarchy as the
oldest form of the state and by arguing against both Hobbes
and the proponents of divine right to the effect that democracy and aristocracy possessed the same moral power to
obligate their citizens and the same sanctity as monarchy.[45]
    What lay behind his toleration of constitutional forms is
indicated by his indifference to further specifications of them.
He recognized the bulk of the usual distinctions—between
the form of the state and the manner of its administration,
between healthy and corrupted variants of each form, between the generic definition of each form and such actual
deviations as patrimonial kingdoms from monarchy and the
denial of suffrage to "not a few" subjects from the norm of a
democracy—but he denied that any of these "accidents or
qualities" constituted another "species" of state and insisted

that "the species of states should not be multiplied on that account." Pufendorf justified his refusal to go beyond the traditional triad in defining the valid forms of the state by arguing that all other variations "alter neither the nature of political power itself nor its particular holder [*subjectum proprium*]." [46] Obviously, then, his sole criterion in judging what was fundamental in the state was the direct and reciprocal relationship between sovereign and subjects for purposes of mutual safety, and he would admit no other diversionary or challenging consideration. Thus he held states to be corrupted either by "human vices" which prevented the ruler or rulers from acting as sovereigns or by "constitutional vices" through which inappropriate laws and institutions prevented the people from fulfilling their duties as subjects, and since both these cases were mere negative functions of the essential political relationship, they manifested, in accord with Pufendorf's intention, no independent political principle.[47]

Pufendorf's general indifference to constitutional forms, then, reflected his desire to apply his primary political insight as widely across the board of political reality as he could. The equal validity which he asserted for monarchy, aristocracy, and democracy to denote the legitimate location of the sovereign power in the one, the few, or the many exhausted the requirements for its most varied application and rendered further distinctions among states even more inconsequential.

And yet it was precisely this problem of constitutional forms that stirred Pufendorf as only the relations of religion and politics were otherwise to do. It stirred him not in the shape of a preference among the traditional forms for a more authoritarian or a more popular source of ultimate political power—an issue which had been crucial before him and would be again after him—but rather in the distinction between "regular" and "irregular" states, that is, between the pure and the hybrid forms of the state in the Aristotelian scheme. For this distinction he argued with a passion and constructed a foundation in fundamental principle that he denied to any other in politics, save that of natural and divine right. He published no less than five treatises on the theme of "irregular commonwealths," including the notorious work on the German constitution, which he wrote in the guise of a traveling Italian nobleman, Severinus de Monzambano, and which he actively defended in the subsequent polemic.[48] Nor, despite his composition of these pieces during the 1660's, can Pufendorf's preoccupation with the theme be dismissed as a mere episode or even as a theoretical phase which would be wholly absorbed into the more basic political concepts of natural law and sovereignty. Not only did he insert an epitome of his doctrine on irregular forms into his mature and systematic *On the Law of Nature* but he devoted part of his final years to the preparation of a new edition of *On the Constitution of the German Empire.*[49]

The question naturally arises: why did Pufendorf, who was otherwise so casual about constitutional forms, make the particular constitutional distinction between regular and irregular forms a fundamental political principle? The magnetism of his sensational work on the German constitution, with its clear, direct, and critical perception of the anomalous internal relations which characterized the actuality of German politics, has established the conventional view that Pufendorf's concern with constitutional forms in this way was a register of his political realism: he was convinced that contemporary political reality could not be comprehended through Aristotelian concepts, with which he identified the "regular" forms of the state.[50] Whether "Monzambano" was thus merely a critical realist or whether he meant to demonstrate the superior applicability of his own *a priori* concept of

[156]

sovereignty, it is certainly true that the result of the work on the German constitution was to furnish empirical confirmation of Pufendorf's political theory.[51] But there are several considerations which indicate a more positive theoretical function for his constitutional doctrine: it was not only a practical elaboration of his political philosophy but also an essential theoretical contribution to it.

First, Pufendorf's theory was not simply a monolith which could be opposed, *en bloc,* to the Aristotelian tradition. It overlapped that tradition and where the two conflicted a gap was opened in the Pufendorfian theory itself. Aristotle distinguished among states by asking to whom political power was distributed and came up with his three pure forms and a fourth, residual, category of "mixed" constitutions. Pufendorf distinguished among the states rather by undercutting the tradition to ask what kind of power it was that was being distributed and his answer coincided with the bulk of the Aristotelian forms. Not only in the healthy but in the corrupted versions of democracies, aristocracies, and monarchies Pufendorf identified the powers exercised by the rulers as sovereign powers, and he even appropriated from the category of "mixed states" those cases in which variations in the manner of administration led Aristotelians to the erroneous classification of what is actually a pure form, equipped with undivided sovereignty.[52] But this left the hard core of mixed states, in which the ultimate political, or sovereign, power was divided and distributed among several independent persons or organs, and it was in reference to these that Pufendorf had to make a categorical and principled constitutional distinction. He was forced to take a fundamental position on this constitutional form because he could not account for it with his doctrine of sovereignty and yet his doctrine of sovereignty was designed precisely to provide a unitary basis for every kind of state. Hence he could not, without undermining the vaunted universality of his political theory, simply slough off this mixed form as non-states. He had, in short, to account, with his theory of sovereignty, for the kind of polity which this theory could not account for.

It was this apparent paradox which Pufendorf's categorical distinction between regular and irregular forms of the state was designed to meet. The regular forms he defined as those in which "the supreme sovereignty, without division or opposition, is exercised by one will in all the parts of the state and in all its undertakings": included in this category were the three traditional forms together with all their corrupted and variant deviations. The irregular form he defined as polities that "vary from a regular state in that not everything proceeds from one and the same will, nor is each and every person to be controlled by virtue of sovereignty." [53] The ambiguity over which this ostensibly logical division of constitutions is built creeps out in Pufendorf's cautious terminology: he uses *civitas,* or the state properly so called, only for the regular forms; both the genus, of which there are regular and irregular species, and the irregular forms themselves are always *rei publicae* or *republicae,* a blanket concept which he is careful not to define but whose aura is best sensed in the archaic connotation of our literal translation into "commonwealth." [54] The ambiguity appears too in his paradoxical characterization of the irregular form as "formless": "Whoever wishes to divide the parts of government will never constitute a state properly so called but only a formless aggregate whose parts are held together not by sovereignty which is the soul of the state, but only by the force of natural agreement." [55] Because the irregular forms are formless they cannot be classified; each case is, rather, *sui generis.*[56] Thus, while Pufendorf had to open the way, in his political theory, for cases of divided sovereignty the theory did not explain them; the theory had rather to be explained by them.

Secondly, then, Pufendorf's treatment of the German constitution was no mere explanation of German politics in terms of his theory; it was embedded in a context which showed his intention to have German politics also clarify the theory. To be sure, his apparent designs upon a chair of German constitutional law at Heidelberg and his biting criticisms of jurists who were applying the Aristotelian categories of monarchy, aristocracy, or mixed state to the German Empire show that his interest in Germany as such was not negligible.[57] He was participating, moreover, in a specifically German constitutional school of historical realists, represented notably in his predecessors Bogislav Chemnitz, who had published his anti-imperial work on the German *raison d'état* in 1643 (*De ratione status in Imperio Romano-Germanico*), and Hermann Conring, whose *Origin of German Law* (*De origine juris Germanici*) had employed German constitutional history to reject the traditional dominion of Roman law in German constitutional doctrine. But if Pufendorf's book on the German constitution falls into this development, the fact remains that in the essays that both preceded and succeeded its publication, the German constitution was simply an example in his general theory of constitutions.

He set forth the theoretical framework which was to support the German observations of "Monzambano" during 1664, when he was just beginning to compose the impressions of that impersonator, in a treatise on Philip of Macedonia. This initial formulation of the theory, revealingly enough, had a negative function. Pufendorf was arguing that Philip's regime was a "limited sovereignty" and therefore a proper state in accordance with his concept of sovereignty. To set off what it was by contrast to what it was not, Pufendorf developed, in opposition to the class of limited sovereignties which explained Philip's state, the concept of "a monstrous com-

[159]

monwealth [*monstrum quoddam reipublicae*]" which "exists" wherever sovereignty is divided and there is no one supreme power.[58] In Monzambano's *German Constitution*, published three years later, the contemplation of German conditions developed this negative relief into the rudiments of an explanatory category. The residents of the category were not yet set in contrast to a logically equipoised class of "regular" states and they were still "monstrous," but they were already also "irregular":

> Just as the health and strength of natural and artificial bodies result from the mutual harmony and connection of their parts, so moral bodies or societies are judged strong or weak according to whether their parts are deemed to be mutually connected well or badly and therefore according to whether they exhibit a well-proportioned [*concinnam*] form or something irregular and monstrous. It appears clearly enough from the foregoing treatment that certain elements in the commonwealth of the Germans do not permit it to be registered among the simple forms of commonwealths as they are usually described by political writers. . . . There is nothing for it but to say that Germany is an irregular body, similar to a monster, if it is measured by the rules of civil science.[59]

When Pufendorf turned, a year later, to the defense of Monzambano against his detractors, the "monster" was gone.[60] He cast his argument in the form of a complete constitutional theory designed to explain all the variants of politics in terms of their unifying bond in sovereignty and representing Monzambano's German analysis not only as an example that irregular commonwealths, one of the main divisions in the theory, exist but also as a case study of how the genre operates. It is convenient, he began, "for demonstrating phenomena in certain commonwealths more clearly, to divide all commonwealths in the world" into simple and composite (of which more later) and each of these again into regular and irregular.[61] And he concluded, after expatiating on the specific points of Monzambano's depiction of the German constitution, with generalizations from the German instance on the degeneration of regular into irregular forms and on the possibilities of the latter's "dissolution"—a standard conclusion for a constitutional theory.[62]

The reciprocal flow of the German analysis into his general constitutional theory reveals Pufendorf's disinclination to rest content with the obvious course that was open to him: to demonstrate, via his theory of sovereignty, that the Aristotelian theorists were wrong in their validation of the German constitution and to accept his own conclusion that this constitution was, in any rational political sense, invalid. The realities of the German situation apparently alerted him to something that pushed him beyond mere theoretical criticism to a positive development of his own theory.

What this something was emerges from the third consideration which made his work on the German constitution more than an application of his concept of sovereignty: he learned from the German case that irregular constitutions not only demonstrate the defects in traditional constitutional theory but also mark actual defects in political reality. The "fluctuation" of the German constitution between the regular forms, he noted, "furnishes a permanent spur to destructive disease and internal convulsions" and is itself "among the chief diseases" from which the country suffers.[63] He concluded from this that the irregular forms in general are "aberrations of states" and belong to those "defects of things which depart

[161]

from their primary idea." They must be studied as much as "the structure of regular states," for we must understand the nature of the defects "if we want to apply them to our uses." [64] Thus Pufendorf's German experience taught him that the problem of irregular forms was a defect not of his political theory but of political existence. His theory was designed to account for constant political relationships behind the variety of facts, but the German case exhibited the existence of facts that did not enter into these relationships. Through political action the facts might be made reasonable and the necessary ambiguity of theory clarified.

But the German study contributed something still more positive: it revealed the one context that would solve his three main theoretical problems: the pairing of regular versus irregular forms of sovereignty as the chief distinction among constitutions; his use of the concept of the state to account for political forms that were by this token not states; and his uncharacteristic call for political action to reform the facts in accordance with his theory—the precise converse of his usual attitude. This context was, to give it a later formulation, the primacy of foreign over domestic policy. By demonstrating this principle, Pufendorf's interpretation of German constitutional history furnished a basis in reality for his general constitutional theory which made the unity of political power, whoever held it, more important than the identity of its holders. In German history, as he saw it, monarchy had degenerated, not into another internal form of the state, but toward a confederation of states. The process was, moreover, practically irreversible, for "the German constitution is so hardened that it cannot be reformed toward a proper monarchy without the destruction of the entire commonwealth." [65] But this development meant a conversion of all the terms of political reference from domestic to international relations, from the choice of the sovereign to his policy.

For all practical contemporary purposes, then, Germany was an irregular commonwealth not so much because the monarch (emperor) had alienated the core of his sovereign powers as because the remnant of those powers was preventing the principalities from exercising their sovereign powers toward the proper external confederate relations.[66]

Nor did Pufendorf fail to generalize the constitutional lessons of the German case. He developed a doctrine of "state-systems [*systemata civitatum*]" as a "cure" for irregularity, "since the irregular forms of many commonwealths so calcify that they cannot be changed to regular without convulsion." He defined a state-system as "several states that are so connected as to seem to constitute one body but whose members retain sovereignty." [67] He then inserted these state-systems, as "composite states," prominently into his theory: along with "simple states" they set up a primary constitutional distinction which became the framework for the subsequent distinction between regularity and irregularity.[68] In the strict sense Pufendorf specified state-systems to include personal unions and confederations, but he admitted also into the category the "looser bonds" among states ranging from bare natural law to the tribal and religious community of nations.[69] Thus it transferred the constitutional problem from the arena of internal political relations to the setting of international relations.

In this setting Pufendorf's constitutional theory lost its ambiguity. The formless "commonwealth" for which he could not account with his internal concept of the state he could account for with his external concept of the state. Even in its tightest and most important type—the confederation—the state-system was precisely such an indefinite commonwealth, but a commonwealth explicable now as a voluntary union of sovereign states. It was constituted by a permanent agreement of sovereigns to the effect that those parts of their

[163]

sovereignty which are concerned with their "mutual safety" are "to be exercised by common consent" but not in such a way that the decisions of the common council can be enforced upon the individual sovereigns against their will or that they can be prevented from seceding when "they hope for more utility from separation than from union." [70] An irregular constitutional form, when measured by such a regular system, is no longer a matter of fundamental political relations but of the facts of sovereign foreign policy, and constitutional reform becomes an exercise of the sovereign will.

Thus Pufendorf developed his constitutional doctrine into a demonstration of the primacy of the state's international position in the determination of its political structure. With this development he externalized the problem of explaining political reality. He had now to deduce from his system the unitary rules that would make sense of international relations, but he had also to deal with the recalcitrant facts of human variety which he had exported out of the internal structure of his sovereign state. The first requirement led him to international law, the second to international history.

IV. INTERNATIONAL LAW

Pufendorf is usually celebrated along with Vittoria, Suárez, Gentili, and Grotius as one of the founding fathers of international law, but it is also recognized that his role was much more one of transmission than of innovation.[71] The reason for this lies partly in the function which it had for Pufendorf: it was the denouement of his general political theory and hence was analyzed not so much in its own terms as for its confirmation of Pufendorf's general doctrine of natural-law sovereignty. Thus it occupied but four brief chapters of *On the Law of Nature and Nations*, winding up the discussion of the sovereign's particular powers. There was yet another, more substantive ground for the superficiality of Pufendorf's international law. Because his regimentation of the internal factors in the state had projected the variability and particularity of human behavior into the international arena, the great bulk of what makes up international relations was for him beyond the realm of law. He himself admitted the hiatus by reserving for future treatment the problem of ascertaining the rules governing international policy: "Since the acts of supreme sovereigns and of independent states often seem to deviate from the rules of duty which private individuals have to preserve in their dealings with one another, it would not be out of place to inquire whether at all, and if so, how far, supreme sovereigns are exempt from the rules of private Law, and how far those acts can be approved, which are commonly said to be done 'for reasons of state.' . . ." [72] This question he never answered, and the only attempt at it was through his histories, where he examined those "acts" themselves. The only international law he adduced to cover them related to the causes of war; he recognized none either for the conduct of wars or for the condition of peace. [73]

The field that Grotius had reserved for international law (*jus gentium*) lost its integrity in Pufendorf: he separated it into a realm of indiscriminate natural law and a realm of natural liberty governed by necessity and convenience. [74] The only international *law* for Pufendorf was the natural law which governed all individuals in a state of nature. "We fully subscribe" to the view "that the law of nature and the law of nations are one and the same thing, differing only in their external denomination. . . . Nor do we feel that there is any other voluntary or positive law of nations which has the force of a law, properly so-called, such as binds nations as if it proceeded from a superior." [75] Since sovereigns are related to one another as individuals in the state of nature, the rules of natural law are basically the same for the conduct of individuals and of sovereigns—that is, they prescribe "peace," in which no one unjustly damages another. In general, then, these laws need no specification for sovereigns. The one kind of situation for which Pufendorf separates out explicit formulations of the natural law for sovereigns relates to the condition of war, since individuals are deprived of their right to war by their organization into states and sovereigns assume special collective obligations in this respect. What this natural international law distinctively prescribes are the rules arising from the supercession by the sovereign of the individual's right to alter his condition either from peace to war or from war to peace.

The most prominent provisions of Pufendorf's natural law in its international "denomination" were those relating to the causes of war: first, the limitation to "just wars" originating in defense against unjust invasion, recovery of a just debt, reparations for past injury, guarantee against future invasion, or special tie to another sovereign who has been injured; and, secondly, the provisions defining the transfer to the state of the guilt for injuries committed by individual citizens.[76]

But on the conduct of warfare Pufendorf recognized no binding international law, because the natural law with which he identified it denied its own competence in the condition of war. "According to the law of nature," whoever violates the duties of peace, "in confessing that he is my enemy . . . allows me a license to use force against him to any degree, or so far as I may think desirable."[77] The only checks which Pufendorf acknowledges have no legal status: the "customs of nations," which are purely voluntary and derive from a fortuitous consensus, and the natural "law of humanity," which dispenses "mercifulness" and is, as we have seen, purely moral, with no binding effect. Natural law has a binding legal effect only over those particular wartime acts that are directly related to the just cause of the war or the establishment of peace—that is, the acquisition "by the law of nature" of "whatever is owed" a warring party in a "just war" and the fulfillment of truces concluded by an "express pact." [78]

Since the natural law is the rule of peace, it would seem logical for Pufendorf to deduce for that condition the binding international law for sovereigns which he denied for war. It would seem all the more called for since he does ascribe international legal force to acts relating to both ends of the transition between peace and war—that is, not merely to causes of wars but to truces, peace-restoring treaties, and the necessity of the victims' agreement after the restoration of peace to the victors' acquisition of both property and subjects during the war.[79] And yet he chose to submit the international instruments of peace to the very different standard of state interests, rooted in the "natural liberty" of the sovereigns. The only peacetime institutions that fall under the law of nature are those which merely confirm "the common duty of humanity" and are usually called pacts of "friendship." But "between those who in their more advanced culture profess the observance of natural law, such treaties are no longer necessary. . . . In general civilized men should almost be ashamed to be a party to a pact the articles of which say no more than that they may not clearly and directly violate the law of nature, as if without such a pact a man would not be sufficiently mindful of his duty." [80] What the natural law prescribes during peace, in other words, exercises no greater sanction upon sovereigns than upon any other individuals in the state of nature, and it consequently authorizes no specifically international law.

To the contrary, Pufendorf's inescapable implication is that the sanction of natural law upon sovereigns is even weaker than its sanction upon other natural individuals. In general, he carefully refrained from grounding effective international agreements definitely in the law of nature, although he had so grounded the obligations of individuals both to make and to fulfill their agreements. He classified all international arrangements that stipulate definite obligations —including commercial treaties, alliances, and confederations—vaguely as instruments which "contain something over and above the duties of natural law, or at least settle and determine them when they seem indefinite." [81] In his subsequent discussion of the particular international instruments he continued to avoid the general question of their sanction, but his specific judgments revealed what he dared not quite admit—that international relations were simply a function of state interests, as defined by the respective sovereigns. Not only did he rest the duration of "permanent" confederations on the sovereigns' calculation of "utility" but he stipulated that since every king "enjoys natural liberty" like any individuals "who live in natural liberty, subject to no other man" he has the right to renounce unilaterally any agreement in which he finds "a flaw," whether of his own or others' making but damaging to his interests. The king also has the right, peculiar to his sovereign status, to withdraw from international agreements of his predecessors that were not made "with the intention of promoting the advantage of the people." [82] Thus sovereigns, in their international posture, enjoy the same liberty as individuals in the state of nature but are not under the same legal obligations.

Why the discrepancy in the otherwise parallel treatment of the relations between natural individuals and the relations between sovereigns? Why the reluctance to equip international pacts with something of the legal status accorded to natural institutions even if not that accorded to the state itself? Pufendorf gave no direct answer to these crucial questions raised by his provocative treatment of international law, but the assumptions of this treatment which derive from his general political theory are clear enough to permit us to answer for him. Sovereigns differ from natural individuals in two essential respects. First, they are only *political* individuals, constituted exclusively by security; consequently they are not bound by, nor can international law consist in, any of the social prescriptions of the natural law that look beyond considerations of security. Secondly, sovereigns differ from natural individuals in their respective relations to one another even within the potentially political realm defined by mutual security: the administration of mutual security by a state is the only way in which self-interested natural liberties can be necessarily related to other-oriented natural obligations, and since by definition a state is appropriate only to an association of individuals and not an association of sovereigns there can be no logical or legal relationship between the interests of state and the universal obligations of natural law in the international field.

Behind this theoretical position lay Pufendorf's undoubtedly valid insight that in his contemporary world the maintenance of external order was guaranteed only by the concentration of a well-defined authority in the unitary government of a regional state. But in his attempt to represent this fact as a rational necessity, he was able, even by his own lights, to show the inevitable organization only of internal political facts into necessary logical relations. When he came to the borders of the state he came also to the frontiers of political and constitutional theory. He came face to face with political facts in fortuitous and actual rather than necessary and rational relations. He crossed the narrow no-man's-land of international law into contemporary history.

[6]

THE HISTORIAN

When Pufendorf was evacuated from Lund during its temporary occupation by Danish troops in 1676, external circumstances favored his conversion into a professional historian, and these same circumstances helped to determine the kind of professional historian he would become. The occasion for his appointment was the death of the official historian at the Swedish court, Johan Loccenius, during 1677, in the very midst of his administration of Charles XI's charge to gather materials for a general history of Sweden. That a scholar of Pufendorf's training and experience should be installed in such a post and function was quite in line with the customs of the age, and consequently it was not simply the specific terms of the assignment but the general context of seventeenth-century historiography that set the conditions for his historical activity.

I. The Problem of History in the Seventeenth Century

The relationship between law and history in the seventeenth century was so intimate that the selection of his most prominent jurist was the natural choice for Charles to make.

Not only had the two preceding Swedish state historians, Loccenius and Bogislaw Chemnitz, mixed historical and legal publications during their tenure—Chemnitz' *On the Reason of State in Our Roman-Germanic Empire* (*De ratio status in imperio nostro Romano-Germanico*) of 1640 had influenced Pufendorf's *On the Constitution of the German Empire* just as his *The Royal Swedish War in Germany* (*Der Königliche Schwedische in Teutschland gefürte Krieg*) of 1648–53 was to contribute much to Pufendorf's Swedish history—but several of the most prominent names of the century made the connection a standard one. Hugo Grotius held a formal appointment as historian for the Estates of Holland for more than a decade and wrote his *Annals and History of Belgian Affairs* (*Annales et historiae de rebus Belgiciis*) in that capacity, while Leibniz, whose doctorate and first important publication were in the field of jurisprudence, found that his post as ducal librarian involved him in the twin tasks of drafting legal memorandums in defense of Hanoverian positions and writing a history of the House of Brunswick. Before he took up this place and again later when he became discontented with it, an alternative which he cherished as appropriate and desirable was a nomination as court historian in Vienna. The connection between law and history was often apparent, moreover, where the relationship was not institutionalized. Jacques-Auguste de Thou and Lord Clarendon were celebrated historians who were also trained jurists; Francis Bacon combined both capacities in his galaxy of talents; and even Hobbes, who reversed the characteristic development of his contemporaries by turning first to historiography and later to theory of law, wrote an introduction to his early translation of Thucydides which developed its meaning for the general study of history.[1]

The process behind the association of law with history in the seventeenth century is plain enough, but it had an impact upon the writing of history that was far more problematical. History was still an institutionally and intellectually dependent discipline. Its growth out of the medieval combination of universal history and chronicle was in the tow of developments in theology, the humanities, and, latterly, jurisprudence. Even before the religious struggles of the early sixteenth century began to stimulate a new concern with the sources and unfolding of church history, the humanistic interest in classical history and historians spread into an analogous concern with the secular sources and career of contemporary states. The humanist tendency to carry over historical motifs from the ancient to the modern arena was stimulated by the institution of the official historian, which went back to fifteenth-century Italy and was picked up north of the Alps around the turn of the sixteenth century along with the other facets of the humanist movement. The Italian humanists, Paulus Aemilius and Polydore Vergil, for example, personified the diffusion when they were commissioned by Louis XII and Henry VII to write general histories of France and England, respectively. It was not long before the practice was naturalized, when such commissions were vested in literarily trained humanists of native vintage, such as England's William Camden and the Bavarian Johannes Turmair (Aventinus), prominent representatives of the mediocre genre of scholars and publicists who wrote official history by commission or profession. But in the northern environment, with its emphasis upon state-making, the predilection for grounding rulers' claims in precedents gave a practical slant to the generic humanist impulse. Gradually jurisprudence replaced classical literary scholarship as the framework of the humanist approach to history.

The rise to predominance during the sixteenth century of the "French mode" of Roman law—in which the application of the humanist approach brought a new emphasis upon the historical understanding of the texts—reached directly into political history through de Thou, who studied under Jacques Cujas, the leading light of the school. Jean Bodin focused his humanistic learning upon the self-imposed prescription to base a universal law upon history, since "in history the best part of universal law lies hidden, and what is of great weight and importance for the best appraisal of legislation . . . is obtained from it." [2] The same kind of political influence that was making jurisprudence the focus of the humanist concern with history in sixteenth-century France made itself felt in the German universities of the seventeenth century, when the law faculties became the loci of secular history.[3]

It was hardly surprising, then, that the humanistic jurist came to write political history and became the favored candidate for the post of official historian. In the absence of an independent historical profession, not only were the lawyers the most appropriate available practitioners of a discipline dedicated to establishing the identity through time of a political community which was being defined in terms of its lawmaking and law-sustaining power, but even theoretically the jurist was the logical executor of the humanist conception of history. In both classical antiquity and the Renaissance a didactic civic function was assigned to history which the jurists had then only to sharpen into a doctrine of political utility. The very term "pragmatic," which became current on the Continent during the seventeenth and eighteenth centuries and which has been draped over the whole of humanistic history to characterize its practical purposefulness, joins its diverse meanings of the edificatory in history (from Polybius) and the political in society (from the *pragmatica sanctio* of Roman law) through the Ciceronian connotation of juristic practice (*pragmaticus*) .[4] Particularly in Germany, where the influence of Melanchthon had helped to channel

[173]

the humanistic impulse into ecclesiastical history, did the belated flowering of secular humanism in historiography take a jurisprudential form.[5]

However reasonable the extension of humanist history into jurisprudence may have been as a response to the growing political specialization of its moralistic purpose, the result was to exacerbate the historiographical problem already present in the genre itself. For between the humanistic urge to seek out the original sources of the past and the equally humanistic urge to draw general lessons for the present and future there was a fateful rift. Given the radical character of the two impulses, the result was an incompatibility between material and interpretation. A single historical work could consist of sources arrayed in undigested blocks (as in Leibniz' *Brunswickian Annals*) or of coherent narratives and interpretations based upon secondary accounts, personal reminiscences, and partisan selection (as in More's *History of Richard III*, Bacon's *History of the Reign of Henry VII*, and Clarendon's *History of the Rebellion*) , or of both sources and narrative connected by such doubtful but standard humanistic practices as the invented oration, the interpolation of Providential judgments, or the focus on contemporary political history with an assumption of automatic relevance. In the case of Grotius, the hiatus was manifest in the distinction between his work on Dutch origins, which emphasized the sources—*On the Antiquity of the Batavian State (De antiquitate reipublicae Batavorum)* and *History of the Goths, Vandals and Lombards (Historia Gothorum, Vandalorum et Langobardorum)* —and his separate work on the Dutch revolt against Spain, *Annals and History of Belgian Affairs,* in which political interpretation prevailed, while Leibniz, in whom the passion for textual criticism and presentation was predominant, never got beyond the medieval period in his Hanoverian history.

[174]

The unifying framework which was missing from humanistic history was supplied by the second major category of
seventeenth-century historiography: universal history. But
here too a scheme which had once provided a satisfying
meaning for historical events now continued to supply a bare
form with little substantive unity. The traditional pattern of
universal history had been religious, anchored in the Providential plan and eschatological purpose of the Christian God
and articulated in the biblical sequence of the Four Monarchies. This tradition still had representatives in the seventeenth century, particularly on the level of popular history.
The outstanding exemplars of this genre were Raleigh's
History of the World (1614) and Bossuet's *Discours sur
l'histoire universelle* (1681). It was not surprising that
Bishop Bossuet should combine "religion and political government" as "the two points around which human affairs
revolve" or that he should have organized them, on the model
of Augustine's two cities, with the concepts of "the great
changes in empires" and "the permanent duration of religion." [6] More revealing was Raleigh's adherence, despite the
infusion of humanistic skepticism and moralism, to the fundamental Christian pattern of Divine Providence working
itself out through the Four Monarchies.[7] But this Christian
scheme of universal history no longer commanded the consensus of historians. Jean Bodin's attack on the organizing
principle of the Four Monarchies had been only part of his
general criticism against the whole theological scheme of
coherence, and by the second half of the seventeenth century
his example was being followed by many academicians who
rejected both the particular doctrine and the general religious approach to historical unity in favor of an empirical
sequence of particular events.[8] This critical historiography
retained the ideal of a universal history but produced no
coherent conception of human history to replace the Chris-

tian *telos* which they no longer saw at work within history. The historians of the late seventeenth century were left in the paradoxical position of clinging to a category of universal history that remained, by default, the residue of the Christian interpretation, and of filling it with a collection of specific secular narratives.[9]

At this stage of its development, universal history could obviously contribute only a conventional framework to secular history. The limits of the relationship were thrown into sharp relief by the more fruitful combination of this religiously based framework with the third main category of seventeenth-century historiography—ecclesiastical history—since here it was obviously appropriate. The largest technical advances in the collection and critical edition of sources occurred precisely in this category, and at least one of the contributing factors lay in the ready availability of a general historical process which conferred meaning upon such labors. Not only were the pioneers of this tendency, the Benedictines of St. Maur and the Jesuit followers of Jean Bolland, the most secure defenders of the traditional historical cosmology, but the direction of their effort to a coherent set of sources that neither required nor received interpretive elaboration revealed the internal workings of an accepted structure. From this chrysalis the method took on an independent life of its own, with the Maurist Jean Mabillon's generalization of it into a science of documents in *On Diplomatics* (*De re diplomatica* of 1681). It was borne into the eighteenth century on the secular applications of it by the Maurists themselves to the sources of French national and provincial origins, by Leibniz to early Hanoverian history, and by Lodovico Muratori to the sources of Italian history.

But if the history of religion could stand as a model for the appreciation and critical appraisal of sources, it was far from enjoying such a status for the more constructive phases of historical writing. Despite its silent service for the improvement of historiographical techniques, on the level of interpretation the mantle of universal history covered religion hardly more adequately than it covered politics. Interpretive ecclesiastical history tended to focus on the religious conflicts dating from the sixteenth century, and for these issues the traditional scheme, with its assumption of Christian integrity vis-à-vis the evanescent and variegated vanities of the temporal world, provided little authority. Interpretive religious history during the seventeenth century was as dominated by confessional utility as secular history was by political, for the rivalry of confessions remained as overbearing an incentive toward history as the rivalry of states. Some of the best-known works in the field were products of ecclesiastical polemics. Sforza Pallavicino's *Istoria del Concilio di Trento* (1656–57) was a papal rebuttal of Paolo Sarpi's work on the same subject. Veit von Seckendorf's *Commentarius historicus et apologeticus de Lutheranismo* (1688–92) was a rebuttal of the Jesuit Louis Maimbourg's *Histoire du Lutheranisme* (1680), and in a second edition he took on Bossuet's tendentious *Histoire des variations des églises protestantes* (1688) as well. Thus, despite the progress in the methods of ecclesiastical historical research the area of what we should now call modern history was as bereft of a unitary historical process that could mediate between source and interpretation in the religious as in the political field. Just as universal history provided no pattern for the states that were divorcing themselves from even the theory of the Fourth, or Roman, Monarchy, so it now provided none to the churches that were dividing the heritage of a universal Christendom. The result was to complete the emancipation of political history which had already been adumbrated in Melanchthon and to throw open the search for canons of meaning in both the political and the ecclesiastical branches of modern history.[10]

Because Pufendorf conformed to these established genres of seventeenth-century historiography, they help to explain both his acceptance as a historian and the format of his historical writing. But since, on the other hand, he was distinctive in the professional coverage which he gave to the whole range of these genres, he helps, in turn, to explain them, by contributing a rationale to the relations among them. He published political histories of national and territorial states; he composed a humanistic version of universal history; and if he did not write ecclesiastical history he worked out the critical and interpretive criteria for the one that he wanted to write. The role which these various historiographical endeavors played in his intellectual development illuminates his thought; the role which his intellectual development played in these historiographical endeavors illuminates the thought of his age.

II. Pufendorf's Juristic History

Pufendorf became a professional historian not only because it was a common practice to appoint jurists to such functions but also because he had already, as a jurist, given public expression to his interest in history. As Monzambano he had surveyed German history. As a member of the Lund law faculty he had delivered lectures on universal history. In both cases his history was derivative: it was a direct application of his political principles and did not transcend the lawful realm of those principles. But at the same time it did manifest the need of his political system for historical support and operated as a transition to the independent history which he was to undertake subsequently. This phase of derivative history thus made explicit the function of history in his theory of natural law and established the implications of his natural-law theory for history.

[178]

In his *Constitution of the German Empire* (1667) Pufendorf placed national history frankly in the service of political
doctrine. His purposes were to demonstrate that the German
political realities corresponded to none of his political principles, that this lack of correspondence entailed the practical
"diseases" of the German political condition, and that the
restoration to normalcy could be accomplished only through
the application of the "reason of state" which was the connecting link between the actuality and the principle.[11] His
sketch of German constitutional history was to furnish the
factual underpinning to the portrayal of the non-conforming
political realities. "Whoever tries to represent so irregular a
state-form without any knowledge of German history and
politics possesses as much talent for it as a donkey has for
playing the lute. . . . Whoever wants to acquire a precise
knowledge of the relationships of the German Empire will
have to investigate how the so-called Imperial Estates have
reached their important power-position."[12]

Thus his account of Germanic origins was designed to
show that the remnants of imperial authority go back to the
actual sovereignty of Charlemagne over Germany but that
the derivation of his title from conquest (for Pufendorf
Charlemagne was ethnically German but politically French)
rather than from legal transfer or from Roman law (since the
"Holy Roman Empire" was only a prestigious title, legally
independent of the original Roman Empire) endowed his
successors with no rightful claim to the sovereign powers
assumed by the territorial rulers.[13] Pufendorf's historical
account of the Imperial Estates was designed to show that
their relationship with the emperor rested on a *de facto*
post-Carolingian independence of the princes which became
de jure in the form of feudal contracts stipulating, in return
for an oath of allegiance, the emperor's confirmation as
imperial fiefs of the territories already possessed by the

princes. Through such a feudal relationship, according to Pufendorf, "the princes lost . . . neither power nor prestige," for it was no political pact but "only a treaty of alliance establishing unequal rights." [14] The consequence for the political relations of his own Germany that Pufendorf drew from this history was that the princes have their powers "by dint of their own rights and not as delegates of the Emperor," since the feudal relationship "does not infringe their power but only determines the manner in which it is acquired and held." [15]

Despite its format, Monzambano's performance was, as commentators have remarked, a work of political theory rather than constitutional law, since its crucial section was concerned not with establishing what the constitutional relationships in Germany were but with measuring these relationships against the forms of the state which Pufendorf had already demonstrated to be politically valid.[16] But if his German constitutional history served this political purpose it served it only at the very limits of his political system. Pufendorf called upon history to account for Germany as an "irregular polity"—that is, precisely that residual category of states for which his political theory could not account. History to him, at this early stage, was a prime auxiliary for grounding in fact contemporary political institutions that were insusceptible to political logic. But it must be emphasized that at this stage it was indeed an auxiliary: through the device of irregularity the facts that history established were brought by indirection back into a logical relationship to the political system.

And yet even now, during this derivative phase of his approach to history, the internal rift which was the bane of humanist historiography showed through. He used original sources and the best of recent authorities—especially Hermann Conring—for the material of his history in the *Consti-*

tution of the German Empire, but these materials simply did not deliver the evidence that he required to make historical fact support the political conception of the irregular state.[17] He was, moreover, perfectly aware of the gap between the actual historical evidence and the political purpose it was to subserve. The historical existence of *"feuda oblata"*—that is, of the contracts in which the princes voluntarily offer their possessions for enfeoffment and consequently retained independent rights in them—he frankly acknowledged to be the keystone of his whole argument. "Without this the phenomena of the Germanic constitution cannot possibly be secured [*salviren*]." In the published work he simply represented such contracts as historical facts from which he unhesitatingly drew political conclusions, but privately he admitted that it was only a "hypothesis [*hypothesis Monzambanea de feudis oblatis*]" for which he expected "some proofs [*testimonia*] from the history of those times to be produced" but which he had not himself found.[18] It was this kind of gap between the sources and the political interpretation of history that helped drive him ultimately into a different approach to the field.

But he did not make this change before he had made another application of politically derivative historiography. Just as he had utilized national history in his *Constitution of the German Empire* to seal the internal frontiers of his political system, he utilized universal history to round off its international limits. His *Introduction to the History of the Great Empires and States of Contemporary Europe* (1682–85) appeared after he had become a professional historian, but it was based upon lectures which he had given while still a member of the law faculty at the University of Lund. The juristic circumstances of its origin molded the whole conception of the work. Pufendorf designed it as a popular textbook for young men of quality whose destination toward "offices of state" makes them the most appropriate students of history, since it is "a most useful science" for such employments.[19] In correspondence with this political function, Pufendorf admitted that he planned his work to cover the history only of nations maintaining "some connection" with Swedish interests and to emphasize "recent" over "ancient" history. "One should always begin with" the earlier history, which has its uses, but the later history is "more useful, especially for those concerned with affairs of state." [20] Thus his *Introduction* became a model for the juristic adaptation of universal history to political utility. He retained the pattern of the Four Monarchies for ancient history, but he divested it of its overriding religious dimension and he reduced it to the status of a brief prolegomenon to the political histories of the modern states.

Pufendorf followed the mode of his century when, like Hobbes and Leibniz, he assigned history to a realm of "facts" whose truth was categorically different from the necessary truths of reason. But where Hobbes applied the distinction to the subordination of history to logic and where Leibniz applied it to the separation of history from philosophy, Pufendorf applied it to the complementing of his political system.[21] To be sure, he believed along with the others that historical truths are logically probable rather than certain, but he also carried out, albeit he did not state, the principle that Hobbes stated and did not carry out: that, epistemologically, history is "absolute knowledge" as opposed to the "conditional" knowledge characteristic of "science." [22] Thus in the very same context Pufendorf attributed to historical fact both logical contingency and "moral certainty," different indeed from the logical certainty of moral science, but still one which "can very rarely deceive us" and which inspires "faith" in the consensus of historians.[23] The intermediate position which Pufendorf theoretically prescribed for history between subordination and indifference to the logic of politics found practical expression in the dual relationship which his written history bore to his politics. On the one hand, the political principles provided the canons of selection, interpretation, and meaning for the facts of history. On the other hand, within this framework of relevance the facts of history provided an independent source of existential reality for the political principles, both by bringing factual support to the truth of propositions and by organizing into forms pertinent to propositions those facts which logic could not reach. The interplay of this dual relationship made up the structure of the general history which Pufendorf embodied in his *Introduction* of 1682.

Pufendorf's sketch of ancient history was frankly prefatory, for he justified it as a description of "ancient Empires, especially the Roman, from whose ruins modern empires and states have grown," but still he used the occasion both to apply and to feed his political system. His history was focused upon ancient politics, and he ascribed the rise and decline of states to the application or neglect of valid political principles and maxims. The Assyrian Empire triumphed because it was the area of the first state and established states are stronger than infant ones; it fell because its sovereign allowed power to devolve upon the provinces. Persia rose because Cyrus monopolized power and fell because his successors neglected to check the power of Macedonia. The Greek city-states, like Carthage subsequently, fell because their desire for conquest outran their "capacity [*Beschaffenheit*]." The Macedonian Empire rose by dint of the military and political abilities of Philip and Alexander; it fell because fast political growth is not stable and the conquests could not be united into a single civil society. Both the rise and the fall of Rome were attributable to its exclusively military constitution, which was in the long run a political evil because the penetration of citizens with martial mores led ultimately to civil war and "the worst kind of monarchy, in which a standing army arrogates sovereignty to itself." [24]

But if Pufendorf's substitution of political for religious criteria of explanation effectively secularized the traditional ancient arena of universal history, this arena still retained enough autonomy to perform a service for the political principles which now shaped it. Two aspects of the section on the ancients bespoke the counteraction of history upon politics. First, Pufendorf's account of primitive society put the imprimatur of historical actuality upon the state of nature which had been but a logical postulate in his political system.[25] Secondly, the retention of the familiar Four Monarchies as the frame of ancient history, abetted by sporadic references to the Flood and to "the Divine Providence which sets for every Empire its goal and limit," reinforced his political maxims with the authoritative mantle of the age-old theme of imperial rise and fall.[26]

The main body of Pufendorf's *Introduction* consisted in the juxtaposed separate histories of the several European states, and in this frankly contemporary context he made the complementarity of politics and history entirely explicit. The far greater detail which Pufendorf put into his modern history in contrast with the ancient made its organization by the politics of kings, wars, and revolutions the more obvious, particularly since he could now be quite open and consistent about the political principle he was applying. The principle was "the interest of state," defined by policies making for balance of power against universal monarchy abroad and making for "the common good of the state" against the "private interest" of rulers, advisers, or factions at home.[27] For the most part Pufendorf articulated this principle through the simple selection of governmental events, which he made into a straight political narrative, as the historically meaningful ones. At crucial points within the narrative, however, he sometimes made explicit the criteria of civil and international order which guided him. Thus he recounted religious struggles entirely as civil disorders, slurring both Coligny and William the Silent as "ambitious" and making frequent allusion to the use of religion as a pretense for political convulsions; his section on the history of the "Papal Monarchy" was an object lesson in the invalid intermixture of religion and politics; and he did not shrink at times from drawing frank historical confirmations of his favorite political maxims, such as his conclusion from the Portuguese revolt against Spain, "what a noteworthy example it is of how easily a country can be lost when the subjects are not attached to the ruler." [28]

But it was in the formal structure of the chapters on modern history rather than in their content, overburdened as this was by annalistic narrative, that Pufendorf's desired relationship between history and politics emerged most clearly. He climaxed the history of each state, which he brought down to the Treaty of Nimwegen (1678–79), with a discussion of the constant factors pertinent to its politics—to wit, its manners, its resources, and its "interest" in respect both to its general foreign policy and to its bilateral relations with the other powers. The analysis of the state's "interest" represents the real conclusion of the work, "since it is the basis on which one must judge whether something is done well or badly in political affairs," and in it history and politics meet. On the one hand, the adduction of the constant factors serves "to elucidate the history"; on the other hand, the constant factors plus the history make up the crucial "true interest" of the state. For this interest is constituted both by the "permanent" factors of geography, resources, and popular disposition, and by the "transitory" factors of the changing situation and strength of neighbors, particularly as measured

[185]

by the actual authority and policies of their rulers. These transitory factors belong to "the province of modern history," which thus contributes the knowledge of the "changeable" to the definition of political interest but must itself be capped by direct political "experience not to be learned from books." [29]

Despite the apparent integration of history into the Pufendorfian political system under the aegis of the "reason" or the "interest" of state, the structure even of this general history showed flaws which adumbrated another role for his new discipline. Over and above the political mold and the sporadic political judgments the bulk of Pufendorf's narrative was in the form of chronicle, without inner coherence, general principle, or real linkage with the notion of "interest" that was supposed to serve as his historical principle.[30] This was particularly glaring in his modern history, for the juxtaposition of territorial histories that succeeded the sequential pattern of the Four Monarchies not only exhibited no real universal connection among them but no general illumination of particular events within them. The political utility of particular states did not cover the variety of historical events, even when these events were politically pre-selected. This lack was manifest in the methodological dimension of the problem. Pufendorf drew the materials for each state in his general history avowedly from "its own historians," and he admitted that he let stand whatever discrepancies there might be between their partial accounts, for "to take up these differences and make a judgment therein is not my job." [31] Thus, just as his German history had shown him how historical reality outstrips internal political categories, so now his international history showed him how inappropriate those categories were to provide general criteria of historical truth. Both lessons underlined the distinctiveness of the historical realm and drove him to the sources as the only valid approach toward what was independent in it.

III. THE PROFESSIONAL HISTORIAN

In 1685, with the publication of the general history of Sweden that composed the second volume of his *Introduction,* Pufendorf marked the transition from derivative to autonomous history. In his dedication to the Swedish Crown Prince, who was later to become famous as Charles XII, he analyzed the process of historical instruction into two successive phases that may stand as an epitome of his own development. First comes "universal history," which teaches "in an easy, sure, and pleasant way" how rulers should behave by showing "the benefits brought by virtue and prudence and the injuries brought by vicious and unwise pride" and by immortalizing good deeds and evil "in the eternal memory of posterity." Then comes the "basic knowledge" of the ruler's own realm and his neighbors', in which "lessons [*Morale*] can be drawn from history" only if the student "knows how to supply what the historian dare not write." [32] The second volume held overtly to the structure of the first—a political history followed successively by the constant factors of land and people and by the general and special "interests" of the Swedish state—but the execution reflected the development of the historiographical assumptions adumbrated in the dedication. Pufendorf announced that he based his account of remote Swedish history upon "the credit of authors who are my guarantors, until I come to recent times, where truth and certainty may be found"; in conformity with this methodological division, Pufendorf imposed his judgments of good and bad government primarily in the sections through the Reformation and adduced, for the subsequent period, copious documentary paraphrases and extracts which he permitted to speak for themselves.[33] The assumptions of this latter phase were henceforward to dominate Pufendorf's work as a professional historian, which evinces incongruous qualities difficult to explain without reference to these assumptions and to their place in his general intellectual development.[34]

Pufendorf wrote his independent history under the pressure of two divergent needs which endowed it with its distinctive form. On the one hand, his passion for certainty drove him into a realm of historical actuality which he now recognized to be categorically distinct from and superior to his political logic in this respect. Thus, he greeted his new profession as a relief from the conflicts which his natural-law system had inspired. "My hope is that I shall be exempted from this kind of feud for the remainder of my life, since I have moved into another kind of study which is not so subject to contradiction." [35] On the other hand, he retained the function of a political relevance for history, arguing that "it is important to acknowledge the former errors of the fatherland so that it may not subsequently be dashed against the same rock" and prefacing his later histories, like his earlier, with references to the function of history in "preserving the memory of great men" and to the model it provided of "justice, security, and peace . . . which every prince should unswervingly follow." [36] The three large tomes and the torso of a fourth which made up Pufendorf's contribution to scholarly history manifested these divergent assumptions both in their external structure and in their inner rationale.[37] Externally, their vast bulk was made up of long and apparently undiluted paraphrases and extracts from archival documents, physically marked off by italics; yet they were without exception located in the period of recent and contemporary history which pointed up their political relevance and purpose. Internally, Pufendorf asserted his historiographical criteria in these works to be, simultaneously, the objective "love of truth" and the political subjectivity of "the historian, who does not expose his own judgment but acts as the public interpreter of the actions and policies of his prince or state whose deeds he reports, and who cannot help expressing their opinions unless he stupidly means to betray and condemn himself." [38]

The format which combined the archival and contemporary emphases in Pufendorf's mature histories yields the obvious inference of a conflict, within his method itself, between the historical material and its political purpose and has raised the question of the predominance of the one or the other as the explanation of their relationship.[39]

On the side of his historiographical autonomy was Pufendorf's technique of composition. Not only did he describe his working day to be filled with "extracting" as well as writing and his method to be "the exhibition of the uncorrupted truth from the authentic sources," but he substantiated these claims with the kind of material he used and the way in which he treated it.[40] He based his account on interminable excerpts and synopses of the diaries, reports, and official texts of declarations, ordinances, and treaties which he found in the archives; he limited his exposition correspondingly to governmental deliberations, negotiations, decisions, and reported events; and he confined the continuity between the documentary relations largely to the external sequence of events and to portrayal of motivations represented by the historical actors themselves within the context of the particular occasions. The results of this procedure were frequently neutral enough to permit the use of material from his Swedish history in the parallel section of his Prussian history.[41]

On the side of contemporary politics as the conditioner of his historiography were Pufendorf's criteria of selection and organization. Not only did he identify, in general, "the maximum light of history" with "public records" addressed to "the practice of arms and civil affairs," but he indicated his "preference for writing about the present war" to composing remoter history and in his actual histories of both Sweden and Brandenburg dealt almost exclusively with seventeenth-century war and diplomacy.[42] Political considerations were responsible for Pufendorf's consistent omissions and distortions of such contemporaneously sensitive historical topics as the Great Elector's friendly relations and alliances with Louis XIV and in his scattered interpolations of political judgments into his historical narration. These interpolations, significantly, were more frequent and insistent in his strictly contemporary history of Elector Frederick III than in the recent history of the precedent Great Elector, and more frequent and insistent in both of these than in the relatively more remote Swedish histories.[43] More important, however, was Pufendorf's habitual organization of his material under the humanistic aegis of figurative rather than literal correspondence to the sources. The solid blocks of extracts and paraphrases turn out, upon comparison with the original documents, to be not precise transcriptions, but a reworking, a revision, a rearrangement, and occasionally an invention of particular items to convey the inner political truth of the whole event.[44]

The crucial concept in the mediation of the two poles in Pufendorf's historical method was undoubtedly the "reason of state," and the consensus of commentators has been to see here the political notion permitting the junction of law and politics. According to this consensus, Pufendorf evinced a genuine historical sense in his passion for the sources and in his ability to immerse himself in them with a minimum of consideration for political secrecy and personal prejudice;

but he made the ensuing historical knowledge serve political purpose through the mold afforded by the reason of state. This was compatible with authentic history through its depersonalization of the relationship between historian and historical agent, and yet it guided the selection and organization of particular historical data into general forms available for pragmatic political use.[45] This judgment undoubtedly has a valid basis, for Pufendorf himself justified his position that the historian's "molding himself to the opinions, feelings, and reasons of his prince" still leaves his function "far different from the function of an advocate or a judge" by explicit reference to the "particular reasons of his state [*peculiares status sui rationes*]" which is "the measure of the prince's actions." [46] But closer analysis shows that the concept operated for Pufendorf not to integrate the historical into the political world but only to make them commensurable. History for Pufendorf was now a discipline distinct and apart; the reason of state applicable to it was a concept different from, albeit related to, the reason of state pertinent to his natural-law politics.

The fact was that as an independent historian Pufendorf drew his criteria from specifically historical considerations, his coherence from what was immanent in the historical process, and his function from precisely that dimension of history which lay beyond the laws of politics. Now he explained his focus on recent and contemporary history by reference not to political utility but to the sources, which for the older periods "do not suffice to supply the proper substance of history" and which only "in this century . . . provide the tools [*apparatus*] of history." "So it is futile to think about a genuine German history of previous centuries, for which nothing remains but to compile chronicles and fragments." [47] But he did evince an interest in this less useful history. He even expressed, subsequently, a qualified intention to treat the "antiquities" of Brandenburg history if he lived long enough.[48]

More important than this acknowledgment of an intrinsic historical truth was Pufendorf's conviction of an intrinsic historical meaning connecting the apparently discrete events of his archival works. Thus he insisted, despite "the variety of events," that his history of the Great Elector "is not to be considered as the life of a single prince but almost as the universal history of half a century," since his "regime occurred in the kind of times and was involved in the kind of transactions which had the greatest importance for the constellation of Europe and on which the fate of kingdoms and commonwealths depended." Political utility might well serve as the intended effect of the history, but not as its principle of coherence. The coherence of the work was grounded in the far-flung network of interests of the Great Elector, in the "constancy of mind" which bestowed a combination of justice and security as "one and the same quality upon all his actions," and in the circumstance which enmeshes each state's "own security" in "the properly adjusted community of Europe [*probe attemperata compages Europae*]." [49] These were connecting factors which Pufendorf deemed rooted in the very conditions of his historical situation. They conferred upon his discrete descriptions of events an implicit historical meaning which made superfluous and irrelevant the deliberate imposition of an explicit political meaning. As he said himself of this meaningful context: "Since, therefore, the evidence so commends this history, I am the less troubled whether it conforms to the external discipline which would keep me from making judgments but would leave such judgments to the academic world." [50] Since, in other words, the meaning is in the structure of the material it need not be imposed by subsequent judgments from the outside.

The substance of this historical meaning Pufendorf tended to subsume under his familiar notion of reason of state, but now this became a historical concept distinct from its former political application. Whereas Pufendorf had previously, in his *Constitution of the German Empire,* derived it from his political theory, making it dependent upon the form of the state and directing it to the realization in policy of a theoretical form, he now derived it from his history to cover precisely those aspects of actuality which the forms of his theory could not cover. As we have seen, Pufendorf concentrated primarily on international relations as the locus of this obstreperous reality, and consequently he now specified history as the source of "the rules [*rationes*] which mediate reciprocally among diverse nations." [51] These rules, moreover, in the form of the "particular reasons of state," must be so derived because they must be applied to "princes and polities" who are not only "exempt from the civil laws" but do not, in this respect, "measure their actions by the common fundamental law [*jus*] of men." [52] Thus Pufendorf called in history to supply the rationale that the law could not supply, but a gap inevitably remained between the political rationale originating in the internal structure of law and the historical rationale originating in the sequence of international activity.

It is in this context that Pufendorf's apparently contradictory theory of history must be assessed. He held both that the historian must "express with his pen the sentiments of the lord he serves" and that he must keep himself "free from prejudice" and be "content to report events as they have happened, without love or hatred" "from the authentic sources, interpolating nothing." [53] Since he expressed both views repeatedly and simultaneously, he apparently saw no incompatibility. But since, on the other hand, he was well aware that the historical reason of state which he sought to represent as "public interpreter" of his prince was a particular and subjective criterion it could hardly serve the requirement that the historian "say nothing false and not omit anything true." For not only did Pufendorf in general restrict himself to the native sources but he made a principle of "not representing the decision and actions of the opposing party except as they have come within the point of view of our own." [54] The reason of state did reconcile the two duties of the historian on the level of the mutual impersonality of writer and agent; but it did not reconcile them on the level either of impartiality or of final truth, and Pufendorf knew it. In almost every instance he accompanied his declaration of his historiographical ethic with the prescription which he had found necessary in his *Introduction*—that judgments be made by the "wise reader"—but now he supplemented it with the description of the law by which the truth delivered by history becomes the basis for the "judgment of honor or dishonor" by posterity to which all sovereigns are subject.[55] Moreover, where the *Introduction* had specified "the lesson" which the reader was to draw for himself as the political conformity of policy to "true interest," the judgment relinquished to the reader and posterity now became the broader one of the moral conformity of actions "to reason and justice." [56] The judgment, finally, was now to be made not simply of foreign rulers—Pufendorf's utilitarian position in the *Introduction*—but of all sovereigns, including one's own. Thus Pufendorf did recognize the necessity of an ultimate judgment upon history, above the particular reason of state and in accordance with the natural law, which could bridge the gap between the dual functions of the historian as the spokesman of subjective political truth of a particular state and as the purveyor of an objective historical truth transcending it—but he denied the historian the right, by virtue of either function, to make it.

What connected the historian's two functions, for Pufendorf, was the location of both in the same realm of particular historical truth beyond the general moral truth of politics. They contributed different sides of this same particular historical truth. As spokesman for his prince, the historian delivered a particularized rationale of his state's international politics which was the only immanent organization of historical events upon which a political judgment could ultimately be based. By the historian's function of delivering "uncorrupted truth" Pufendorf meant simply to guarantee this particularized rationale of history against the imposition of a general rationale, either by the historian's own judgment or by political restrictions on the sources to be used and the events to be reported.[57] Behind this doctrine lay Pufendorf's belief that the function of the historian was to establish the certain existence of particular truths; that the general principles of "reason and justice" could, in the field of international politics, find historical existence only as particular reasons of state; that the actors in history can embody and the historian deliver only particular truths in this sense; and that the final judgment upon these truths by the application of general principles can be made only by anonymous "readers" or future "citizens" who, because of their place and time, are neither historical actors nor historians and can, as observers, transcend the usual limits of history.[58]

But there was one important exception to the critical distance which Pufendorf maintained between internal politics and international history and between the general and particular truths which they entailed. Where religion entered history Pufendorf let the bars down. On these occasions marked for him especially by the revocation of the Edict of Nantes and by the English Revolution of 1688, he entered, uncharacteristically, upon protracted narratives of domestic history.[59] More revealing, not only did these narra-

[195]

tives abound in the kind of moral and political judgments which he otherwise forbade historians to make and which by and large he refrained himself from making, but for this field of history he acknowledged such judgments in principle. When he declared his willingness to write a history for the then German emperor, he specified his desire to treat the "noble and pious war" against "the barbarians" (the Turks), since to do so would not require the "moderation" which the history of "other wars" in Europe calls for. He even indicated, in contrast to his usual working habits, that it would not be necessary in this case to go through all the relevant records in the imperial archives for the elucidation of the causes of the sovereign's actions.[60]

The theme of religious conflict had always attracted Pufendorf. The description and analysis of the confessional struggle in Germany made up the conclusion and climax of his *Constitution of the German Empire,* on the ground that the policies which he had proposed to bring the political reality of Germany into line with her "reason of state" as a defensive confederation "and all others which might be required for the welfare of Germany could only be executed and made practical if the governments perceived the advantages of good intentions," to which the chief obstacle is "the diversity of religion." [61] This early focus on religious institutions reveals the crucial role which religion was to play for Pufendorf, first in politics and then in history: it provided a linkage between particular acts and general norms which could be guaranteed in no other way. The transition from the political to the historical context of this role appeared in the *Introduction,* his general history, for not only did the religious struggles in each state evoke the largest concentration of his judgments upon history but he lifted the chapter on papal history, which was distinguished from the rest as a straight political argument from history on behalf of political sovereignty, out of the main corpus to give it prior and separate publication.[62]

Such was the background of Pufendorf's exceptional treatment of religion in his professional history. As his point of view shifted from rational to factual truth his need for an immanent coherence within the realm of particular facts became the greater, and so we find an ever increasing emphasis upon religion in history to fill this need. The untypical stress upon the integrated and interpretative domestic histories of French and British religious conflicts in his history of the Great Elector has already been remarked, and in his last work, on the history of the Brandenburg Elector Frederick III, the concern became predominant. It took the form of an obsession with the English Revolution of 1688, to which he returned time and again until it comprised fully a third of the uncompleted volume. Both in its proportions and in its substance the treatment marked a development over Pufendorf's earlier consideration of the same theme. He repeated indeed, in his *Frederick III,* the relevant sections of the *Great Elector,* with their interpretations of the specific events, but then he went beyond them to interpret the revolution as a whole in the light of the general rules of politics.[63]

Religion now provided him with the long-sought connection between historical documents and political principles. He announced as his starting point the French efforts "to impose a yoke upon Europe and destroy the churches and the property of the Protestants" and made his running theme the disjunction between Catholicism and the reasons of state against the conjunction between Protestantism and the reasons of state. Thus James "preferred to subvert the religion and laws of his people" rather than "follow the character and reasons of his state [*indolis rationesque sui Regni*]," while the English people "executed their rightful duty, under the pressure of necessity, of guarding the safety of the state through which their religion, liberty, life, and property are secured." [64] Pufendorf permitted himself such general interpretations only rarely, but they informed his crucial particular explanations. Thus, the "counsels of the priests" and the "deceptions of the French" combined to divert James from the true reasons of state, and correspondingly the concerns for both "the Protestant religion and the laws" kept William and the English notables faithful to the true reasons of state.[65] Protestantism functioned as the bond between historical and political truth that enabled Pufendorf to pursue the narrative, usually without commentary of his own, from within the Orangist point of view in full confidence that portrayal from its angle and explanation in its terms represented not only a relative political but also an absolute historical truth. Religion permitted him to break through the barriers of history within which politics had confined him. By virtue of it, the sources provided their own interpretation; the events of domestic history were integrated by a common theme and became meaningful; the particular reasons of state became measurable by a substantive criterion of a general European interest as the political balance of states acquired a deeper confessional foundation; and the historian could consequently follow the Protestant tie beyond his own state to the representation of an alien prince and state which was valid by reason of its conformity to an ultimate truth.

In his correspondence Pufendorf confirmed the striking impact which the English revolution had upon him and set into even bolder relief than in his formal history the reasons for such an effect. The ostensible main point of his discussion—that the revolution was caused not by the reformation in religion but by the misgovernment of James in violating the laws, institutions, and liberties of the realm—simply confirmed Pufendorf's long-held secular principles of politics and does not account for his new-found excitement.[66] What did account for it was the answer which the combination of history and positive religion provided to the fundamental relationship between freedom and authority that had been left problematical in Pufendorf's political theory.

Hitherto, within the framework of his secular moral and political doctrine, Pufendorf had found only in the authority of the sovereign a certain means of directing the diversity of voluntary individual acts toward the public order that was necessary to morality, but he had been unable to find in this authority a certain means for reconciling this order with the persistence of individual liberty that was equally requisite to morality. Now the reconciliation that had escaped him in logic was born in actuality from the juncture which he looked for in the success of the revolution: "the good of public liberty and the Protestant cause." [67] He denied the applicability of the divine-right doctrine to the case but he also did not attempt to make use of his own doctrine, for he recognized that actuality was contributing an inimitable solution. If the Prince of Orange succeeds, he wrote, and has to defend this "fact" with "principles," then "those will have to be found who will defend it with the pen and then a great revolution in Europe is to be expected." [68] That the fact came before the principle was Pufendorf's explicit ground for not having sought to deduce the rightfulness of the revolution from political norms. "I see in all the histories that such things are usually judged à la Turk, where the successful event is called the vote of heaven." [69] It did not hurt Pufendorf's notion of Protestantism as an internal qualification of liberty to notice the approval of the revolution by the Elector's court, and the alignment of absolutist Brandenburg and revolutionary England under a common Protestant aegis led him to reassert the balance of freedom and authority implicit in his political system.[70] The appearance of revolution as orderly fact enabled Pufendorf to assert what he could not previously deduce without reservation: sovereignty is defined by law in such a way that violation of liberties under the protection of the law releases citizens from allegiance to the ruler and validates the election of a new sovereign.[71] It was in this context, where the interests of Protestantism rekindled Pufendorf's investment in liberty, that he gave vent to his most radical expressions of political relativism, justifying republicanism and elective monarchy along with the more orthodox forms of the state as equivalent objects of obedience so long as what is involved is a "state that does me good." [72]

The crucial role of religion in conferring a general meaning upon Pufendorf's political history was a measure of the way in which the development of Europe was outgrowing his strictly authoritarian categories. The same need that led him to focus upon religion in general history also led him, late in life, to a concern with religious history proper. The function of positive religion in spanning the gap between political theory and historical practice showed him the necessity of establishing the historical reality of the creeds and churches that bore this function. In this genre, revealingly enough, the careful delimitations which he imposed upon his secular history fell away: Pufendorf plotted ecclesiastical history in the grand style, from Christian origins to the present, and he did not doubt either that in this endeavor a historian could "empty himself of all prejudices drawn from his own sect" or that "the whole fate of our church" could be shown.[73] In both his criticisms of and his prescriptions for ecclesiastical history, which he came to consider "the noblest piece of erudition," he insisted, as in his professional political history, that the scholar "will have to go to the sources themselves—that is, not only the old authors of ecclesiastical histories but the conciliar acts and patristic writings," but from these he expected the historical scholar to write of "the propagation of religion, the administration of the Church, the origins, progress, and destruction of heresies, the origins of councils and the progress of the hierarchy," to correct for the theological "faults" of the Church Fathers in multiplying heresies, and to search for "all the priestly and doctrinal intrigues" which "constitute a good part of this history." [74]

And yet, despite his enthusiastic recipes, Pufendorf himself never wrote serious ecclesiastical history. This abstention was not rooted in any disinclination to enter the religious arena, for he bypassed its history to invade theology proper. The fact was that the larger interpretative freedom which he allowed to ecclesiastical history could not entirely compensate for the inherent limitations of history as such in providing a certain grounding for general political truth. He recognized the distinction between the theologian whose concern was for the treatment of religious "truth" and the historical scholar who had to guard against sectarianism. [75] But the function which he attributed to religion in establishing a coherence within history rested precisely upon its ultimate truth, which could only be implicit in history. So it was that Pufendorf extended his purview from the positive reality of history to the positive truth of religion.

[7]

THE THEOLOGIAN

Just as the pursuit of a rationale for the external relations among states led Pufendorf to cross the line from jurisprudence into history, so did the pursuit of the rationale for the internal relations within states lead him across the more treacherous divide separating natural law from theology. Outwardly, the two excursions were under quite different auspices. Whereas the professional jurist became the professional historian and deliberately shifted his standards to meet the different kind of knowledge appropriate to this new métier, the natural-law theorist of politics drifted gradually into the realm of Christian theology which, in his concern for the integrity of the natural law, he had loudly forbidden himself. He never avowed himself a theologian, and he dressed his late writings on religion in the mantle of the relations between church and state or of a special jurisprudence, such as "covenant law [jus feciale]." And yet the undeniable fact was that toward the end of his life he was expounding Christian doctrine and had joined to the vocation of history the avocation of theology. Despite the difference in his attitudes toward them, moreover, the two pursuits performed analogous intellectual functions: they ordered the realms of positive fact which his political system assumed and his jurisprudence required. The coincidence of his confessional preoccupation and his new historical profession underlined his intellectual relocation in a realm of truths categorically different from his former realm of necessary universal truths. It was this relocation that saved the formal validity of his political and legal system.

I. THE PROBLEM OF SECULARIZATION IN THE SEVENTEENTH CENTURY

Whatever the formalities that serve to reconcile the apparent discrepancies in Pufendorf's thinking, it seems natural to ask whether his late turn to positive religion did not actually signify a regression from the secularization of thought in which he had so prominently participated. But to affirm this would be to misunderstand the process of secularization, for the fact is that at this stage of the process its most prominent representatives were capping their intellectual careers just as Pufendorf did, with an accounting to theology. Descartes climaxed the creative decade that witnessed his breakthrough in the realms of method and of physics with his application of its consequences to theology in the abortive metaphysical treatise of 1629 that ultimately became his *Meditations on Primary Philosophy* of 1641.[1] However doubtful the validity of Hobbes's own religiosity in *Mr. Hobbes Considered in His Loyalty, Religion, Reputation, and Manners,* which he published in 1662 to defend himself against the charge of atheism, what remains indubitable is his theory's need for religion. Hence, his long address first to "the Natural Kingdom of God" and then to the scriptural exegesis of "the Principles of Christian Politics" marked the conclusion of his political system in both *De Cive* and *Leviathan.*[2] Spinoza published his *Theological-Political Treatise* in 1670, suspending the completion of his

Ethics to define the nature of a biblical faith that would be compatible with it. Toward the end of his life Leibniz expounded an explicit theology to frame his principles of nature in the *Theodicy* (1710) and *The Principles of Nature and of Grace Founded on Reason* (1714). John Locke, finally, evinced not only the contemporaneity but the surprising homology of his development with Pufendorf's. He rounded off the successive commitments to a philosophy (the *Essay concerning Human Understanding,* 1690) and a political theory (the *Letter on Toleration* and the *Two Treatises of Government,* 1689 and 1690, respectively) which sought to divorce knowledge and politics from theological assumption and scriptural authority with the *Reasonableness of Christianity as Delivered in the Scriptures* of 1695, in which he extended his rational system to the exposition of positive Christianity.

It can be maintained, with truth, that these reckonings with religion are explicable simply as the efforts of secularizers to demonstrate the external relations of the autonomous philosophical and political systems which they had developed with the Judeo-Christian tradition that had been rejected from these systems but could still be conceded validity in its own sphere. It can be further maintained that this concern for coexistence holds both for those who, certainly like Hobbes and perhaps like Descartes, were prudently propitiating the majority of old believers and for those who, like Spinoza and Leibniz, were working out the relations of the two independent realms for their own unity and peace of mind.

If this were all, then the categorical judgments about secularization need be tempered only by tactical and psychological qualifications. But this was not all. In each case there was also a gap, or a tension, or a demand, within the philosophy or political theory itself, that called for God. These strains set limits of varying essentiality to the secularization of thought—religious limits which should be identified if the process of secularization is to be properly understood.

The most modest infringement of the secular attitude was the postulation or demonstration of the Good or the First Cause or the One as a logical necessity of a philosophical or political system, to establish an ultimate unity or authority for it. When such an entity is conceived on the analogy of personality, as God, to signify the integral union of self-consciousness, reality, and creativity in a perfect whole—and it generally was so conceived in the seventeenth century—the explication of the necessary existence and qualities of such a being may be called natural theology and may be characterized as theology without religion. Whether in the form of Descartes' and Leibniz' derivation of divine attributes from His "supreme perfection" or Hobbes's, Spinoza's, and Locke's derivation of the sanction for natural law from "the power of God" and "the measure that God has set to the actions of men for their mutual security" in His "Natural Kingdom," the initial autonomy of philosophy and politics was compensated by the inclusion of the Divinity within the purview of nature and reason.[3] Certainly the substitution of a descriptive, mechanistic, and derivative connection for a formal, teleological, and primary coherence diminished the natural functions of divinity and was a significant step toward a more secular mode of thought, but still the very persistence of a natural theology, rooted as it was in scholastic tradition, braked the tendency toward secularism. This limitation was intensified by the equal persistence, in the seventeenth century, of natural theology's function as a prelude to considerations of supernatural theology.

The second degree or level of theological consideration is the crucial one for seventeenth-century thought: here the logical functions of divinity were articulated into the attributes of a personal God and the way thereby opened from natural theology into positive religion. The key to this intermediate level lay in the dovetailing or even the coincidence of the qualities presumably deduced from God as "the final reason of things" with the God of Christian revelation. Descartes exemplified the dovetailing, and Leibniz the coincidence of natural and Christian qualities.

The ambiguous character which informs this level of religiosity is reflected in the combination of Descartes' own disclaimer that "I have never intermeddled with theological studies" with the growing consensus of recent commentators that he did.[4] The resolution of the difference lies precisely in Descartes' tacit postulation of an intermediate level between rational metaphysics and positive religion, for by his eschewal of theology Descartes meant what "we are . . . taught in the Holy Scriptures," whereas the religiosity now commonly imputed to him refers to the Christian postulates required by his philosophy. Thus, for his metaphysics and his ethics the verdict is that Descartes used the substance of positive Christianity, albeit without the title, to root the ultimate certainties of which his method of philosophical doubt had deprived him. In his physics his mechanical principles required not simply a prime mover but a theological reinterpretation of God in terms of an infinitude, a transcendence, and a sovereign inscrutability to execute Descartes' belief that "the opinions which have seemed to me the truest in Physics, those that proceed by consideration of natural causes, have always been those which best accord with the mysteries of religion." It is hardly surprising, then, to find Descartes' rational truths forming a kind of continuum with those of Revelation: "I have tried to prove by natural reason that the soul is not corporeal; but . . . it can only be known through faith whether it is to ascend above."[5]

The Christian theology that was implicit in Descartes'

philosophy became explicit in Leibniz. Like Descartes he refrained from a systematic exposition of Christian theology, but he went far beyond Descartes in the positive identification of the "supreme perfection" required by natural reason with the personal God of the Christians. As against Descartes' reliance upon inscrutable transcendence, Leibniz' God, even when "founded on reason," acquires deduced qualities of omnipotence, omniscience, supreme goodness, supreme justice, and supreme lovableness.[6] The personal connotation of these qualities is clear from Leibniz' dictum that "universal justice is the same for God and for men; only the facts differ in the respective cases."[7]

Leibniz, moreover, found a place for revelation in the very structure of reason itself. Rational truths, he maintained, included both those that were "eternal"—that is, logically necessary—and those that were "positive," and these positive truths, in turn, included *a posteriori* truths of "experience," with which "faith is comparable, since faith . . . depends upon the experience of those who have seen the miracles upon which revelation is based and of the credible Tradition which has passed them on to us. . . ." The truths of scripture thus fall for Leibniz into the realm of contingent existence—realities dependent upon the free choice of God—and faith becomes epistemologically parallel to the principle of sufficient reason, which Leibniz devised to account for such contingent "truths of fact" in nature. Like this principle, faith "explains" the existence of things without having to "comprehend" how they come to be. Like this principle, it can be invalidated only by a conflict with the logically necessary eternal truths. But because faith is parallel rather than subject to the principle of sufficient reason it does not fall under the latter's criterion of probability; rather does it bear its own motives of belief which are "above reason"—that is, sufficient reason—but "not against reason"—that is, demonstrative reason. The parallel of sufficient reason and faith under the common sway of necessary reason is not perfect: it holds for the independence of faith from sufficient reason, but not conversely. The probabilities of sufficient reason become "false reasons" on occasions of conflict with faith.[8]

The function of Leibniz' tortured argument, reconstructed here to exhibit the implicit structure which, in view of its flaccidity, he dared not articulate, was to accord a distinctive place in philosophy for the truths of Christian revelation by conferring on them sufficient compatibility with logic to make them philosophically relevant and by retaining sufficient "positive" or existential finality to guarantee their ultimacy and remove them from further rational analysis. By virtue of the first of these purposes Leibniz could claim that the nature of God and man (in relation to the problem of evil) was knowable by reason and faith together, which "harmonize what the light of nature and the light of revelation teach"; by virtue of the second he could claim that through this harmony he had made "reason serve faith."[9] Thus he could simply assert the Christian attributes of God, deduce their logical implications, and in this philosophized form use them to validate such crucial metaphysical positions as the pre-established harmony and the perfectibility of this best possible world.

The natural and the ambiguous levels of theologizing were the bases, tacit or explicit, for the third and most intensive level of this activity among the secularists of the seventeenth century: the crossing of the self-imposed frontier into scriptural exegesis itself. It is true enough that Hobbes, Spinoza, and Locke, the most notorious sponsors of this apparent paradox, engaged in scriptural exegesis with the avowedly critical and apparently negative purpose of demonstrating, in good secularizing style, the indifference of theology to both philosophy and politics. In Spinoza's terms, "the Bible leaves reason absolutely free, . . . Revelation and Philosophy stand on totally different footings. . . . Theology is not bound to serve reason, nor reason theology, but . . . each has her own domain." [10] And yet, for each of these thinkers the apparent confirmation from the Christian theological side of a separation already consummated from the philosophical or political side actually covered a constructive effort to turn the relationship of mutual independents into one of mutual complements. The commensurability lies along two dimensions, one signifying a projection of the natural into the revealed realm, the other an extension from revelation into natural philosophy and politics.

The first of these connections lay in the common affirmation of reason as a necessary criterion for the interpretation of scripture. In Locke's extreme formulation, "Reason is natural revelation . . . ; revelation is natural reason enlarged by a new set of discoveries transmitted by God immediately, which reason vouches the truth of . . . , that they come from God." [11] Spinoza started with a more modest formulation: "I found nothing taught expressly by Scripture, which does not agree with our understanding, or which is repugnant thereto," but then proceeded to the assertion that from the one and only precept of faith—obedience to God—"all other doctrines of the faith can be deduced . . . by reason alone," and even to the general principle that "as the highest power of Scriptural interpretation belongs to every man, the rule for such interpretation should be nothing but the natural light of reason which is common to all." [12] Hobbes, in turn, declared that in treating scripture "we are not to renounce our Senses, and Experience; nor (that which is the undoubted Word of God) our natural Reason. For they are . . . not to be folded up in the napkin of an implicit faith, but employed in the purchase of Justice, Peace, and

[209]

true Religion." He did not shrink, consequently, from calling his exegetical procedure "true ratiocination." [13]

In this paradoxical application of reason to revelation for the purpose of separating reason from revelation the seventeenth-century intellectuals faced the issue which brought to a head the general problem of the secularists' masquerade as Christian theologians. The problem was to reconcile the theological validity of their reason with their rejection of the reason embodied in the bulk of traditional theology. The obvious distinction would be between their critical use of reason and the syllogistic constructs of dogma, but although the secularists did apply such a distinction when they pointed out the contradictory implications of traditional theology, they did not dwell upon it. Indeed, they could not, since they themselves went beyond criticism to the employment of reason in the construction of religious doctrine. The reason that they justified in theology was a reason that was parallel and analogous to the reason that they applied to nature; it was a reason, then, that analyzed the materials of scripture into general relations that were reducible to a single principle. Spinoza was most explicit about the twin exercises of reason:

> The method of interpreting Scripture does not widely differ from the method of interpreting nature—in fact, it is almost the same. For as the interpretation of nature consists in the examination of the history of nature, and therefrom deducing definitions of natural phenomena on certain fixed axioms, so Scriptural interpretation proceeds by the examination of Scripture, and inferring the intention of its authors as a legitimate conclusion from its fundamental principles. . . . As in the

examination of natural phenomena we try first to investigate what is most universal and common to all nature . . . and then proceed to what is less universal; so, too, in the history of Scripture, we seek first for that which is most universal, and serves for the basis and foundation of all Scripture, a doctrine, in fact, that is commended by the prophets as eternal and most profitable to all men.[14]

It is, perhaps, not surprising that the philosophical progressives of the seventeenth century should have thought the rational methods of analysis and synthesis in which they took such pride to be as applicable to revelation as to nature. What is striking, however, and revealing of an intellectual motive beyond pride in the general instrumentality of reason is the substantive construction, in the theological realm, of a doctrinal pattern homologous with the pattern of truths in the natural realm. Thus Hobbes derived from scripture a "signification" of the "Kingdom of God" that was a precise counterpart, in revelation, of the human commonwealth in nature—

a Kingdom properly so named, . . . a commonwealth, instituted (by the consent of those who were to be subject thereto) for their civil government, and the regulating of their behavior, not only towards God their King, but also towards one another in point of justice, and towards other nations both in peace and war; which properly was a Kingdom, wherein God was King, and the High Priest was to be (after the death of Moses) his sole Viceroy, or Lieutenant.[15]

[211]

Spinoza derived from scripture the reduction of faith to the single precept of "obedience" just as he had derived from nature the reduction of phenomena to the single concept of "substance." The distinction in religion between "the dogmas of universal faith or the fundamental dogmas of the whole of Scripture" which are "absolutely required in order to attain obedience to God" on the one hand and all other doctrines, about which "everyone may think . . . as he likes" on the other corresponds to Spinoza's distinction between the adequately knowable "series of fixed and eternal things" and the inadequately knowable "series of particular and mutable things" in his epistemology. It also corresponds to the distinction, in his politics, between the transfer of the individual's whole power to the body politic as the embodiment of reason and the retention of "a certain number" of his "natural rights"—particularly, those of "free judgment" and "freedom of speech" and of "religious belief." [16]

Locke, finally, performed a similar operation upon scripture, but within the overlap of critical methods Locke's scriptural theology reflected precisely the larger proportion of empiricism in his philosophy and liberality in his politics as compared with the rationalism and democracy of Spinoza's natural model. Although both critics elaborated political theories distinguishing between the outer or practical side of religion which was the concern of the body politic and the inner or contemplative side which remained within the sphere of individual natural rights, Locke assigned all that had to do with salvation on the outer as on the inner side of religion to the latter sphere, leaving to the magistrate only the sector of the outer side bearing on civil peace, while Spinoza assigned the whole of the outer side to the sovereign for the purposes both of civil peace and salvation.[17] Locke's relocation of the line between the individual and the community toward the individual, as well as his analogous relocation

of the epistemological line between the particular phenomenon and general truths toward the phenomenon, had as its
exegetical correspondent the reversal of the fundamental
doctrines which Spinoza and he found in scripture. Where
Spinoza made obedience the main precept and faith its
corollary, Locke made belief in Jesus as the Messiah the main
precept and obedience its corollary.[18] This reversal had as its
consequence a further theological discrepancy of prime importance: whereas for Spinoza obedience was a basic category
requiring subscription to its entailed dogmas regardless of
their status as rationally demonstrated truth, for Locke the
belief in Jesus' mission merely certified entailed dogmas
whose truth had always been accessible to natural reason.
Hence Locke's theology confirmed a larger capacity and civil
right for the individual in matters of religion than did
Spinoza's, whose larger doubts of the individual's natural
reason and larger attributions to the discrete sphere of biblical obedience confirmed his embodiment of reason in the
sovereign.[19]

But if the secularists' Christian theology mirrored the
structure of their respective philosophies and politics, it was
not merely a function of them. The reflection of nature in
revelation demonstrated, to be sure, the relevance of the
latter to the former, but it was accompanied by a reverse
connection, projected from revelation into nature, which
demonstrated an independent function for Christian theology in putatively secular philosophies and politics. What
this connection and this function were emerges first from the
secularists' notion of what was distinctive in revelation and
secondly from the needs of their philosophy and politics
which the distinctive quality of revelation filled. On the first
count, it is clear that despite the provision of a prominent
role for reason in Christian theology and despite the careful
matching of revealed dogma with philosophical principle,

the secular theorists were stridently insistent upon the ultimate disjunction of the two realms. Spinoza carried the
disjunction furthest with his categorical declaration that

> philosophy has no end in view save truth; faith
> . . . looks for nothing but obedience and piety.
> . . . The sphere of reason is . . . truth and wis-
> dom; the sphere of theology is piety and obedi-
> ence. The power of reason does not extend so far
> as to determine for us that men may be blessed
> through simple obedience, without understand-
> ing. Theology tells us nothing else, enjoins on us
> no command save obedience: she defines the dog-
> mas of faith . . . only insofar as they may be nec-
> essary for obedience, and leaves reason to deter-
> mine their precise truth. . . . By theology I here
> mean, strictly speaking, revelation, insofar as it in-
> dicates the object aimed at by Scripture. . . .[20]

The canon for the interpretation of scripture is therefore
nothing but the language and history of scripture itself, and
when we interpret "we are at work not on the truth of
passages, but solely on their meaning." [21] Neither Hobbes nor
Locke went so far as to separate thus explicitly truth and
meaning, knowledge and faith—for Locke, indeed, faith
bestowed knowledge [22]—but they agreed that there was a
fundamental difference in the respective operations of the
mind in the two realms. Hobbes qualified his position that
the natural faculties, and particularly "our understanding
and reason, are everywhere constant in their operation," with
the injunction that in their application to scripture, we must
will to "captivate" them "to the Words" so as to "forbear
contradiction" and not try to sift out "a philosophical truth
by logic of such mysteries as are not comprehensible." [23]

Locke, similarly, recognized the distinctive quality of "the truths revelation has discovered," and warned that "it is our mistake to think, that because reason confirms them to us, we had the first certain knowledge of them from thence. . . . The contrary is manifest. . . ." [24]

But upon closer examination it appears that not all or even most of revelation is thus distinctive. In Spinoza's terms, it is *"the basis of* theology" that "cannot be investigated by the natural light of reason" and that makes "revelation . . . necessary," but "we should . . . make use of our reason to grasp with moral certainty what is revealed. . . ." [25] The other secularists concurred in the concentration of faith upon a single pole of revelation—faith in Jesus as the Christ. They made rational judgments upon scripture in order to separate out this pole of faith; from it they made rational deductions in order to construct a theology; but they admitted that only the faith itself, and not the letter or the doctrine, was necessary to salvation.

The care which the secularizing intellectuals of the seventeenth century took to isolate one cardinal tenet of faith and to denigrate the rest of the revealed realm indicated their relative unconcern with theology as such and bespoke their urgent need for an irreducible single tenet of faith, extensible into the natural realm. The generic character of the need, and consequently of the extension, becomes visible in the insistent uniformity with which practical obedience is associated with faith. While the precise relationship of the two lessons of revelation varied, as we have seen, with the particular character of the philosophical and political theory, the combination of them in any form demonstrated, as a common feature of the age, the role of positive religion in anchoring the rational morality that mediated between philosophy and politics.[26]

In the cases of Hobbes and Spinoza, both of whom attributed to obedience an independent status as an absolute precept of revelation and connected it with the obligations of the subject in an authoritarian political system, the natural function of a supernatural principle is transparent. For both, "God's law" or "the Divine law," which is what scripture commands men to obey, is nothing but "the laws of nature," which are "seated in right reason" and have now also "been promulgated by the Divine Majesty as the laws of his celestial kingdom through our Lord Jesus Christ and the Holy Prophets and Apostles," and "the laws of our several sovereigns": "For our Savior Christ hath not given us new laws. . . . The laws of God therefore are none but the laws of nature, whereof the principle is that we should not violate our faith, that is, a commandment to obey our civil sovereigns. . . ." [27] Thus the function of faith was to furnish a natural ethic with a supernatural sanction for the purpose of providing the discursive logic of secular obligations with a final authority that was positive and beyond all logic. Hobbes gave literal expression to this function of revealed religion when he indicated that the moral rules known by reason from nature were merely natural "inferences" until "they were brought by God into the Holy Scriptures": only this scriptural source made logical inferences into binding "laws properly so-called." [28]

Nor was the juncture of obedience and positive religion by authoritarians like Hobbes and Spinoza an indication simply of a consistent *ad hoc* application. That the liberal Locke made a similar juncture demonstrates the broader paradoxical consistency of a calculated resort to revelation in order to acquire for reason a reality that only unreason could confer. If obedience was not a primary basis or concomitant of faith for Locke, still it was a necessary consequence of the belief in Jesus that was the primary basis of faith.[29] The law which "the revelation of the Gospel" prescribes for men's obedience, moreover, is the same "eternal, immutable standard of right" which "the light of reason" and "the light of nature" first "revealed to all mankind, who would make use of that light." [30] It was only because "natural religion, in its full extent, was nowhere, that I know, taken care of, by the force of natural reason" and because "human reason unassisted failed men in its great and proper business of morality" that "the world stood . . . in need of our Savior and the morality delivered by him." This failure of reason was in part a defect of knowledge—"it never from unquestionable principles, by clear deductions, made out an entire body of the 'law of nature' "—but, what was more important, since the want of knowledge was a want of its totality and since by implication the totality of knowledge breeds obligation to its rules, the defect of knowledge became a defect of authority:

> It is true, there is a law of nature: but . . . who ever made out all the parts of it, put them together, and showed the world their obligation? If there was not it is plain there was need of one to give us such a morality. . . . Such a law of morality Jesus Christ hath given us in the New Testament; but by . . . revelation. We have from Him a full and sufficient rule for our direction, and conformable to that of reason. But the truth and obligation of its precepts have their force, and are put past doubt to us, by the evidence of his mission. . . . Here morality has a sure standard, that revelation vouches, and reason cannot gainsay, nor question. [31]

What the Christian faith delivers, then, is simply a positive ultimate sanction of moral laws that are discernible, albeit actually not discerned, by deductions from "principles of reason, self-evident in themselves." Hence the deliberate target of the Christian revelation is, according to Locke, "the greatest part of mankind," "the people," "the poor," for whom "hearing plain commands is the sure and only course to bring them to obedience and practice," since they "cannot know, and therefore they must believe." [32] Just as religious faith, in the eyes of other secularists, turned concepts into precepts for execution by sovereigns, so here it performed the same alchemy for individuals: however various the political purposes, the underlying pressure to carve from revelation a single reality that combined the finality of fact with the tolerance of logic and to install it at the apex of moral philosophy was a common and fundamental qualification of secularization in the seventeenth century.

II. POLITICS AND RELIGION IN PUFENDORF

Pufendorf's theological concerns, then, were far from idiosyncratic. The rationalists with whom he was aligned, thinkers for the most part far more rigorous than he, not only reintroduced at the capstone of knowledge the divinity they had eliminated from its foundation but even applied their vaunted reason to biblical exegesis for the purposes of isolating a principle which was frankly inaccessible to reason alone and then appropriating that principle. This context illuminates the internal necessity of an intellectual process that would perhaps be less apparent in Pufendorf's own more syncretistic approach, but if the context helps thereby to explain him, he in turn, by the very virtue of what is distinctive in his approach, contributes otherwise to the understanding of his environment.

What was distinctive about Pufendorf, within the rationalist school, was his orientation toward the broadest possible applicability of his principles to the facts of contemporary life. Others, such as Hobbes and Locke, were similarly oriented for the *derivation* of their principles,[33] but, once derived, the subsequent development of these principles took place under the aegis of a logical formality that masked any further existential influences. In Pufendorf, on the other hand, the integration was looser, the seams more apparent, the existential influences more identifiable. With him not only may we learn something more in general about the interplay of fact and principle but, because he articulated the development of natural-law politics to Christian theology into a series of stages responsive to a succession of different existential influences, we may also learn something more about the *process* leading from secular to religious modes of thought in the seventeenth century.

An additional kind of context, consequently, becomes relevant for Pufendorf—and indicative of him—over and above the general fact of Christian faith to which the primary thinkers had resort. Where they used it as the prevalent form of positive reality in which they rooted their secular logic and their secular institutions, he went beyond the general fact to cope with the religious institutions and the religious logic— the confessional dogmas—that were also prevalent positive realities in the world around him. He registered the actual qualification which the persistent vitality of Christian churches, practices, and attitudes brought to the intensified secular concerns of the seventeenth century. Far more explicitly than his fellow secularists did he see in positive religion a whole domain of discrete organizational and doctrinal facts rather than only a supreme principle of factual existence in general; far more contrived and graduated in consequence was his establishment of the relationship between the natural logic of politics and these extra-logical existences that were at once independent of and relevant to it. Where the philoso-

[219]

phers could ultimately settle the body of nature upon a theological skeleton, Pufendorf had always to adjust the relations of two parallel bodies.

What we may look for, then, in the pattern of Pufendorf's theology is a development that was similar in form to that of his great contemporaries but increasingly divergent in substance. Like them, his quest for a final unifying principle that would guarantee the reality of rational truth pushed him first from natural theology to the hybrid doctrine that specified the natural functions of Christian faith, and then from this ambivalent position into Christian theology proper. But unlike them, he remained ever attentive to the reality embodied not only in Christian faith but in Christian institutions as well. He moved from one stage of his theologizing to the next, ever seeking to anchor in an ultimate positive reality both the general principles of reason with which he explained and the particular facts of state and society which were to be explained.

Pufendorf's starting point, like that of so many of his contemporaries, was a rational system of natural law which at once excluded faith and required God—or, in his terms, renounced "theology," both "dogmatic" and "moral," and admitted "natural religion." [34] On the one hand, he distinguished categorically between the "separate studies" of natural law—based on reason, common to all men, addressed to "this life," located in "external actions"—and theology— based on revelation, appropriate only to Christians, addressed to salvation in a future life, and located in the "internal movements" of the mind. He resented, consequently, the scholastic absorption of philosophy into theology, and he abstained, in turn, from the absorption of theology into his philosophy. "The articles of faith concerning the fall of Adam, the origin of sin, the sacrifice of Christ, faith, the justification of man, etc., can and ought no more to be determined by the discipline of natural law, which is ordered to the understanding of all peoples, than the mystery of the Trinity by physics." [35] On the other hand, however, he appealed to natural religion as the necessary logical basis of natural law. For if its precepts "are to have the force of law, it is necessary to presuppose that God exists, and by His providence rules all things. . . ." This necessity is, to be sure, in the first instance ethical, or requisite for the conversion of natural description into prescription, but it is also ultimately metaphysical, for it postulates the creative and preservative principle behind the orderly universe upon which morality is imposed.[36]

But even at this early stage, when he was avowedly still working within his strictly delimited realm of nature, Pufendorf was impelled to venture beyond the affirmation of natural religion to the assertion of propositions which predicated a recognition and an interpretation of revelation. The overt intent of such propositions was tactical—to argue the compatibility of his natural-law system with the teachings of revelation—but to accomplish this mutual toleration he had to admit reciprocal connections between the two spheres. In order to show that a natural-law precept could not be opposed to a scriptural principle on the same subject Pufendorf revealed that some of his natural-law precepts were themselves constructed "by abstracting from that knowledge which is drawn from the Sacred Scriptures." [37] Then, in order to maintain that scriptural principles could not be opposed to his natural-law politics he not only inferred from scripture the negative proposition that "our Savior and the apostles" introduced nothing "new" in the way of political principle but ventured the positive scriptural interpretation that the "genuine" Christian doctrine supports the "sociability" and "tranquillity" attributed by natural-law precepts to states.[38]

In his chief theoretical and polemical works Pufendorf

scarcely went beyond such general claims of biblical confirmation, since the appeal to scripture as evidence for the
Christian respectability of an ostensibly secular and rational
system of universal politics was both an embarrassing infringement on his own delimitation of the fields and a
dangerous double-edged instrument. And yet, during this
very period of his concern with the natural law, utilizing a
different format, he initiated the theological elaboration of
his political argument from scripture. In a separate essay
whose title—"On the Harmony of True Politics with the
Christian Religion"—showed the persistence of his tactical
concern he supplied specific biblical testimony for his argument that "true politics, deduced from genuine principles
and legitimately applied, never opposes . . . but rather co-
operates amicably with the Christian religion," which, in
turn, "does much in states to make politics realize its purpose
the more easily," and to this extent the essay was simply an
attempt to prove what he had elsewhere only asserted.[39] But
from the purely tactical point of view the advantage of
scriptural support for his political principles was balanced by
the perils of Pandora's Box. The substance of his argument
reveals an urgency that goes far beyond considerations of
intellectual diplomacy. It reveals a deeper, more internal,
and more compelling ground for his exegetical excursion:
the postulation of God's existence, which was the admitted
apex of Pufendorf's natural-law doctrine, itself required
stabilization, and this could come only from a source beyond
nature and law. Natural-law politics turns out, in Pufendorf's
treatment, to be harmonious with the teachings of Christian
revelation for the best of all possible reasons—because it
needs them. It was characteristic of Pufendorf that his overt
desire for accommodation should find faithful reflection in
the immanent problems of his thought.

The context of the essay yields a preliminary indication of

the intellectual function of what we may call Pufendorf's Christian political theology. He published it in the same collection as his treatises on patriotism and irregular state forms. This conjunction assigns his scriptural arguments to the general preoccupation which dominates these treatises: his examination, at the peripheries of his political system, of the relations between the realm of law and the realm of actuality, and the construction of devices to direct men's particular heterogeneous acts into his rationally pre-established legal channels. Pursuant to this preoccupation, Pufendorf used scripture as an extra-legal source of principles that explains men's actual submission to the laws of politics beyond what might rationally be expected of them. Thus the Bible provides the supreme validation of the *fact* of civil sovereignty, while leaving to reason and nature the *process* of its establishment and operation. Its injunctions for men to honor and love their rulers, to remember their ultimate responsibility before "the divine tribunal" for their actions, to carry out their duties for their own sakes even where there is no fear of punishment for transgression, and to enact "benevolence, humanity, and charity, without hope of return"—these are scriptural principles which lead men to obey the natural law in areas where it has little practical effect.[40]

At this initial phase of his theologizing, Pufendorf's notion of religious support for the final authority of natural law was primitive and literal. It was frankly authoritarian, reinforcing the power of the sovereign, who was the executor of the natural law. He articulated this orientation not only in his acceptance, as politically valid, of particular biblical prescriptions of obedience to kings because they "exercise divine authority on earth" but in the whole cast of the essay, which identified "true politics" with the situation in which "citizens love their present status, acquiesce in it, . . . and do not incline to innovation." [41] But his interpretation of scripture along these lines, however selective, raised problems which he could not avoid. He could and indeed did gloss over them for the nonce, but they undermined his footing and were to drag him down, further and further from the political terrain on which he started, into the quicksand of theology.

The first of these problems had to do with those political and social precepts of biblical Christianity which ran counter to the authority of sovereigns. Pufendorf acknowledged the New Testament principles of pacifism and humility, but he used arguments about the existence of non-Christians and bad Christians in the world, as well as citations on the duty of "even a true Christian to repel unjust violence" and a defense of Machiavelli in this context, to rule such principles inapplicable to politics, to make a Christian virtue out of military bravery in defense of the state, and to grant Christian approval to "dissimulation" and such others of "those arts which are useful and necessary in view of the malignity, stubbornness, and stupidity of men." [42] Pufendorf backed his selection of scriptural references for this position not only with the usual rationale on the frailty of the human condition but with arguments mixing religious and natural considerations. Thus he held that with its approval of civil government the "Christian religion" also approved the means necessary to it and that "Christian virtues [like pacific submission to injury] must not foment evil in others." [43] But he acknowledged that the problem of the *pure* Christian ethic was difficult, and if he did not admit that he had not resolved it to his satisfaction, its status as unfinished business was subsequently uncovered when it became the dominant concern in the next stage of his theological development.

But "On the Harmony of True Politics with the Christian

Religion" adumbrated more than the potential disharmony between politics and Christianity. The concluding section of the essay betrayed the line of thought that was to lead Pufendorf to his final breakthrough from the political function of Christian exegesis into dogmatic theology proper. He sought his clinching proof of the concord between true politics—defined as obedience to sovereign authority—and the Christian religion in the necessary connection between such politics and the *true* Christian religion. He sought, that is, not simply to associate his political principles with Christian political precept but to anchor them in the general truth of the total Christian dogma. This he attempted through the negative demonstration of the connection between subversive political principles and those "Christian sects" which have degenerated "from the original purity of the religion." [44] His argument here specified not so much the sectarians whose theology was reputedly a function of their revolutionary politics but the churches whose theological systems transcended politics—the Catholics and the Calvinists. But the proof of his proposition was obviously incomplete. What he did argue was the opposition of these churches to his authoritarian principles of "true politics." He castigated the Catholics for their belief in an independent "sacred power" which created turmoil in the state, for their exemption of clergy from the obligations of citizenship, their transfer of wealth out of the state, and their assessment of citizens by observance of ritual rather than of natural law. What he condemned in the Calvinists was, analogously, the love which so many of them (he had the English Puritans particularly in mind) showed for democracy, their hatred of kings, their apocalyptic denigration of civil magistracy, and the judgment of actions in accordance with individual conscience. The only "Calvinist dogma" which he rejected was that of "fatal necessity," but his standard was again political—the dogma's effect in negating the free will required for judgment by a civil court.[45]

Pufendorf's purpose was to show that these were errors "no less in religion than in true politics" and, indeed, that the latter were the consequence of the former. What he actually argued, however, was the *petitio principii* that religious error was the logical consequence of political error. Of his original purpose the only trace was the underlying assumption that both Catholic and Calvinist dogma were somehow erroneous and that their unspecified dogmatic errors demonstrated the errors of their political ways. In the protracted sequel to the essay on "Harmony" which resumed the argument against the papacy this political conditioning of Christianity was explicit: here he admitted that he was leaving the validity of Catholicism as a religious doctrine to the theologians and was simply demonstrating its inconsistency with the nature of civil sovereignty.[46] This treatise, *The History of Popedom,* which he published in 1679, was a piece of the general European history that he was to bring out three years later. As such it represents a coincidence of his growing interests in history and religion that reflects the urge, common to both, for grounding his theory in the authority of the actual. But the treatise itself, written under the influence of Pufendorf's reassuring impression that the interests of state would prevent both a concert of Catholic powers against Protestants and the suppression of Huguenots by Louis XIV, still identified his political principles with the ruler's authority, and its tendency, as in the essay on "Harmony," was still to prove Christianity's support of it: according to Christian revelation, "every Christian may yield an exact and perfect obedience to every command of the secular power, as long as such commands do not recede from the Law of Nature, right reason, and the necessities of the state, . . . for it [revelation] does require in us a strict observation of all the precepts of the law of Nature." [47]

Thus what appeared to be, at the start, a simple plea for the orthodox religious implications of his secular political doctrine opened out, under the pressure of the doctrine's inner need for roots in an independent actuality, into a call for the thorough exegesis of generic Christian political principles and, beyond even this, a dogmatic theology and ecclesiology that would support them.

Pufendorf's response to the first of these calls—the call for an internal exposition of Christian politics—drove him into the next stage of his theological development. Not until the revocation of the Edict of Nantes served as a practical demonstration of the theoretical difficulties inherent in the narrow authoritarian approach to the problem of politics and Christianity did he resume the discussion on a broader basis. The event reminded Pufendorf that his system of natural law involved something more than a mere doctrine of authority, and in view of this larger conception the Christian principles which had seemed simply troublesome to the authoritarian approach took on a more positive aspect. He used the concrete issue of the relations between church and state to reopen the fundamental theoretical discussion of the relations between natural-law politics and revealed Christianity. When he published his main work on the issue in 1687, he entitled it, accordingly, *On the Relations of the Christian Religion to Civil Life,* and if he began and ended with the explicit address to the specific problem of church and state— "how far the ecclesiastical power extends which the clergy claims for itself and how much authority accrues to the civil sovereign in religious matters"—his path between the question and the answer took him far afield into the realms of natural law and revelation.[48] His system of natural-law politics provided no demonstrable application to the actual issue

[227]

of church and state and consequently he had to adduce the generic implications of positive Christianity for politics before his political principles became applicable to it. His answer to the church-state issue proved so complex, hybrid, and even inconsistent, with its mixture of toleration and intolerance, religious individualism and political ecclesiasticism, that it obviously refers, for its explanation, to the tenuous connections which he forged between the underlying realms of politics and religion.[49] His own position on the immediate issue was clear enough: he was far more interested in keeping the church out of the state than the state out of the church.[50] But because his natural-law politics called for an access of positive religion he could not defend this position without taking revealed Christianity into account, and thence came the complication of the issue.

Pufendorf started *On the Relations* with an apparent recapitulation of his natural-law doctrine on religion—in this context, natural religion—but now that he had the whole of his doctrine under review rather than only its authoritarian effects, the work developed a set of conflicting conclusions which, in view of the general and logical form of the doctrine, took on the aspect of an antinomy.

On the one hand, the generic worship of God the Creator is a part of the individual's "natural liberty." It must be exercised by himself, need not be exercised in association with others, is alien to "human authority" and "forceful remedies" save through the pacific parental instruction of children, and is not a factor in the institution of civil societies. Since religion arises from a source both "prior" to and "higher" than civil sovereignty and is irrelevant to the "cause of security" for which men submit their wills to the will of the sovereign, it is not altered by the establishment of sovereignty: "citizens do not submit their will to the will of the sovereign in matters of religion." [51]

[228]

On the other hand, the sovereign not only takes over, as "father of his country," the paternal duty of inculcating piety in his political children, but, since "piety toward God is the basis of probity and honor toward men," of "the sanctity of promises and covenants," and of "the bond between rulers and citizens," the sovereign qua sovereign has both "the duty" to ensure the proper cultivation of natural religion by the citizens and "the power to punish whoever commits external acts subverting it in whole or in significant part." [52]

The only exit from the paradox which Pufendorf's political logic afforded him was the classification of religion under the general category of human opinions—equivalent to "opinions on doctrines of physics"—which were by their very nature "as acts stemming from an internal movement of the mind through an intrinsic impulse not susceptible to external compulsion" and which were subject to coercion by the political sovereign only when "under the mask of religion" they stirred up "dangerous political factions or conspiracies." [53] Obviously, such a rule did not suffice for the deduction of political rules either about churches as particular institutions or even about positive religion. First, natural religion had to do with the individuals only, since religious association was irrelevant to it. Second, the logical distinction between immune "internal" and punishable "external" actions was abridged by Pufendorf's explicit "exception" from the former of punishable "open" "negations of God," "inventions of plurality of Gods," "worship of false Gods or images," "blasphemies against God," or "the worship and compacting with demons," and by his immunizing of "a diversity of external rites" as an innocuous social division which must be tolerated by the sovereign.[54] The logic of his natural-law doctrine set the outer limits of possibility for the problem of politics and religion but furnished no clear line of explanation or application to the realities within them.

[229]

It was thus as much a requirement of his own logic as a substantive stage in his anthropological history of humanity when Pufendorf then turned to revelation for "the fulfill-ment of that more sublime end which is unattainable by the worship afforded by natural reason alone." [55] But now, unlike his previous treatments of the Christian faith, Pufendorf's exegesis was dedicated not so much to demonstrating its support for political authority as its complete indifference and otherness from everything political. The antipolitical Christian values that he had had to explain away now became the standard determinants for the relations between religion and the politics based upon natural law. The reason for this significant change in emphasis was a shift in Pufendorf's point of view: he was now, at this stage of his argument, considering revealed Christianity not for its relations to the state but in itself, for its internal relations to its own external organization.

Only in this context can we understand Pufendorf's argu-ment that Christian doctrine propagates values and endorses institutions which are antithetical to the principles of poli-tics. It is not simply that "the union of the faithful under Christ their King constitutes a realm that is not of this world," with the King located "in the heavens" and its "citizens" consisting of all those, "diffused throughout the world, who embrace the doctrine with a vital faith," and that therefore "civil sovereignty is superfluous in this realm be-cause it can do nothing for solid piety." [56] Equally important was the converse negative relationship, that "virtues and attitudes which Christ requires as appropriate to his kingdom do little for the virtues of a citizen in a worldly state": the Christian realm tolerates "hostile citizens within its fron-tiers," the worldly state does not; in the Christian realm the citizen is "worthless" who defends his legitimate rights against the attack of a fellow citizen, while in the worldly state it is proper for each citizen to defend his rights; unlike the worldly states, in the realm of Christ unequal labor brings equal reward; the application of industry to the increase of property which is one of the leading marks of good citizenship in the worldly state is among the last for the kingdom of Christ; while Christ prescribed the renunciation of possessions, the security of property is a chief cause for the foundation of worldly states; the pre-eminence of one man above another which is required for government in the worldly state is the basis of ambition and the need for revenues is the ground for avarice, both of which qualities are condemned in the Christian realm; Christ prescribes, finally, that his doctrine cannot be forced upon anyone, while the founders of states have for their rule to oppose force with more force.[57]

Pufendorf's purpose in adducing, with approval, this set of antipolitical Christian maxims was to demonstrate from revelation the regime of absolute individualism in the internal organization of the Christian religion as a necessary consequence of its otherworldly purpose:

> Christ adopts no external support for advancing his doctrine. Men are forced to understand and embrace it by no human power or decree. Whoever can accept it, accepts. . . . God does not desire to drag men into heaven by the collar, . . . but it pleases Him to propose the means of salvation in such a way that it is in the power of man to reject it and be the cause of his own perdition.[58]

The role of both Christ and his apostles, consequently, is that of the "teacher," and it comports neither directly nor indirectly with any kind of sovereign or compulsory power over men.[59] The anarchism of this invisible church, moreover, pertains to its visible organization as well. In scripture, as well as "church [*ecclesia*]" is used indiscriminately for "the whole multitude of the faithful everywhere" and for "the assemblage [*coetus*] of the faithful of a province, a town, or even a private household or family." [60] "In either sense" of the term, the same meaning prevails, consistent with its original Greek signification of a concourse of citizens acting by voluntary consent. It is in the nature of "a private association [*collegium*]," instituted not by any antecedent covenant of men with one another but by "the submission of every individual, each for himself without regard for other men, to Christ's terms of salvation" and structured, consequently, so loosely as to preserve the priority of the individual's "obligation to Christ," which is "more effective and more valid than any bonds of necessity among men": scripture prescribes no form for the church beside the "simple division into teachers and pupils [*doctores et auditores*]," a division which bestows no function on the teachers beyond explanation and persuasion and no obligation on the pupils to "submit their will and faith" on the means of salvation or to obey statutes and contribute money save by the voluntary consent of all; scripture prescribes, moreover, no binding forms of adjudication between churches, whether in the form of a single head, a special tribunal, or a council.[61]

Pufendorf's obvious target in this exegesis was the Roman Catholic Church, and his ostensible purpose was to show that scripture authorized no cognate political organization of the church such as he saw in Catholicism. But in demonstrating the voluntaristic, antipolitical character of the church itself, he created for himself the new and more difficult problem of reconciling it with the political character of the state. For non-Christian sovereignties his problem was not difficult, since the scriptural provisions for the "primitive church" which furnished his norms of church organization had themselves been composed under and attuned to this political condition. The juridical concept of the private association (*collegium*) which had served as a model for the internal structure of the authoritative primitive church served also to define its generic relation to the heathen state. To the definition of a voluntary society uniting several men for the transaction of "some particular business" he added, in this context, "without prejudice to the authority of sovereigns over them." The non-political character of the church meant both that as a matter of fact it did not supersede or amend the prevalent civil status of subjects and sovereigns and that as a matter of law its statutes and discipline must not violate the civil laws.[62]

But to this status which the primitive church shared with other legitimate private associations—and which coincided with the principles of the natural law—Pufendorf added a distinctive dimension. In contrast to the professors of "the human sciences, who cannot arrogate to themselves the function of teaching publicly without the express or tacit consent of the civil sovereign and who must keep silence at the pleasure of the latter," the Apostles' authority to teach the Gospel, derived from Christ, "was not subject to the civil sovereign and they were bound neither to keep silence nor to change their doctrine at his command; if they disobeyed his decrees they were not accounted guilty of any offense against his sovereignty [*majestatem*]." Since, indeed, the Apostles' exercise of their mission could be forbidden "by no human interdict," not only were such interdicts by civil sovereigns "rightly disobeyed" but they were accounted "violations of God's sovereignty." [63] Moreover, this right of establishing Christian churches without the consent of the civil magistrate applied not only to the Apostles but to whosoever of "the faithful"—even "two or three"—"desired to assemble in

[233]

the name of the Savior." [64] In short, as Pufendorf made clear in another context, the general similarity of the church to any private association "which is in the state but yet which the state does not dispose over at will" is qualified by the important difference that where other private associations may originate as a concession from the state, "the freedom of the church has a higher source." [65]

Nor was this higher autonomy of mere historical interest for the model of the primitive church. Pufendorf insisted— probably to preserve the present relevance of his anti-Catholic argument—that the conversion of civil sovereigns and entire polities to the Christian religion changed nothing of this fundamental relation between the Christian church and the state. "Since the Christian religion does not need the state, nor the state the Christian religion," the conversion alters neither the power of the sovereign nor the religious obligation of the Christians in the church. "The New Testament contains nothing enjoining sovereigns to a special duty concerning the Church." [66]

With this affirmation Pufendorf found himself in a most uncomfortable intellectual position. He had established in his natural law a political relevance of generic religion and a lawful possibility of its political regulation which his view of scriptural authority denied for the actuality of the Christian church. The dilemma was a result of conflicts both among his practical desires and within his theoretical requirements: on the practical level he sought at once to buttress political authority in general and to forestall oppression from Catholic political authorities in particular; on the theoretical level he sought to ground his natural-law politics in an ultimate indisputable actuality and yet to safeguard its independence. He did bludgeon his way out of the dilemma, but it was at the cost of rational integrity. He shifted his attention from the realms of reason and revelation to the ill-assorted institutional facts of church and state, made of these facts a kind of intermediate realm between reason and revelation, and strained both his political and his ecclesiastical logic to account for them. The fact of the Christian ruler now became his lodestar and from it he traced various lines of rational argument back to natural law and to revelation, selecting them for the cover which they might give to the peculiar constellation of practices in the existing state-church system. When, after admitting that neither natural law nor scripture yielded an adequate basis for gauging the authority of the Christian sovereign over the Christian church, Pufendorf maintained that such authority would have to be "deduced either from the inherent character of the civil sovereign, or from the character of the Christian religion, or from the voluntary transference by the Church itself," he was using the weakest kind of disjunctive. He picked among these sources for deductions most appropriate to the practice, and the result was an inconsistency that was reconciled only in the facts themselves.

The logical conclusion of Pufendorf's natural-law politics had been a civil religion. The logical conclusion of his scriptural exegesis was a system of free churches. In order to make these divergent conclusions converge under the category of the Christian state, he had to admit a logical leap between the doctrinal and factual requirements of Christianity: he asserted that the relations of the Christian church and the Christian state had reference only to already established churches and not to the foundation of churches—an admission that set the Christian churches in a universe of discourse far different from the state, where political logic related the structure of states precisely to the principles of their foundation.[67] Within the category of already existing churches, Pufendorf had previously, in his *History of Popedom,* essayed a logical arrangement of political authority and

[235]

Christian liberty in the neat division of ecclesiastical structure into the "external direction [*directorium*]" and the "ministry [*ministerium*]" of churches. He assigned the "direction," consisting in the appointment and supervision of clergy, the administration of church property, physical support and maintenance, and the adjudication of disputes among clergy, to the civil sovereign, and the "ministry," consisting of teaching, preaching, and the administration of sacraments, to the clergy.[68] But by 1687, with the more positive approach to the religious claims of Christianity, evinced in his *Relations of the Christian Religion to Civil Life,* the integrity of even this derivative distinction was dissipated by the unreconciled reassertion of its two sets of constituent principles, the authoritarian set drawn from the generic character of state and religion, and the libertarian set addressed to the specific truth of a particular religious confession. Apparently, only duality, rather than synthesis, could do justice to contemporary practice.

In the final formulation of his position on church and state in the *Relations,* consequently, Pufendorf proceeded not from the principles themselves but from the actual concrete forms of the issue—the extent of sovereign power over appointments, statutes, dogmas, dissidents, etc.—and assigned the various appropriate principles to them *seriatim.* The categories to which the principles belong thus appear hybrid and discontinuous, but, when unraveled, they take the familiar Pufendorfian pattern of deducing two parallel sets of propositions from a general category, the first giving substantive expression to its universal truth and the second extending it to explain the particular qualifications and deviations of practice.

The general category under which Christian church-state relations falls is that of the "association [*collegium*]," in which Christians, like members of churches and states universally, bear two "aspects [*personae*]"—the Christian and the civil—which, having separate orbits and ends, neither collide nor mingle but rather retain their separate distinct obligations. On this level, the sovereign who is a member of a Christian church "possesses no more authority than the common soldier." [69] From this definition Pufendorf moves to the specific areas of church-state relations and finds mixed therein principles reducible to the general category of the Christian association by two different lines of ratiocination. First, there are the principles that are universally applicable to religious associations: included herein are the rights of the prince to inspect the proceedings of the church for abuses that violate the civil laws; to punish such doctrinal threats to the state as idolatry, blasphemy, and violations of the Sabbath; and positively to reform churches when their religious "errors and abuses" are prejudicial to civil authority.[70] The obverse side of these same universal principles confers upon the citizen the right to his own religious convictions, since faith lies beyond the competence of the state, and even, within the bounds of civil order, to the toleration of religious dissent in the form of separate churches, particularly when such dissent has a legal basis in civil contract or fundamental law.[71]

But Pufendorf also interspersed a second set of principles, derived from the positive institutional connection of the Christian association with the Christian state, and in this application his universal principles underwent considerable modification. The religious requirements of the state were now identified not only with a definite faith—Christianity—but, because of the sovereign's membership in a particular confession within that faith, with a particular Christian church, and this specification of the relationship altered all its terms of reference, since now the realm of the lawful intersected the realm of the actual. Thus, because of the actual "conjunction of the duty incumbent upon any Christian with civil sovereignty," the sovereign must include in his general obligation to defend his citizens from aggressions the defense of the Christian church from "insult," and he must include in his general obligation to support religion the financial support of the Christian church.[72] By virtue of this conjunction, moreover, the ecclesiastical discipline of church members, which now affects their civil status in a Christian state, falls within the province of the sovereign, as does the right to enact and repeal church statutes making for the external "dignity and order" of the Christian church and even to endow them with "the force of civil law." [73] This general Christian function formed only the outer circle of his institutional powers and obligations. The sovereign, who had originally been supposed to wear an entirely separate "aspect" as one simple Christian among others, now acquired a special "prerogative," as "the principal member" of his particular Christian church, and this prerogative endowed him with a preponderant voice in the appointment, disciplining, and dismissal of clergy in that church.[74]

But the *Relation*'s most striking modification of Pufendorf's original separatist principles on church and state was yet to come. When the two new institutional powers of the Christian sovereign—the inclusion of external Christian organization in the valid functions of the ruler and his preponderant internal role within the congregation of a particular Christian church—were combined, the result was, for Pufendorf, an accretion of political authority which eviscerated his previous distinctions. Within the church the ruler was now assigned crucial doctrinal powers that crossed the line between the external and internal sides of church organization: he could convoke church synods for the resolution of conflicts on dogma and enforce their decisions; he could compel "the compendia of Christian doctrine, catechisms, symbols, confessions, etc., to conform with the Holy Scriptures," provide, where such a "public formula" of Christian faith did not exist, for its composition by "the most skilled theologians," and compel the clergy's subscription to it.[75] It was at this point that the separate categories of the civil sphere, the generic Christian religion, and the particular confessional church converged in Pufendorf's advocacy of the state church. He conferred upon the ruler the power, based upon "his care for the public tranquillity," to compel the conformity of all "private and public doctrine" with his particular articles of Christian faith and to affix, as penalties for non-conformity "unless reasons of state persuade rulers otherwise," loss of civic rights, the imposition of "silence" on matters of the Christian religion, and—in case of public contumacy—expulsion from the realm.[76] For "lest it be thought that we confer infinite license on all kinds of heresies, . . . we declare that it is greatly to be desired and endeavored for there to be but one faith and religion in the state, and that such as is congruent with the doctrine of Christ and the Holy Scriptures of the Apostles, since it contributes much to the tranquillity of the state." [77]

Now clearly there was a conflict in tendency between this institution of a state church and Pufendorf's general convictions that "our faith, aroused by the Holy Spirit, consists in a trustingness of the heart" and "the internal habit and movement of the spirit" without which "public recitation" and "compliance with any kind of rites and corporal motions" are "no religion at all"; that "Christian doctrine is not to be propagated by force"; and further that since "dissent concerning the articles of religion does not *per se* disturb the tranquillity of the state, . . . conscientious dissidents" not only "can be tolerated" but at times "are obliged to be tolerated." [78] The conflict of principles was not head-on, to be sure, for Pufendorf was careful to keep an inner core of religion free from any temporal interference. He emphasized, *passim,* that his sovereigns were neither bishops nor ministers; that they had the right to administer and enforce arbitration, discipline, and the legislation of doctrine by the clergy rather than to undertake such ecclesiastical functions directly; that, analogously, their right to repeal and enact ecclesiastical statutes was limited to the *"external"* order of the church—"to those things that surround [*circumstant*] religion"—which mediately or immediately affect their civil authority and did not warrant the addition of civil sanctions to "Christian dogmas" or indeed of any compulsion "to force their acceptance," since "the very nature of Christian doctrine requires" propagandizing by teaching alone.[79] Even the penalties lawfully affixed by sovereigns to derelictions from the "public formula" of Christian faith in a state church were bounded in this sense, for they entailed only negative penalties, prescribed only "refutation" as persuasion toward positive compliance, and could not abridge the right of emigration.[80] But however softened, the conflict of principles between the sovereign's ecclesiastical authority and the individual's "freedom of conscience" was theoretically patent in the plurality of religious roles attributed to the sovereign and in the vacillating concept of temporal sanctions. But it was on the practical issue of toleration for public non-conformity in dissenting churches that the conflict became, for Pufendorf, inescapable.[81]

Pufendorf could resolve the problem of toleration only by going beyond considerations of law and logic to find recourse in particular fact and ultimate reality. First, he located his criterion of religious toleration, as he had of political history, in the reason of state, conceived as the constant measure for the variety of specific human actions. Thus the first test for toleration consists in the calculation, according to "common sense and natural reason," of whether "the number of dissenters is so great that they cannot be expelled without significant weakening of our state or if serious detriment would be caused the latter by their settling in another state." [82] Although he clearly had the Huguenots in mind here, the most striking application of this empirical principle was Pufendorf's advocacy of mutual Catholic-Protestant toleration despite his own explicit argument about the politically divisive and subversive character of the Catholic church. He argued that the basis of Catholicism lay in the special practical interests of its clergy rather than in its religious doctrine, and his proposal for Catholic toleration of Protestants was simply on the ground that they had no such separate practical interests.[83] To buttress his opposition to the Protestant proscription of Catholics, Pufendorf finally excluded the question of right from toleration, limited the latter to concession, and simply recommended it, as a wise policy, to the discretion of the ruler.[84]

But it was an ultimate reality, transcending the level of law, capping the level of facts, and more secure than either, that was the ultimate source of Pufendorf's ambiguous principles. In terms of this locus, and only in terms of this locus, does his tortuous argument take form and make sense as a matter of rights rather than policy. On this level his position was simple enough: the "true" Christian doctrine, together with the church organized around it, should not tolerate and must be tolerated. Time and time again Pufendorf prefaced his variable decisions on the issue of toleration with the requirement of prior theological discussion, and each time his decision was predicated on the assumption that the dogmas relating to the "main heads of the Christian religion" were knowable and that their partisans should prevail—an assumption which penetrated through the veils surrounding the civil order and sincerity in religious belief, which were his ostensible standards. Thus the sovereign has the right to convoke, direct, and execute the decrees of synods for the settlement of religious controversies, but this power can and should be exercised "no further than the nature of Christian doctrine permits"—a degree that Pufendorf predicates but does not specify.[85]

As Pufendorf developed the problem into the dilemma of the Christian subjects who, on the one hand, "cannot be required to submit their faith to the faith of the sovereign or, even if they conform voluntarily, be rendered certain of salvation" and, on the other, dissent from "the publicly accepted doctrine" of the state church, his answer varied with his predication of where the religious truth, measured by "demonstration from the Holy Scriptures," lay. When Pufendorf argued for the authority of the sovereign over the dissenters' rights of religious profession and civil residence, he postulated that ecclesiastical unity in the state referred "not to any kind of religion" but only such as were "true and ancient—that is, faithful to the Holy Scriptures." He postulated, moreover, for the imposition of sanctions on the dissenter, that "he has been surely and properly refuted," whether he accepted such refutation or not.[86] When Pufendorf turned about and argued for the right of dissenters to toleration, his only certain ground, over and above factual considerations of *ratio status,* was the converse postulation of doctrinal truth on the separatist side. Toleration was due not only to existing dissenting groups but also to those who undertook to secede from "communion with the sovereign" in his established church, when "they could demonstrate clearly that it persists in sinful error." "It is of no concern to sovereigns whether a citizen holds the same faith as they or not—at least when we presuppose that he would be professing error with the prince. . . . Whatever injury is inflicted by the prince upon citizens—at least to the orthodox who are prepared to demonstrate their doctrine from the Holy Scriptures—is to be accounted an unjust and illegitimate act." The sovereign does have the authority to withhold civil rights at his discretion but to molest the citizen no further because of difference of religion "when his error has not been demonstrated." The rule " '*cujus est regio eius est religio*' " does not apply "unless the princes could presuppose the truth of their religion." Otherwise, "territorial authority [*ius territoriale*] did not legitimate the compulsion of subjects to embrace false dogmas; where the dictum was turned by heterodox princes upon the orthodox it worked serious damage to the true religion." [87]

Thus Pufendorf found combined in religion the answers to the two superficially distinct problems of his political system. This system hung suspended between two kinds of realities; it was closed off at the bottom from the variety of actual institutions and practices which it presumably rationalized and closed off at the top from the ultimate positively existent unity upon which the reality of the system was contingent. Unlike his own approach to history, which was addressed to the penetration of the first of these separations, and equally unlike the religiosity of his natural-law colleagues who reduced faith to final principles addressed to the second, Pufendorf's religion comprehended a whole realm which satisfied both needs at once in the form of a particular institutionalized church founded on the one true dogmatic version of the Christian faith. Within the political framework of church and state that outlined his universe of discourse he could indicate *that* such a true church and doctrine existed and that it was authoritative. *What* they were he did not yet specify. But certainly their identity was implicit throughout. Only his own Lutheranism could ground the complex and problematical relations between politics and religion which he was ostensibly demonstrating.[88] What remained was for him to make the implicit explicit, to expound

the substantive truth of the Lutheran doctrine which alone
could harmonize the authoritarian effects with the libertarian ground of his natural-law doctrine. It was to this
exegesis that he finally turned and it was in this exegesis that
his long quest for certainty incarnate found rest.

III. THE THEOLOGY

At first glance Pufendorf's venture into the field of Christian theology proper seems simply a further application of his
politics to the problem of church and state. Undeniably there
was a political dimension in the circumstances. The format of
his theology was a program for the unification of the Protestant churches.

In 1679, when he was in the employ of the Lutheran
Charles XI of Sweden, Pufendorf had found such a program
of unification "extravagant," on the grounds that we mortals
have no authority to "presume on our own to make any
article fundamental or problematic" and the matter is best
left to "Divine Providence." But now, a decade later, when
he moved into the service of an undogmatic Calvinist Elector
of Lutheran Brandenburg, he undertook the exposition of
it.[89] The English revolution of 1688, with its Catholic Ja-
cobean background, sharpened Pufendorf's susceptibilities to
the ambiguities of his position on toleration, and he began
his work on theology, *The Divine Law of the Covenant,* with
a reconsideration of the whole problem—of "political" as
well as "ecclesiastical toleration." [90] The agency which he
proposed for the enactment of a unifying theology was an
assembly which would include representatives of the state as
well as of the clergy and laity, an arrangement which testified
to the persistence of his concern for civil peace even in the
formulation of Christian doctrine.[91] But easily the most
spectacular demonstration of the continuity between Pufen-

dorf the jurist and Pufendorf the theologian was his argument for the exclusion of Catholicism from the program of
Christian unity, an argument that carried over the fundamental assumption of his political thought into the realm of
religion. The unity of the Catholic and the Protestant
churches is impossible, not because of differences in religious
belief or doctrine but because of temporal interests. "Where
the dissension is about domination and liberty, there cannot
on either side be any wish except domination over the
other." [92] He based this conclusion on the general proposition
that "there is no reason" for conflicts on principles, since
differences of opinion "are mitigated by time and ultimately
vanish," while conflicts about "worldly advantage," concerning "God the Belly" as they do, are insuperable.[93] *Mutatis
mutandis,* this subscription to the malleability of principle
and the stability of practical interests can stand as Pufendorf's
political confession.

And yet, over and above these indubitable connecting
links, Pufendorf's theology also represented a decisive break
with the political universe of discourse which, in one way or
another, had bound the whole of his previous thought. It was
a break, moreover, of which he was well aware. When, in
1688, he confessed his dream of doing "a meditation on the
rational divine worship of Christians," he cherished the
purpose of "proving to the world that I had as much concern
with true piety as the black-coats," and when he completed
the first draft of it toward the end of 1690 he evinced not only
a self-consciousness and an unwonted modesty at tackling
such a theological subject "as a layman" but also his pride in
"posterity seeing that I did not think only of worldly intrigues, which truly have ended by nauseating me as the
vanity of vanities." [94] It was also a period of his life when he
exhibited an intense interest, both critical and constructive,
in ecclesiastical history and developed a sympathetic concern

for German Pietism.[95] He even requested that the manuscript of his "meditation," which was to become the posthumously published *Divine Law of the Covenant,* be submitted to Philipp Spener, for his comment, and he promised to proceed in accordance with that Pietist leader's judgment.[96]

The structure of the *Divine Law* confirms this external evidence of the distinct status which Pufendorf assigned to his theology. The introductory re-examination of toleration ended in the delimitation of that politically conditioned concept and in the assignment of the subsequent theology to quite another category. Not only did he withdraw the religious liberty which is held as "a right"—including dissent by a politically significant number of subjects, purchase of such right, and a "ruling religion" in conflict with a new "religion of the ruler"—from the purview of political toleration, considered now purely as a concession by sovereign discretion, but he depreciated toleration in general into a category of action that "suspends the effects but does not remove the cause" of conflicts.[97] The motive that spurred his theology was rather that of "reconciliation," with the distinctive function of removing the causes of conflict by establishing a positive and indisputable religious truth. Ecclesiastical toleration was accorded the subordinate role of accommodating those Christian doctrines that remained in dispute but were unnecessary for salvation.[98]

The coexistence of a persistent political connection and of a transcendent religiosity in Pufendorf's final theology manifested more than a psychological inertia in regard to the one or an intellectual atavism in regard to the other. The two dimensions were internally related in the theology. Together, they made up its very structure. Their complementary functions enabled Pufendorf to close his career fittingly with a theology that established the ultimate certainty heretofore

denied to his natural-law politics and yet was itself coherent
with this natural-law politics.

The function of Pufendorf's transcendent faith in Christian revelation was to provide an absolute ground for a
particular set of Christian doctrines. On this level, manifested in the identification of the "fundamental" as opposed
to the "indifferent" articles of Christian faith, Pufendorf was
uncharacteristically rigid and positive. He rejected any process of compromise, comprehension, or toleration in the affirmation of the dogmas necessary to salvation: the declaration
of a dogma to be fundamental or indifferent "does not
depend on the discretion of men, but a firm basis is required
so that it is manifest whether an item belongs within the
essence [*ratio*] of faith or outside it." This "firm basis" is
afforded by the demonstration of "the true religion" from
scripture.[99] Pursuant to this dictum, Pufendorf's unified theology, despite its pretensions to "impartiality," was in fact a
rationale of Lutheran doctrine through biblical exegesis.
Although he verbally relegated such divisive issues as predestination and the meaning of communion to the tolerated
category of indifferent articles, his actual argument explicitly
vindicated the dogma of "the consent of the human will" to
"faith" as against "any predetermination or predestination"
and included as fundamental the Lutheran doctrine that in
the Lord's Supper "not only the bread and wine but at the
same time and conjointly the body and blood of Christ are
present . . . , on account of which conjunction the attributes
of the body of Christ and the bread, of the blood of Christ
and the wine, are reciprocally predicated of both."

Pufendorf worked this exegetical sleight of hand by the
simple expedient of identifying indisputable biblical doctrine with the Lutheran position without so labeling it and of
identifying the Calvinist position with "problematical," "fig-

urative," and consequently "indifferent" adumbrations upon it. Thus "the consent and acceptance by men" of divine worship is scriptural, but predestination is not mentioned in scripture and is not fundamental; the real presence is the simple sense of the scriptural Lord's Supper, but the Calvinist "spiritual" or "symbolic" interpretations are "subtle" speculations on the manner of the presence which may be left undecided. Although Pufendorf did not admit the coincidence, the fact of the matter was that the putatively non-partisan fundamental articles of faith which he deduced on these points were essentially reiterated as Lutheran tenets with additional arguments in the later sections where he treated of conflicting, indifferent, and contingent dogmas. He assigned to this inessential kind of dogma what was additional in Lutheranism but what was integral in Calvinism.[100]

The format of reconciliation notwithstanding, Pufendorf revealed privately that "the target" of his *Divine Law of the Covenant* was precisely "the foundations of Calvinism," and particularly the "Calvinist palladium" that "our salvation is . . . by absolute decree," a dogma which he confessed he "abhorred." [101] This confession lay bare the focal point which explains the sectarian Lutheran turn which he gave to his theology. What he needed and what he sought in religious faith was an absolute and positive ground for morality, whose "imposition" by man was the precondition of Pufendorf's entire theoretical system. The faith appropriate to this purpose he found only in the Lutheran combination of the decisive role of divine grace with the negative liberty of men to resist it:

> God does not wish to impose these divine benefits
> on men who are unwilling or reluctant to receive
> them; nor can this be done without the destruc-

tion of morality. . . . Morality would be completely extinguished and men would be drawn to
their highest goals like machines. . . . If the
physical act in men's conduct is so predetermined
that it cannot fail to exist and if through that existent physical act man cannot participate morally
in it, I cannot conceive that men have more liberty
than water flowing within its channel . . . , in
whose motion also no constraint appears.[102]

It was around this particular proportioning of authority and
freedom in religion, which echoed the similar proportion in
his natural-law politics, that Pufendorf endorsed, as fundamental, the traditional dogmas of the Trinity, the personal
union of divinity and humanity in Christ, justification by
faith, and the efficacy of the sacraments. Because the relations
between authority and freedom in his version were more
balanced and delicate than those of his natural-law contemporaries, he was far more inclusive and particular about the
fundamental dogmas which, by association, linked them to
the absolute truth of Christian revelation. Without such
dogmas, "nothing remains but a correct moral philosophy,"
but what he wanted was the independent support which an
articulated positive faith brought to such a philosophy.[103] Not
Christianity as such but only the appropriate Lutheran version of it would do.

But if Lutheran doctrine provided the ultimate grounding
which Pufendorf's system of natural-law politics required,
this system in turn entered into his theology to produce
the mediation to morality which the transcendent Lutheran
faith required. He applied to his theology the pattern of
thought derived from his natural-law theory for the purpose
of making the particular, positive, and inward truths of reve-

lation relevant to the general, logical, and external canons of human behavior. He performed this construction in two related steps.

First, Pufendorf applied to theology the *method* which he had worked up for deriving general natural laws from particular observations, but now to the end of demonstrating generally acceptable religious truths from particular religious institutions. He undertook, that is, to use what was common to the particular Calvinist and Lutheran confessions as propositions whose general truth was proved by their necessary place in a system of deductive logic. "I should judge that it would do most to abolish controversy if someone tried to build those dogmas about which there is mutual agreement into a complete system of theology, without gaps or mutilation but continuously from the same principles and bound together from beginning to end." [104] It was precisely this that Pufendorf ostensibly undertook to do, and it was consistent with this logical criterion of religious truth that he excluded from the start, without any examination of their scriptural validity, all those confessions which dissented on "fundamental articles" or the whole "system of doctrine" and consequently afforded no common basis for deduction from "the same principles." [105]

But actually, albeit tacitly, Pufendorf crossed this politicized criterion, which based fundamental dogma on the agreement of Lutherans and Calvinists, with his criterion which prescribed the proof of fundamental dogma from scripture. The conjunction of these two planes of argument produced particular Lutheran doctrine in the form of a generally valid logical system. Specific Lutheran dogmas were clothed in the mantle of coherent general propositions and the Calvinist dogma that Pufendorf personally "abhorred" was dismissed in this context as a heterogeneous particular whose truth could consequently not be demonstrated.[106] The idea of resolving religious differences by thus arranging "Christian theology in the form of a proper art through continuous ordered demonstrations, so that naturally by the premising of necessary definitions and if need be of postulates, and then by indubitable axioms, the articles of the Christian religion necessary and sufficient for salvation are demonstrated in the mode of mathematical propositions" goes back in Pufendorf at least to 1681.[107] It stems, consequently, from the period in which Pufendorf was still under the influence of the natural-law system in which he had applied this method to the achievement of a consensus on the principles of politics, and it was from this secure base that he proposed and ultimately carried out its translation to theology.

Having guaranteed the relevance of religion to nature through the medium of an identical rational method, Pufendorf proceeded to the second stage of the connection. This consisted in dressing the method with an appropriate substance, also drawn from the model of natural law and assuring that the articles of faith would be not only rationally comprehensible but ethically applicable. To channel the faith that was necessary for salvation into the action that was necessary for the moral and social order—that is, to dovetail religion and morality—Pufendorf chose as the central concepts of his theology cognates of the concepts that had served him so well within the realm of nature for the dovetailing of morality and politics: the pact and the law. He had used a series of pacts (or, more precisely, two pacts and a "statute") to assure the continuity of moral consent as a component of obedience to the law, and now he applied the same instrumentality—multiple pacts in logical series—to assure the continuity of religious faith as a component of obedience to moral law. He even employed, as a rule, the same term—*pactum*—in both the political and the religious contexts to underline the factor of contractual consent that was common to both, although his alternative use of the adjectival *feciale* for the religious instruments added the flavor of "covenant," with its fideistic connotation.

Pufendorf made the "covenant" God's chosen and characteristic expression of his mutual relations with man. God's generic purpose in this choice was "that the consent and acceptance of men might be added to the proposal made by God and that thence a mutual obligation and closer union might arise between God and man." [108] Pufendorf's own purpose in thus exalting the covenant is clear from his emphasis upon it as the contradiction and refutation of the doctrine that men are "saved or damned by the force of some absolute decree." [109] The covenant was his way of fixing a dimension of human liberty in the absolute realm of faith. But in his religious as in his political scheme of things human liberty was but a dimension, and he was faced now, even more urgently than he had been in the realm of nature, with the task of bringing it into conformity with the lawful order of reality. The task was more urgent, first, because in religion, unlike politics, an individual could never enter a covenant save for himself alone and consequently no sequence of integration was possible; secondly, because the gap which remained in his natural-law politics between particular acts of will and general conformity to law had, on the religious level, finally to be filled. [110] To solve his problem, Pufendorf applied once more his system of multiple contracts but addressed now to the end of complementing the external sanctions of the natural sovereign with the internal compulsion of the Christian man toward the fulfillment of the law.

Pufendorf's sequence of covenants was a development not in the ends of the covenants but in the capacity of men to fulfill a constant end. The tailoring of this sequence to the profound moral need of his natural system was established by his disclaimer of knowledge, even from revelation, of the initial covenant—that of God with prelapsarian man, a human condition which he had deemed irrelevant to his politics.[111] It was confirmed by his characterization of the conditions of the following covenant between God and immediate postlapsarian man as "observance of natural law toward God and other men" and by his prescription that the subsequent divine covenants with the Jews and with all mankind through Christ (including here a double covenant of the Father with the Son and the Son with the people) continued to stipulate "the obligation to sanctimonious life and morals as inseparably assigned by God to human nature." [112]

The same law—the love of God and neighbor—rules in the regenerate as in the primitive human condition; Christ is not the giver but the fulfiller of this law, which remains as necessary as ever, since the service of God in righteousness is the purpose of redemption.[113] What has changed is the necessity of human conformity to the law. From this point of view the sequence of covenants witnesses an increasing human capacity, assisted by God, for such conformity. The original covenant manifested God's direct revelation of His purpose to men. The postlapsarian primitive and Jewish covenants engaged men additionally through the promise of a Savior. Through the misuse of their freedom men violated both. With the coming of Christ the Savior, however, the way to fulfillment becomes regular and certain. Christ has fulfilled the law for men, and through faith in Christ, which brings a union with Him on the order of "a moral conjunction by which many coalesce in one moral body and participate in certain rights and benefits from this coalition," "a new disposition, a new inclination, new forces are imposed and excited in our spirit by the Divinity"—a change which affects "the intellect and the will." Fulfillment of the law follows therefrom necessarily as a fruit of faith, but it is a necessity

[253]

that is at last joined integrally to liberty, for it is a necessity that stems not from "the compulsion of the law" but from "the free spirit" following the ways of Christ.[114] And so it is that "if there is ever to be a better condition of human life, it is to be expected from nothing but the earnest and universal cultivation of Christian piety." [115]

With this final link Pufendorf closed the circle of his thought. The religion which he had expelled from the order of nature ended by performing for it a combination of services which only an extra-natural order could perform and by receiving from it an essential service in return. Revealed Christianity surrounded the lawful world of nature and of nature's articulation into human politics with a realm that provided both an ultimate principle of unity and an embodiment of it in established institutions. Between these poles the laws of nature could draw authority from the undeniable reality of the first and transmit it to the undeniable reality of the second. By virtue of these natural laws men could reduce to order the plurality of authorities and the variety of human rights whose existence remained independent of those laws. They could explain what they could neither replace nor reform. With this aggressive respectability Pufendorf could finally rest content. All the objects of his divided loyalties were equally blessed.

EPILOGUE

I. Post-mortem

Cultural immortality can be of two kinds. There is the creation that never loses its identity: its author continues, as an individual, to speak to us across the ages. There is also the creation that submerges its identity in a larger movement; its author speaks to us through the anonymous assumptions that have entered into the general fabric of subsequent epochs. As a humanist, Pufendorf sought the undying literary fame of the first. As a practitioner, he achieved the collective status of the second. The overt form of his production, with its hypostatization of principles above time as well as above locality and sect, seemed appropriate to an unending discourse with humanity. His actual emphasis upon their application reduced their stature, as changes in the conditions with which he had associated them laid bare their merely relative validity. The history of Pufendorf's influence is the story of his passage from the higher to the lower level of immortality in the judgment of the posterity to which he looked.

Certainly the external signs of Pufendorf's reception furnish impressive evidence of the *fact* of his impact. However tentative and inconclusive the additions of editions must be where the numbers of copies and the character of the consumption are uncertain, the figures for Pufendorf's main works are sufficiently striking to give a reliable, if general, indication of a remarkably pervasive distribution. For the *De jure naturae* and its epitome, *De officio hominis et civis,* listings can be found of no less than thirty-five editions of the original Latin, thirty-nine editions in French translation, and fourteen editions in English, as well as sporadic publication in German, Italian, and Russian.[1] To the five German editions of Pufendorf's general history, the *Introduction to the History of the Great Empires and States of Contemporary Europe,* there should be added five more in Latin, ten each in French and English, and a Russian translation in 1718. Such advantage was taken of the pseudonymous *On the Constitution of the German Empire* to multiply reprints that the count of editions has even less meaning than usual, but its broad dissemination is apparent in the contemporary estimate that by 1710 some three hundred thousand copies had been printed in Germany alone (French, English, and Dutch translations had already revealed a foreign market as well).[2]

There are other, more qualitative signs of Pufendorf's effect upon succeeding generations. He became standard fare in the educational curriculums of the eighteenth century. Not only were his main works used as university textbooks but he was included prominently in some of the most famous educational projects.[3] Locke proposed Pufendorf's *On the Law of Nature* for the training of young gentlemen in both civil law and the principles of politics, indicating not only his preference for it over Grotius' *On the Law of War and Peace* but his flat evaluation of it as "the best book of that kind."[4] The young Rousseau would dispose of the field of "morality and natural law" by assigning both Grotius and Pufendorf, since "an upright and reasonable man should know the principles of good and evil and the foundations on which the

[256]

society of which he is a part is founded." [5] Diderot recommended Pufendorf's *On the Duty of Man and the Citizen* for higher education in "particular morality," and the *Encyclopédie* advised its readers similarly to study *On the Law of Nature* for the best index to the contents of international law. [6]

The influence of Pufendorf is traceable, finally, in subsequent legal and political theory. The most obvious line of descent goes throuh the succession of German legal theorists for whom, as "the father of natural law," Pufendorf inaugurated the preponderant school of eighteenth-century jurisprudence whose outstanding exemplars were Christian Thomasius and Christian Wolff. [7] But his impact upon this field extended beyond Germany to such popularizers as the Swiss Jean Barbeyrac—Pufendorf's best-known editor and French translator—and Jean-Jacques Burlamaqui and to such outstanding jurists as Blackstone and Montesquieu. Burlamaqui confirmed his admission that his concept of sovereignty "coincides in the main with Pufendorf's system" with copious citations. [8] Blackstone not only took his prefatory exposition of general natural-law principles primarily from Pufendorf but supported his explanation of particular personal and property rights and torts with references from the same authority. [9] Such references are not to be found in Montesquieu, but he explained their absence in an unpublished blanket acknowledgment of his debt for borrowings on the account of the *Esprit des lois:* "I thank Messrs. Grotius and Pufendorf for having executed what a great part of this work required of me, but with a degree of genius which I should not have been able to attain." [10] In general, despite the absence of natural law from the universities of eighteenth-century France, "for about a century the Grotius and Pufendorf of Barbeyrac represented in France, along with Burlamaqui, the philosophy of law. . . . It was to these authors that writers usually referred around 1750 when they wanted to treat of political questions." Not only France but Britain, and not only jurisprudence but economics: as a primary supplier of materials for Adam Smith's framework Pufendorf assisted at the birth of modern economics.[11]

In the larger realm of political thought, Pufendorf's influence ranged even further. It entered into the ideas of all the "enlightened" monarchs who dominated the politics of the eighteenth century. Peter the Great ordered *On the Duty of Man and the Citizen* translated into Russian, and *On the Law of Nature* was, along with Grotius, Beccaria, and Montesquieu, an unacknowledged source of Catharine's *Instruction* of 1765.[12] Prussia's Frederick the Great cherished no high opinion of Pufendorf, but willy-nilly, like the rival Joseph II of Austria, he had been trained in his political ideas both directly, through prescribed youthful reading of *On the Duty of Man and the Citizen,* and indirectly, through Christian Wolff, the one German theorist whom Frederick did respect.[13] More remarkable was the serious attention paid Pufendorf by the two patron saints of modern political philosophy, Locke and Rousseau, who not only recommended him for the education of others but used him centrally in the elaboration of their own ideas. Locke owned Pufendorf's basic works, was familiar with the latter's doctrine from the time of the *Elements of Universal Jurisprudence* (1660), and revealed his indebtedness not only in his early, unpublished essays on the law of nature but even in the famous *Two Treatises of Government.*[14] In the words of Locke's most recent authoritative commentator, "of the writers he consulted when engaged on his book, Samuel Pufendorf was perhaps of the greatest use to him, in spite of the fact that their views on constitutional matters were in such contrast. He took advantage of Pufendorf's arguments, he reproduced his positions. . . ."[15] Rousseau knew both *On the Law of Nature* and *On the Duty of Man and the Citizen,* and so intensive was his exploitation of them that "if we propose to search out the sources of Rousseau's political thought, it is incontestably to Pufendorf *(De jure naturae)* that we must turn." [16] One expert has even suggested "the most probable hypothesis . . . [is] that Rousseau was conscious of all that he owed to Pufendorf and that he cherished toward him the sentiments of a pupil for his first teacher." [17]

Nor did Pufendorf's political effectiveness stop at the geographical limits of the European community. In the form of Barbeyrac's French and Basil Kenet's English translations, his works crossed the Atlantic and entered into the early growth of American political literature. Introduced by John Wise, the Congregational preacher who, ignorant of Locke, took "Baron Puffendorff for my chief guide and spokesman" in *A Vindication of the Government of the New-England Churches* (1717), Pufendorf's name was spread liberally through the obscure political writings of the colonial period until he became an authority in the great debates attendant upon the Revolution and the consolidation of the new nation.[18] During the years before the Revolution he can be found buttressing the arguments of Otis, Samuel Adams, Hamilton, and Jefferson.[19] During the years following the founding of the republic he was still in circulation, again assisting Hamilton, Jefferson, and now Madison to affirm the rights of the new state.[20]

The catalogue of heirs is imposing, and it is ample testimony of Pufendorf's contribution to the corpus of modern culture. But when we pass from the fact to the substance of this contribution, the picture changes. Its features shrink as general impressions become definite forms, and not only the man's effect but the man himself is illuminated thereby. If we turn now from the "that" to the "what" of Pufendorf's influence, we find that he acquitted himself of his self-imposed task only too well. His very success in using his principles to account for a wide variety of existing institutions led to the diffraction of those principles. Both the infinite applicability of his ideas and the change in the form and direction of his influence through time testified to the dissolution of his intellectual system and to the resulting submersion of his historical identity.

First, the striking diversity of political purposes to which Pufendorf's works were put went beyond the usual manipulation of the products of one generation by its successors. So adaptable was his doctrine and so indiscriminate the use made of it that it was adduced to support every political tendency and hence stood for none itself. Through Locke, Rousseau, and the Americans Pufendorf operated as an authority on "the natural rights of men" for the revolutionary theorists of the eighteenth century.[21] Through Barbeyrac, Burlamaqui, Blackstone, Montesquieu, and the Encyclopedists, he contributed to the balance of rights and duties in the theory of moderate constitutionalism. Through the German school of natural-law jurisprudence and the modernizing monarchs of central and eastern Europe he fostered the definition and concentration of social power in the hands of the political sovereign. And finally, to match the extremity of his democratic contribution through Wise and Rousseau, such authoritarian regimes as the French Restoration and German Nazism could find a place for his doctrine of civic and "communal" duty.[22]

Now it is quite clear that the rationalized absolutism which characterized the theory and practice of monarchy in the eighteenth century was closest to Pufendorf's own political position. It is also clear that the admission of practical constitutional limitations upon a sovereign power supreme in its proper field was a common assumption during the eighteenth century for which Pufendorf could and did also provide a warrant. To this extent both the broad scope and the undifferentiated quality of his influence is explicable by the persistence for more than half a century of the hybrid conditions which nurtured equally the claims of sovereigns, aristocracies, and commoners and which kept Pufendorf's kind of unfocused theory the standard vehicle of a diffuse political aspiration.

But secondly, the fact remains that Pufendorf was also built into theories of resistance and of mixed government which ran counter to his most cherished principles. The feature of his work which made this effect possible and which was reflected in it was not so much its flexibility as its solubility. The integrity of his system was sufficiently loosened by his insistence upon its applicability for his principles to be detached from one another and employed separately. Thus Locke and the Americans appropriated the ideas of natural liberty and natural law pertinent to the relations among individuals and among sovereigns in a state of nature but neglected the philosophical appurtenances and rejected the philosophical consequences with which Pufendorf had surrounded them.[23] Rousseau took the general ideas of a binding natural law and of moral entities for his doctrine of the general will and he also took Pufendorf's specific limitation upon property rights, but he rejected the whole notion of the state of nature as the locus of the natural law and he also rejected the alienation of liberty to both the lord and the sovereign.[24] Barbeyrac and Burlamaqui, the most assiduous popularizers of Pufendorf for the eighteenth century, reproduced his theories both of natural law and of sovereignty, but they diluted his authoritarian inferences by replacing his exceptional *de facto* concessions to the resistance and limitation of sovereignty with regular Lockian rights to them. Blackstone, similarly, adopted Pufendorf's notion of sociability as the basis of a binding natural law, but this did not

[261]

prevent him from celebrating the "mixed government" which the former abhorred.[25] Diderot's acknowledgment of Pufendorf's version of natural law went along with the rejection of its moral basis in the command of a superior.[26] Even among the absolutists, selection rather than distillation was the rule for the treatment of Pufendorf. Under both Peter and Joseph, it was particularly his provision for the sovereign's authority over church administration that was singled out for use. Not only did Peter frown upon *On the Relation of the Christian Religion to Civil Life,* which contained a defense of internal religious liberty, but the "enlightened" monarchs as a group soft-pedaled the substratum of original individual rights which underlay Pufendorf's explicit doctrine of sovereignty.[27]

The posthumous dissolution of Pufendorf's carefully articulated system was the outer sign of the historical process which submerged his personality into a larger collective identity—the general school of natural law. The crucial modulation within this process took place during the very period that marked the apogee of his influence. If the eighteenth century is viewed as a development through time rather than a block of time, then the categorical change in the character of Pufendorf's reception becomes traceable within it. The turning point comes around the middle of the century. Its quantitative index is the abrupt termination in the publication of his works after 1759.[28] The meaning of this index is revealed in the qualitatively different status which Pufendorf's system was accorded before and after this turning point: where it had been welcomed as a standard form of the otherwise inchoate theory of natural law, it was subsequently demeaned to an unspecified component in an articulated theory of natural law. The integrity imprinted upon the doctrine by the theorist was rejected in favor of the objective integrity imprinted upon it by generally accepted propositions.

For Pufendorf's own generation and its immediate successors, he, along with Grotius, had stood for acceptable natural-law doctrine. Whatever the changes they wrought upon his principles, whatever the selection they made from it, political theorists and jurists from Locke through Montesquieu took his system as the framework of the natural law and worked within it or out from it. Barbeyrac represented the extremity of this relationship when he worked out the cardinal points of his own natural-law doctrine in the form of a running commentary upon his translation of Pufendorf, but for the group as a whole Pufendorf's articulation of the natural-law approach to morals and politics, even more than Grotius', set their point of departure. Christian Thomasius made the position explicit when he deliberately undertook to complete Pufendorf's work.[29] But, unlike those of Grotius and Hobbes, Pufendorf's framework was not solidly enough joined to maintain itself against the historical pressure put upon it. To build theory upon Pufendorf meant to resolve his irresolute duality of state and individual, order and freedom, and the intellectual careers of even his disciples showed the opening cracks in the monument he had left behind. If Thomasius viewed his own early work as a gloss upon Pufendorf, his later development toward an emphatic empiricism and ethical individualism moved him into quite another universe of discourse, appropriate to the dawning Enlightenment.[30] Barbeyrac himself evinced no such dramatic shift, but he nonetheless effected something similar: the Pufendorf that was read by many of the western Europeans and Americans was not the original but Barbeyrac's version of it, which magnified its internal problems into perceptible inconsistencies and correspondingly strained

[263]

the bases of the system. Thus John Adams could make reference to Pufendorf in support of constitutional resistance to tyranny through a citation that was in fact of Barbeyrac's rather than Pufendorf's composition. It was an instance of Barbeyrac's converting into a rival principle one of Pufendorf's reluctant reservations to his authoritarian political doctrine.[31]

By the middle of the eighteenth century the derogation of Pufendorf from a primary to an ancillary cultural factor was well on its way. The social and intellectual conditions that had provided the actual basis of his principles had changed sufficiently for the principles themselves to present an unsatisfactory basis of explanation. The *Encyclopédie* sounded the keynote when it pronounced much in Pufendorf "not appropriate to our customs [*mœurs*]," and preferred Burlamaqui's as "the most recent, most precise, and most methodical work on natural law." [32] Christian Wolff, another eighteenth-century protagonist of natural law, found Pufendorf's "proofs [*rationes*]" inadequate and his "basic principle of natural law . . . an imperfect sort of standard," and decided that he must therefore derive for himself the obligations and rights "from the essence and nature of man." [33]

In general, the crystallization, during the second half of the eighteenth century, of diverse claims into outright conflict among rulers, aristocracies, and commoners manifested a political and social change that outmoded Pufendorf's effort to organize them under the concept of sovereignty. The shift from the preoccupation with order to the concern for freedom manifested a change in intellectual temper that outmoded his catalytic use of sociability in human nature to convert natural rights into civic duties. Henceforward, the emphasis in natural-law thinking was not to subsume rights under duties but to adjudicate or synthesize them. For this purpose the theory of natural law became an anonymous system, with its principles of balance drawn from many sources but with Locke and Montesquieu predominant.[34] Pufendorf continued indeed to be cited, but as one in a series of authorities reduced to their lowest common denominator and adduced for their presumed support of a particular principle or program.

Only in one field did Pufendorf retain a historical identity, and that was the field of international law. The *Encyclopédie* epitomized his system as a "very useful" representative survey of the field, and once the Revolution was consummated it was for his dicta on this subject that Americans turned to him.[35] Even here, starting from Christian Wolff and Emer de Vattel around the middle of the eighteenth century, authorities on international law preferred Grotius' principle of a special international natural law binding upon the community of states to Pufendorf's rejection of an international society and his identification of the natural law immediately with the rights and interests of each sovereign.[36] But, in general, the conditions of international political relations have changed so remarkably less than those of domestic political relations since Pufendorf's day that the international application which he made of his doctrine has retained much more of its relevance and consequently, in the guise of a generally valid principle, has better withstood the test of time.[37]

Apart from Pufendorf's fate as a historical personage, there remains the more difficult question of his actual contribution, whether identified or not. Certainly he helped, along with many others, to construct the notion of a higher law, rooted in the needs and capacities of common humanity, which both authorized and limited the exercise of political power. In this formal aspect the destiny of his contribution is bound up with the destiny of the natural-law theory: it declined along with the theory at the end of the eighteenth century and has its part in the legacy that has set some kind of general standard for what rulers may or may not do in particular. But between the vagaries of Pufendorf's literal reputation and the anonymity of his generic contribution was the specific tendency of what was absorbed from him albeit not nominally identified with him. The range and character of his literal reputation point to his larger role as the outstanding mediator between the authoritarian and liberal stages in the development of the modern natural law. Grotius and Hobbes stood at one end of the process; Locke, Montesquieu, and Rousseau at the other. Each associated himself with a set of transcendent principles and acquired a permanent historical identity along with them. Pufendorf's role, effective through the complexities of his political theory and confirmed in the restless development of his own career, was to reveal, through sundry *ad hoc* qualifications and dualisms, the inapplicability of authoritarian principles in their categorical forms to contemporary European society and thereby to prepare men's minds for their fundamental theoretical revision. Through the compromise of theory Pufendorf sacrificed integrity of principle, and incidentally his own immortality, but he nonetheless performed the invaluable social service of showing men the shape of their ideas in the mirror of reality.

II. A Recipe for Compromise

Pufendorf's abiding achievement was to set up a model for the compromise of theory. The rules for such a procedure may well stand as the relevant residue of his total performance. Let us violate the business ethics of the historian's craft and extract these rules in the didactic form appropriate to a lesson of history.

Remember throughout that your purpose is to rationalize things as they are, not to reform them. Your task is to make as tight a connection as possible between general principles and particular institutions. Although you may exercise some freedom of choice on both sides of the desired conjunction, for the best results you should limit this freedom by the requirements of a good fit. It is advisable that you start from a set of theoretical principles, however out of style such a point of departure may currently be, for an initial concern with institutional facts is more politic for the radical who is suspected of indifference to them than for the compromiser who must establish his commitment to ideals. Your theory must be one that claims validity by virtue of its inner consistency, but you must not forget to use two of the most fashionable versions of the theory and to adopt primary principles from both. Only by doubling your principles will you have the logical flexibility that is indispensable to your purpose. Thus if you start with such pairings as the individual *and* society for your ultimate units, interests *and* duties for the bases of your ethics, liberty *and* equality for your political values, you can refer to the one or the other term in each set as the rationalization requires.

Begin now to work toward contemporary practice by means of deductions from the primary principles. Although you are not yet concerned explicitly with the actual institutions that are the channels of contemporary practice, it is essential that even at this early stage you make tacit choices among them and arrange them in an order of priority to fix in your own mind a steady direction for your reasoning. Keeping your priority list ever present, make the deductions toward your order of institutions in a definite pattern. At each stage two propositions must be deduced from an established principle. One proposition must be analytic: that is, it must assert a logically necessary implication of the principle. The other proposition must be synthetic: that is, you must abstract a quality from your institutional order and subsume

[267]

it under the category posited by the principle operative at that stage. The relationship between the propositions will be such as to render them weak alternatives: that is, a relationship of either-or that implies both-and. In this way the logical necessity of the analytic proposition is extended to the distillation of experience in the synthetic proposition. The synthetic proposition then becomes the established principle for the next stage of the deduction, and the development toward the order of existence can proceed. This method, like so many sequential operations, sounds much more difficult when it is taken apart for inspection than it is in the actual doing. It is a matter simply of viewing experience along the plane of some category and of dividing it into two parts, with one part applying to that sector of experience immediately appropriate to the category, the other part organizing the rest of experience from the viewpoint of the category, but both parts being logical consequences of the category. For example, if you start from the principle that all men have inherent rights as men, then you might deduce from this the proposition that inherent rights are inalienable or alienable, the disjunctive form of the co-ordinate propositions: some rights are inalienable, and the other rights are alienable. Whatever specifications are made of either proposition, the argument would then proceed from the principle that men have certain alienable rights.

But you will find that however much experience you may pack into the synthetic propositions there is a limit in your development toward the explanation of existing institutions beyond which theory cannot take you. Since the theory deals in general truths—that is, in the necessary connections or, at its most concrete, in the probable relations among the classifiable qualities of existent things—it cannot justify the particular things themselves. You will have accounted for the ordering of your institutions but not for their existence.

Indeed, as you have undoubtedly realized by now, the general truths of your theory have assumed rather than proved the validity of your cherished institutions. You must now drop your theorizing, preferably with the demonstration of some such open-ended concept as general welfare, harmony of interests, reason of state, or any other general principle with a practical postulate, and turn to your high-priority institutions. Your task now is to construct an inductive chain of reasoning from the facts back toward your theory by developing, through the empirical study of particular institutions, their possession of the qualities which determine their place in the general order of theoretical truths. This can now be done through one of the social sciences or it can still be done, as it was in Pufendorf's day, through history. In either case your real difficulty will attend this phase of the operation. If you work through a social science the inductive series will almost certainly connect with the general order of theoretical truths but the series will still show a gap between the particular activities of definite institutions and the class of qualities to which they presumably contribute. If you work through history you will probably be able to identify particular institutions and find their common denominator with others equally identifiable, but a gap will almost certainly remain between this limited conclusion and the level of generality required for the theoretical ordering of institutions.

When all else fails, you can always turn to God.

NOTES

INTRODUCTION

1. Leibniz to Kästner, Aug. 21, 1709, in Ludovici Dutens, *Leibnitii Opera Omnia* (Geneva, 1768), IV, 3, p. 261.

2. For such habilitations see especially Hans Welzel, *Die Natur-rechtslehre Samuel Pufendorfs* (Berlin, 1958); Erik Wolf, *Grosse Rechtsdenker der deutschen Geistesgeschichte* (4th ed.; Tübingen, 1963), pp. 311–70; Friedrich Meinecke, *Die Idee der Staatsräson in der neueren Geschichte* (Munich, 1924), pp. 279–303; Karl Obermann, "Vorkämpfer der Menschenrechte," *Aufbau,* III, 15–19.

3. Welzel has noted Pufendorf's preference for the mediatory over the highest principles. *Op. cit.,* p. 7, n. 18.

CHAPTER 1

1. Samuelis Pufendorfii, *Eris Scandica, qua adversus libros de jure naturali et gentium objecta diluuntur* (Frankfurt, 1744), p. 170.

2. *Ibid.,* p. 14.

3. Pufendorf to Paul von Fuchs, January 19, 1688, in Konrad Varentrapp (ed.), "Briefe von Pufendorf," *Historische Zeitschift,* LXX (1893), 27–28; Pufendorf to Thomasius, October 31, 1691, in Emil Gigas (ed.), *Briefe Samuel Pufendorfs an Christian Thomasius* (Munich, 1897), p. 61.

4. A composite assessment from Heinrich von Treitschke, *Historische*

und politische Aufsätze (Leipzig, 1897), IV, 202–304 *passim,* and Erik Wolf, *Grotius, Pufendorf, Thomasius* (Tübingen, 1927), pp. 64–73.

5. See especially Jacob Grimm and Wilhelm Grimm, *Deutsches Wörterbuch* (Leipzig, 1860), II, 538; Regine Pernoud, *Histoire de la bourgeoisie en France* (Paris, 1962), II, 77–80.

6. Marc Venard, *Bourgeois et paysans au XVIIe siècle* (Paris, 1957), p. 33.

7. Thus Seyssel's classification of the bourgeois into a national "middle estate" as early as the sixteenth century. Claude de Seyssel, *La monarchie de France* . . . (new ed.; Paris, 1961), pp. 123, 125.

8. R. H. Gretton, *The English Middle Class* (London, 1917), pp. 124–27; F. W. Maitland, *The Constitutional History of England* (new ed.; Cambridge, 1963), pp. 290–91; Pieter Geyl, *The Netherlands in the 17th Century,* Part II, *1648–1715* (New York, 1964), pp. 191–93.

9. See Werner Sombart, *Der Bourgeois: zur Geistesgeschichte des modernen Wirtschaftmenschen* (Munich, 1913), pp. 177–81.

10. Pernoud, *op. cit.,* II, 7–76.

11. Charles Normand, *La bourgeoisie française au XVIIe siècle* (Paris, 1908), pp. 17–18, 245; Charles Morazé, *La France bourgeoise, XVIIIᵉ-XXᵉ siècles* (Paris, 1946), pp. 64–65; Venard, *op. cit.,* pp. 117–18.

12. Pernoud, *op. cit.,* II, 63–66; Gretton, *op. cit.,* p. 131; Geyl, *op. cit.,* pp. 191–93.

13. E.g., the French Bodin, de Thou, Gassendi, Pascal, Jurieu; the English Bacon, Selden, Cumberland, Burnet.

14. Sombart, *op. cit.,* pp. 183–85; Gustave Huard, *L'Evolution de la bourgeoisie allemande* (Paris, 1919), pp. 184–96; Heinrich Bechtel, *Wirtschaftsgeschichte Deutschlands: vom Beginn des 16. bis zum Ende des 18. Jahrhunderts* (Munich, 1952), pp. 62–67, 332, 341–343.

15. E.g., Hans Motteck, *Wirtschaftsgeschichte Deutschlands* (Berlin, 1957), I, 256–57.

16. For the Thirty Years' War, see Walther Günther, *Grundzüge der sozialen und wirtschaftlichen Entwicklung in Deutschland im Zeitalter des Dreissigjährigen Krieges* (Berlin, 1931), *passim,* but especially p. 99. On prewar period, see Friedrich Lütge, *Studien zur Sozial- und Wirtschaftsgeschichte* (Stuttgart, 1963), pp. 336–95, and *Deutsche Sozial- und Wirtschaftsgeschichte* (2d ed.; Heidelberg, 1960), pp. 287–98.

17. Hugo Rachel and Paul Wallich, *Berliner Grosskaufleute und Kapitalisten* (Berlin, 1938), II, 11–23; Percy Ernst Schramm, *Kaufleute zu Haus und Übersee: Hamburgische Zeugnisse des 17., 18., und 19. Jahrhunderts* (Hamburg, 1949), pp. 119–33.

18. For this fundamental change in bourgeois mores from the end of the seventeenth century, see Bernhard Groethuysen, *Die Entstehung der bürgerlichen Welt- und Lebensanschauung in Frankreich* (Halle, 1930), II, 4–8; Morazé, *op. cit.*, pp. 65–78.

19. For Pufendorf's biography, see especially Treitschke, *op. cit.*, and Paul Meyer, *Samuel Pufendorf: ein Beitrag zur Geschichte seines Lebens* (Grimma, 1894).

20. For Pufendorf's unqualified confession of Lutheran faith, see his *Eris Scandica,* pp. 18–19.

21. Especially the Saxon theologian Valentin Alberti.

22. Meyer, *op. cit.,* pp. 8–9.

23. Pufendorf to Thomasius, June 19, 1688, Varentrapp, *loc. cit.,* LXX, 31.

24. Treitschke, *op. cit.,* IV, 205.

25. Meyer, *op. cit.,* pp. 10–11.

26. Pufendorf to Weigel, April 17, 1659, Varentrapp, *loc. cit.,* LXXIII (1894), 66.

27. Thus two of his major works were entitled: *Idea matheseos universae* (1669) and *Arithmetische Beschreibung der Moralweisheit* (1674).

28. Dedication in Samuelis Pufendorfii, *Dissertationes academicae selectiores* (Uppsala, 1677).

29. Pufendorf to Weigel, April 17, 1659, Varentrapp, *loc. cit.,* LXXIII, 66.

30. Samuel Pufendorf, *De jure naturae et gentium libri octo,* English trans. by C. W. and W. A. Oldfather (Oxford, 1934), II, v.

31. *Jo. Laurenbergii Graecia antiqua* (Amsterdam, 1660) and *Jo. Meursii miscellanea laconica* (Amsterdam, 1661).

32. The case is argued positively in Gerhard Oestreich, "Justus Lipsius als Theoretiker des neuzeitlichen Machtsstaates," *Historische Zeitschrift,* CLXZXI (1956), 69, and *idem,* "Calvinismus, Neustoizismus, und Preussentum," *Jahrbuch für die Geschichte Mittel- und Ostdeutschlands,* V (1956), 155–56.

33. Samuel Pufendorf, *Elementorum jurisprudentiae universalis libri duo,* English trans. by W. A. Oldfather (Oxford, 1931), II, dedication.

34. The so-called *Wildfangstreit,* in which Karl Ludwig reasserted a medieval right of the Palatinate to levy a serf-tax on immigrants from neighboring areas. It led, in 1664, to actual armed conflict between the Palatinate and the surrounding Rhenish towns and knights.

35. Pufendorf, *Eris Scandica,* p. 63.

36. Appendix of H. Bresslau's edition and translation of Severinus von Monzambano (Samuel von Pufendorf), *Über die Verfassung des deutschen Reiches* (Berlin, 1922), p. 130.

37. Pufendorf, *De jure naturae,* II, v.

38. Treitschke, *op. cit.,* IV, 220.

39. "De obligatione erga patriam" and "Dissertatio de Philippo Amyntae filio," both published in the *Dissertationes academicae selectiores* (Lund, 1675).

40. Pufendorf's preface to a posthumously published edition, in Fritz Salomon's edition of Severinus de Monzambano, *De statu imperii Germanici* (Weimar, 1910), p. 164.

41. Pufendorf, *Verfassung des deutschen Reiches,* pp. 4–5.

42. Pufendorf, *Elementorum,* II, 165.

43. Pufendorf, *De jure naturae,* IV, v.

44. Pufendorf, *Eris Scandica,* pp. 18–19, 106–7.

45. *Ibid.*

46. Samuelis Pufendorfii, *Dissertationes academicae selectiores* (Lund, 1675), pp. 20, 25.

47. Samuel von Pufendorf, *De officio hominis et civis juxta legem naturalem libri duo,* English trans. by Frank Gardner Moore (New York, 1927), II, iv, v.

48. Pufendorf, *De jure naturae,* II, vii.

49. The dedication is unaccountably missing from the Oldfathers' translation of *De jure naturae.* For it, see the Frankfurt edition of 1744, I, xxiii–xxv.

50. *Ibid.,* I, vi.

51. Pufendorf did publish a revised and enlarged edition of his *De jure naturae* in 1684, and he furnished some revisions for a new edition of his Monzambano in the same year. From 1688 to 1692 he worked desultorily on the new edition of the Monzambano which he designed

for posthumous publication and which was actually published by Paul Gundling for the Berlin Academy in 1706. These later residues of Pufendorf's juristic phase were unimportant and do not essentially violate the division between the two stages of Pufendorf's career.

52. Treitschke, *op. cit.*, IV, 269.

53. His *Dissertatio de occasionibus foederum inter Sueciam et Galliam* (1680).

54. *Commentariorum de rebus Suecicis libri XXVI ab expeditione Gustavi Adolphi Regis in Germaniam ad abdicationem usque Christinae* (Utrecht, 1686); *De rebus a Carolo Gustavo Sueciae Rege gestis commentariorum libri VII* (Nuremberg, 1696). Although published posthumously, the manuscript of the latter work was completed before Pufendorf left Stockholm in 1688.

55. Pufendorf to Pregizer, October 3, 1691, Varentrapp, *loc. cit.*, LXX, 209–10; Pufendorf to von Fuchs, January 19, 1688, *ibid.*, pp. 28–29.

56. *Ibid.*, pp. 27–28; Pufendorf to von Seilern, March 5, 1690, *ibid.*, pp. 43–44; Pufendorf to Charles XI, August 5, 1691, *ibid.*, p. 207.

57. Pufendorf to von Fuchs, January 19, 1688, *ibid.*, pp. 26–27; Pufendorf to Thomasius, March 24, 1688, Gigas, *op. cit.*, p. 19; Pufendorf to Von Hessen-Rheinfels, July 8/18, 1690, Varentrapp, *loc. cit.*, LXX, 196.

58. Samuelis Pufendorfi, *De habitu religionis Christianae ad vitam civilem* (Bremen, 1687), preface.

59. *Ibid.*, preface and pp. 6–7. The reference to the revocation is indirect but unmistakable.

60. See for example his proposals for the philosophical reorientation of Christian theology in his letter to his brother Esaias, Feb. 24, 1681, in Christoph. Matthaei Pfaffii, *Introductio in historiam theologiae literariam notis amplissimis* (Tübingen, 1724), I, 398–402.

61. On the scholarly side, see Pufendorf's elaboration upon *De habitu's* juristic descussion of the legal nature of the "church" in his letter to Thomasius, April 9, 1692, in Gigas, *op. cit.*, pp. 66–67.

62. Pufendorf, *De habitu*, preface.

63. On Pufendorf's doctrine of toleration, see Friedrich Lezius, *Der Toleranzbegriff Lockes und Pufendorfs* (Leipzig, 1900).

64. "I think that I can be more useful to my country (*patriae*) if I live in Berlin than if I live in Stockholm." Pufendorf to Pregizer, July 29, 1687, Varentrapp, *loc. cit.*, LXX, 22.

65. For his disinterest in remoter history, see Pufendorf to Pregizer, October 3, 1691, *ibid.,* pp. 211–12.

66. He resented the use of the promised fee, which he had anyhow deemed niggardly, as a lure for his return to Sweden. Pufendorf to von Dahlberg, October 14, 1691, *ibid.,* pp. 212–13; Pufendorf to von Dahlberg, May 25, 1692, *ibid.,* pp. 218–19; Pufendorf to Friese, undated, *ibid.,* LXXIII, 63; Treitschke, *op. cit.,* IV, 270.

67. Pufendorf to Pregizer, October 3, 1691, Varentrapp, *loc. cit.,* LXX, 210; Pufendorf to von Dahlberg, October 14, 1691, *ibid.,* p. 214.

68. *Ibid.,* p. 212.

69. *Ibid.* Also, Pufendorf to Friese, undated, *ibid.,* LXXIII, 62–63.

70. *Ibid.,* p. 63; Pufendorf to Charles XI, August 5, 1691, *ibid.,* LXX, 208.

71. Pufendorf to Pregizer, October 3, 1691, *ibid.,* p. 209.

72. Both works were published posthumously: *De rebus gestis Friderici Wilhelmi Magni Electoris Brandenburgici commentariorum libri XIX* (Berlin, 1695) and *Jus feciale divinum sive de consensu et dissensu Protestantium exercitatio posthuma* (Lübeck, 1695). The latter is usually known by the literal and misleading translation, *Divine Feudal Law,* trans. by Theophilus Dorrington (London, 1703).

73. *De rebus gestis Friderici III Electoris Brandenburgici, post primis Borussiae Regis libri III complectentes annos 1688–1690* (Berlin, 1784). For Pufendorf's surprising focus on the English Revolution of 1688, see Hans Rödding, *Pufendorf als Historiker und Politiker in den "Commentarii de rebus gestis Friderici Tertii"* (Halle, 1912), pp. 13–16.

74. Pufendorf to von Dahlberg, October 14, 1691, Varentrapp, *loc. cit.,* LXX, 213–14; Pufendorf to von Dahlberg, May 25, 1692, *ibid.,* p. 217; Pufendorf to his son-in-law, October 11, 1693, *ibid.,* p. 228.

75. Pufendorf to Thomasius, February 25, 1688, Gigas, *op. cit.,* p. 13.

76. Pufendorf to Thomasius, November 1, 1690, *ibid.,* pp. 48–49.

77. Pufendorf to von Fuchs, January 19, 1688, Varentrapp, *loc. cit.,* LXX, 29; Pufendorf to Charles XI, August 5, 1691, *ibid.,* p. 206.

78. Elector Frederick William to Pufendorf, February, 1686, *ibid.,* p. 28, n. 2; Pufendorf to von Dahlberg, May 25, 1692, *ibid.,* p. 219.

79. *Ibid.,* pp. 219–20; Pufendorf to von Fuchs, January 19, 1688, *ibid.,* pp. 27–28; Pufendorf to son-in-law, October 11, 1693, *ibid.,* p. 228.

80. Pufendorf to von Seilern, March 5, 1690, *ibid.,* pp. 41–44.

81. Pufendorf to Thomasius, February 25, 1688, Gigas, *op. cit.,* p. 13; Pufendorf to son-in-law, October 11, 1693, Varentrapp, *loc. cit.,* LXX, 228–30.

82. Pufendorf to Thomasius, March 14, 1688, Gigas, *op. cit.,* p. 14.

83. Pufendorf to Thomasius, March 24, 1688, *ibid.,* pp. 18–19.

84. Pufendorf to Thomasius, February 27, 1692, *ibid.,* p. 6.

85. Pufendorf to Thomasius, no date (probably 1687), *ibid.,* p. 74; Pufendorf to Thomasius, August 28, 1689, *ibid.,* p. 40; Pufendorf to Thomasius, March 24, 1688, *ibid.,* pp. 18–19.

86. *Ibid.,* p. 19.

87. Pufendorf, *Eris Scandica,* p. 14.

88. Pufendorf, *Elementorum,* II, xxviii; *De jure naturae,* II, iv, vi.

89. For Pufendorf's intermediate position, note his formulation when he explained that he could not expatiate fully "in matters of religion. I want of it nothing more than for my own use . . . , as revealed in my small treatises on the Spiritual Monarchy of Rome [an anti-papal tract] and the *De habitu.*" Pufendorf to von Hessen-Rheinfels, July 8/18, 1689, Varentrapp, *loc. cit.,* LXX, 196.

90. Pufendorf to Rechenberg, October 20, 1688, *ibid.,* p. 39; Pufendorf to von Hessen-Rheinfels, November 1, 1691, *ibid.,* pp. 214–16; Pufendorf to Thomasius, January 7, 1693, Gigas, *op. cit.,* pp. 71–72.

91. Pufendorf to Thomasius, December 1, 1688, *ibid.,* pp. 32–33.

CHAPTER 2

1. Pufendorf, *Elementorum,* II, xxix. *De jure naturae,* II, 25. Emphasis supplied.

2. Pufendorf, *Eris Scandica,* p. 173.

3. René Descartes, *Discourse on the Method of Rightly Conducting the Reason and Seeking for Truth in the Sciences,* in *The Philosophical Works of Descartes,* trans. by Elizabeth S. Haldane and G. R. T. Ross (New York, 1931), I, 86, 89.

4. Thomas Hobbes, *Leviathan* (reprint of 1651 ed.; Oxford, 1909), pp. 8, 11.

5. Baruch Spinoza, *A Theological-Political Treatise,* in R. H. M. Elwes (ed.), *The Chief Works of Spinoza* (New York, 1951), I, 8, and *On the Improvement of the Understanding, ibid.,* II, 3.

6. Descartes, *Method,* in *Works,* I, 92–93.

7. For the identity of essence and existence and the discard of all intermediaries but intellect, see Spinoza, *Ethics,* in *Works,* II, 70, and Harry Austryn Wolfson, *The Philosophy of Spinoza* (New York, 1958), I, 218–22. For parallel orders of essence and existence see Descartes' argument that God creates essences just as he creates existences. Norman Kemp Smith, *New Studies in the Philosophy of Descartes* (London, 1952), pp. 178–80.

8. Smith, *op. cit.,* pp. 63–65; Descartes, *Rules,* in *Works,* I, 3–15.

9. Thus Descartes: "Since the principles are clear and nothing must be deduced from them but by very evident reasoning, we have all sufficient intelligence to comprehend the conclusions that depend on them." *Principles of Philosophy,* in *Works,* I, 210. See also Spinoza's first "rule of life": "To speak in a manner intelligible to the multitude," since "it is a part of my happiness to lend a helping hand, that many others may understand even as I do, so that their understanding and desire may entirely agree with my own." *On the Improvement of the Understanding,* in *Works,* II, 6–7.

10. Descartes, *Method,* in *Works,* I, 89.

11. Descartes, *Meditations on First Philosophy,* in *Works,* I, 134.

12. Wolfson, *op. cit.,* II, 340.

13. Descartes, *The Principles of Philosophy,* in *Works,* I, 238–45; Spinoza, *Ethics,* in *Works,* II, 45–46. Descartes, it should be noted, also uses "accidents," as an undefined weak disjunction ("modes or accidents," in *Meditations,* in *Works,* I, 162) or instead of "modes" ("accidents of mind," *ibid.,* p. 141). But the context shows that he uses "accidents" when he discusses the *distinction* between perceived variations and unified substance and uses "modes" when he discusses the *subordination* of perceived variations to unified substance, and it was the latter relation that he increasingly emphasized.

14. For the relations of modes to substance as parts to the whole, see Wolfson, *op. cit.,* I, 61–75; as effect to cause, see Descartes' third meditation in *Meditations,* in *Works,* I, 157–66.

15. Spinoza, *Ethics,* in *Works,* II, 45. Modes, it follows, can only be conceived through some attribute of substance. *Ibid.,* p. 65. Whether Descartes too had added conception to his definition of substance as independent being is a matter of textual dispute. It is, however, implied in the argument of his third meditation. See also Smith, *op. cit.,* pp. 314–15, and Gottfried Wilhelm Leibniz, *Principles of Nature and of*

Grace, Founded on Reason. in *Leibniz: Philosophical Writings* (New York, 1934), p. 21: "There must necessarily be simple substances everywhere . . . ; consequently, the whole of nature is full of life."

16. Wolfson, *op. cit.,* I, 74.

17. Smith, *op. cit.,* p. 358.

18. Descartes, *Rules,* in *Works,* I, 9.

19. Hobbes, *Leviathan,* p. 64.

20. Descartes, *Principles of Philosophy,* in *Works,* I, 211; Smith, *op. cit.,* p. 31.

21. Hobbes, *Leviathan,* p. 122; see also Raymond Polin, *Politique et philosophie chez Thomas Hobbes* (Paris, 1953) , pp. 129–50.

22. Spinoza, *Ethics,* in *Works,* II, 129, 189.

23. Pufendorf, *Elementorum,* II, xxviii; *De jure naturae,* II, 3, 26.

24. Pufendorf, *Eris Scandica,* p. 341.

25. For his initial identification of his career with philosophy, see Pufendorf to Weigel, April 17, 1659, in Konrad Varentrapp (ed.) , "Briefe von Pufendorf," *Historische Zeitschrift,* LXXIII (1894) , 66. For his later excursions into philosophy, see Pufendorf, *De jure naturae,* II, Book 1, and his "Specimen controversiarum circa jus naturale ipsi nuper motarum," in *Eris Scandica,* pp. 170–75, 218–56.

26. *Eris Scandica,* pp. 344, 350. For a general discussion of Pufendorf's method see also Hans Welzel, *Die Naturrechtslehre Samuel Pufendorfs* (Berlin, 1958) , pp. 11–18.

27. Pufendorf, *Elementorum,* II, xxix, 209. For the metaphysical basis of definitions, see his *De jure naturae,* II, 3.

28. Pufendorf, *Elementorum,* II, 210.

29. For Descartes' *dementis,* see *Principles of Philosophy,* in *Works,* I, 222; *Rules,* in *ibid.,* pp. 32, 42–45. Also Smith, *op. cit.,* pp. 66–69. For Pufendorf's acceptance of the syllogism as the standard instrument of deductive logic, see *De jure naturae,* II, 22–23.

30. For Pufendorf on linguistic consensus, see *De jure naturae,* II, 457–90.

31. *Ibid.,* pp. 22–24.

32. Pufendorf, *Elementorum,* II, 209. "Theoretical" and "practical" here are used in their philosophical senses of referring to knowledge of nature and precepts of action, respectively.

33. Pufendorf, *De jure naturae,* II, 26–37.

34. Pufendorf, *Elementorum*, II, xxix.

35. Welzel, *Naturrechtslehre*, pp. 14–15; Pufendorf, "Dissertatio de statu hominum naturali," *Dissertationes academicae selectiores* (Uppsala, 1677), pp. 458–59.

36. Descartes, *Reply to Second Objections*, in *Works*, II, 58–61.

37. Pufendorf, *De jure naturae*, II, 34–36.

38. *Ibid.*, p. 203.

39. For this outline, see the 1744 Frankfurt edition of the *De jure naturae*, I, xl. It is probably the work of the editor, Gottfried Mascovius.

40. Pufendorf, *De jure naturae*, II, 379–427.

41. *Ibid.*, p. 454, italics mine. That this procedure was not tailored to an individual case was indicated by Pufendorf's repetition of his statement about it in reference to the "origin and nature of human government," which had to be examined before investigation could be made of the "law and precepts of the law of nature and nations" which "presuppose it." *Ibid.*, p. 839.

42. *Ibid.*, pp. 864–75.

43. Pufendorf, *De officio*, II, 126.

44. Pufendorf, *De jure naturae*, II, 34–35. In another context (pp. 108–10) he seems to argue to the contrary, that "permissions are excluded from laws in their proper sense," but from his discussion it is clear that here he has in mind substantive permissions in *civil* law.

45. *Ibid.*, pp. 32–33. In another context Pufendorf cites Grotius to the effect that "equity can have no place in natural law," but the elaboration of the argument makes the opposite point (pp. 817–18).

46. *Ibid.*, pp. 1133–34.

47. On this general point, see Erik Wolf, *Grosse Rechtsdenker der deutschen Geistesgeschichte* (4th ed.; Tübingen, 1963), p. 317, and Hans Welzel, *Die Socialitas als oberstes Prinzip der Naturrechtslehre Samuel Pufendorfs* (Heidelberg, 1930), pp. 12–17.

48. On the metaphysics, see below, pp. 73–81; on natural law and theology, see below, pp. 218–54.

49. Pufendorf, *De jure naturae*, II, 26–36, 159–62, 180–83.

50. Pufendorf, *Eris Scandica*, p. 367.

51. Pufendorf, *De officio*, II, vii–viii.

52. *Ibid.*, pp. vi, 21–27; *De jure naturae*, II, 162–63, 525.

53. See chap. vii below.

54. Pufendorf, *De jure naturae*, II, 23.

55. *Ibid.,* pp. 36–37; *Eris Scandica,* p. 362.

56. Pufendorf, *De jure naturae,* II, 23, 26. I have translated *"veras reapse"* as "actual," rather than the Oldfathers' "true in fact."

57. Pufendorf, *Eris Scandica,* p. 367.

58. *Ibid.,* p. 343.

59. Even within this limited context, Pufendorf's use of the term was confusing, although this confusion is extraneous to our discussion. Not only did he admit that he himself sometimes misused "hypothesis," in its proper logical sense of an inadequately proven proposition, by applying it to genuine axioms but he recalled the familiar logical distinction between a hypothesis and a hypothetical proposition, validating his employment of the latter on the ground that he made no deductions from it. None of these usages, however, corresponded to the "hypothetical precepts of natural law" discussed below. See *ibid.,* pp. 356–58, 369.

60. Pufendorf, *De officio,* II, 19.

61. For the substantive course of this development, see chaps. vi and vii below.

62. Pufendorf, *Eris Scandica,* pp. 361, 366.

63. Pufendorf, *De jure naturae,* II, iv; Samuelis Pufendorff, *Einleitung zu der Historie der vornehmsten Reiche und Staaten zo itzigen Zeit in Europa sich befinden* (Frankfurt-am-Main, 1682) , preface.

64. Pufendorf, *De jure naturae,* II, 1014–15.

65. *Ibid.,* pp. 36–37; *De officio,* II, vi.

66. Ernst Salzer, *Der Übertritt des grossen Kurfüsten von der schwedischen auf die polnische Seite während des ersten nordischen Krieges in Pufendorfs 'Carl Gustav' und 'Friedrich Wilhelm'* (Heidelberg, 1904) , p. 8; Pufendorf, *Einleitung,* preface.

67. Samuelis Lib. Bar. de Pufendorf, *Jus feciale divinum sive de consensu et dissensu Protestantium* (Lübeck, 1695) , pp. 11, 68.

68. *Ibid.,* p. 83.

69. A favorite term of Pufendorf to denote the autonomy of the method pertinent to each discipline. E.g., *Eris Scandica,* p. 361.

70. Pufendorf, *De jure naturae,* II, 37.

71. *Ibid.,* pp. 202–3. In *Eris Scandica,* the usual phrase is "the nature of things and men." (E.g., p. 215.)

72. Pufendorf, *Eris Scandica,* p. 265.

73. *Ibid.,* pp. 213–15; *De jure naturae,* II, 201–3.

74. Pufendorf, *Eris Scandica,* pp. 214, 264, 304–5. Cf. Welzel, *op. cit.,* pp. 16–17.

75. For this discussion see Pufendorf, *De jure naturae,* II, 38–51, 56–57; *De officio,* II, 3–5.

76. Pufendorf to Thomasius, June 19, 1688, Varentrapp, *loc. cit.,* LXX (1893), 31.

77. Pufendorf scorned metaphysics in the sense of *Metaphysicae,* the discipline of the scholastics, but he accepted it in the sense of *Philosophiae primae.* Pufendorf, *Eris Scandica,* p. 351; *De jure naturae,* II, 3.

78. See explanatory footnote in *De jure naturae* (Frankfurt, 1744), I, 4.

79. Pufendorf, *De jure naturae,* II, 5–6.

80. Pufendorf, *Eris Scandica,* p. 29; *De jure naturae* (Frankfurt, 1744), I, 5. The Oxford translation is misleading here.

81. Pufendorf, *De jure naturae,* II, 5–6.

82. For this discussion, see *ibid.,* pp. 66–68, and *Elementorum,* II, 3–5.

83. Pufendorf, *De jure naturae,* II, 70–86.

84. *Ibid.,* pp. 6–10; *Elementorum,* 8–17.

85. Pufendorf, *De jure naturae,* II, 27–30.

86. Pufendorf, *Eris Scandica,* p. 87.

87. *Ibid.,* pp. 364–65.

88. *Ibid.,* pp. 78, 242.

89. *Ibid.,* pp. 245–47.

90. *Ibid.,* p. 195.

91. Pufendorf, *De jure naturae,* II, 184; *Eris Scandica,* p. 81.

92. *Eris Scandica,* p. 187.

CHAPTER 3

1. Pufendorf, *Dissertationes academicae selectiores* (Lund, 1675), p. 3.

2. Pufendorf, *De jure naturae,* II, 24.

3. For this discussion, see *ibid.*, pp. 52–64; *De officio*, II, 5–7; *Elementorum,* II, 230.

4. For this discussion, see Pufendorf, *De jure naturae*, II, 18–19, 88–115.

5. Thus *lex* connotes law as command, *jus* as reason. *Ibid.*, pp. 89, 101, 179, 201.

6. Pufendorf, *De officio*, II, 13; *De jure naturae,* II, 103–12.

7. *De jure naturae*, II, 110–11, 118–27.

8. For the previous orientation, see esp. *ibid.*, p. 40; for the later orientation, *ibid.*, pp. 145–53.

9. *Ibid.*, p. 224.

10. Pufendorf, *Eris Scandica,* pp. 177–78; *De jure naturae* (Frankfurt, 1744) , I, 150–51.

11. *De jure naturae* (Frankfurt, 1744) , I, 159, 165.

12. *Ibid.*, pp. 150, 160.

13. Pufendorf, *Eris Scandica,* pp. 179, 357.

14. *Ibid.*, pp. 45, 178–80; *De jure naturae* (Frankfurt, 1744) , I, 151.

15. Pufendorf, *Elementorum,* II, 233–34.

16. *Ibid.*, p. 242.

17. Pufendorf, *De jure naturae* (Frankfurt, 1744) , I, 150, 202–3.

18. On this point see Hans Welzel, *Die Socialitas als oberstes Prinzip der Naturrechtslehre Samuel Pufendorfs* (Heidelberg, 1930) , pp. 13–17.

19. Pufendorf, *De jure naturae* (Frankfurt, 1744) , I, 151, 203.

20. *Ibid.*

21. Pufendorf, *Eris Scandica,* p. 356.

22. Pufendorf, *De jure naturae* (Frankfurt, 1744) , I, 155.

23. *Ibid.*, p. 203.

24. *Ibid.*, p. 224; *De officio*, II, 19–21.

25. For this discussion, see *De officio*, II, 21–27.

26. Pufendorf, *Eris Scandica,* p. 111.

27. Pufendorf, *De jure naturae,* II, 233. Italics added.

28. For the discussion of this point, see *ibid.*, pp. 231–309; *De officio*, II, 28–36.

29. On this point, see *De officio*, II, 37–47; *De jure naturae*, II, 346–78.

30. *De jure naturae,* II, 168–73.

31. For this discussion, see *ibid.*, pp. 379–401; *De officio*, II, 48–55.

32. Pufendorf, *De jure naturae*, II, 390–93.

CHAPTER 4

1. Pufendorf, *De jure naturae*, II, vi; *Eris Scandica*, pp. 167–68.

2. Pufendorf to Thomasius, November 1, 1690, in Emil Gigas (ed.), *Briefe Samuel Pufendorfs an Christian Thomasius* (Munich, 1897), p. 48.

3. For Pufendorf's argument against Grotius' refusal to apply logic to morals and law, see Pufendorf, *De jure naturae*, II, 34; against Grotius' subscription to the traditional doctrine of divided sovereignty, *ibid.*, II, 1021–22, 1176–77; against Grotius' subscription to the traditional confusion of sovereignty and property, *ibid.*, II, 585.

4. For Pufendorf's argument against Hobbes's exclusive individualism in the state of nature, see *ibid.*, II, 170–73, 219; against Hobbes's denial of viable political authority in a limited monarchy, aristocracy, and democracy, *ibid.*, II, 1031–32, 1071; against the anarchic dangers of Hobbes's single pact, *ibid.*, II, 980. For a convenient epitome of Pufendorf's position on the state of nature, particularly in relation to Hobbes, see Iring Fetscher, "Der gesellschaftliche 'Naturzustand' und das Menschenbild bei Hobbes, Pufendorf, Cumberland, und Rousseau: ein Beitrag zur Standortbestimmung der politischen Theorie Rousseaus," *Schmollers Jahrbuch für Gesetzgebung, Verwaltung, und Volkswirtschaft*, LXXX (1960), 650–65.

5. Pufendorf, *De officio*, II, 90–91.

6. In Pufendorf's terminology, "pact," since he uses "contract" only for agreements involving property and money.

7. On property, see *ibid.*, pp. 62–86; *De jure naturae*, II, 524–765.

8. Pufendorf to Thomasius, Dec. 1, 1688, Gigas, *op. cit.*, p. 32.

9. E.g., Pufendorf's discussion of prescription. After he had rejected the origin of the institution in civil law and more hesitantly in natural law he finally concluded that it arose from "the tacit agreement [*tacita conventio*] of nations." Pufendorf, *De jure naturae* (Frankfurt, 1744), I, 637–49.

10. On matrimony, Pufendorf, *De officio*, II, 94–96; *De jure naturae*, II, 839–909.

11. Pufendorf expressed the opinion that desertion and adultery would

be repugnant to natural law on the formal ground of violation of contract, but, as in the case of polygamy, he subsumed his discussion under the proviso that he was setting forth "what is usually stressed on both sides, leaving the decision to those who know how to weigh the force of arguments." *De jure naturae,* II, 875.

12. On the family, Pufendorf, *De jure naturae* (Frankfurt, 1744), II, 69–92.

13. *Ibid.,* p. 82.

14. On slavery, *ibid.,* pp. 934–46.

15. *Ibid.,* p. 96.

16. Pufendorf, *De jure naturae,* II, 826; *De officio,* II, 90.

17. *De officio* p. 91.

18. Pufendorf, *De jure naturae* (Frankfurt, 1744), II, 22, 82, 95, 211.

19. *Ibid.,* pp. 4, 109.

20. *Ibid.,* pp. 109, 118–19, 133–34.

21. *Ibid.,* pp. 75–76.

22. *Ibid.,* pp. 14, 142–43.

23. *Ibid.,* pp. 22–23, 82, 92–93; *De officio,* II, 103.

24. Pufendorf, *De jure naturae* (Frankfurt, 1744), II, 112–19.

25. Pufendorf, *De officio,* II, 103.

26. *Ibid.*

27. When the term "state" is used here and henceforward without qualification it is synonymous with political society (*civitas*), as against its modified use to signify a natural, civil, or political state (*status*).

28. *Ibid.,* pp. 104–5; *De jure naturae,* II, 954–55.

29. *Ibid.,* pp. 165–76.

30. Pufendorf, *De officio,* II, 92.

31. See above, pp. 89–91.

32. Pufendorf, *De jure naturae,* II, 955.

33. He conceded two extraneous exceptions: only a social contract is needed for a monarchy in which the ruler has made a pact with each member of the society individually before the social contract is drawn, and only a single unspecified contract is needed for an individual joining an established state. *Ibid.,* p. 977.

34. *Ibid.*

35. Pufendorf, *De jure naturae* (Frankfurt, 1744), II, 133–34.

36. *Ibid.*, p. 134.
37. Pufendorf, *De officio*, II, 107.
38. *Ibid.;* Pufendorf, *De jure naturae* (Frankfurt, 1744), II, 134.
39. *De jure naturae* (Frankfurt, 1744), II, 163, 189.
40. *Ibid.*, pp. 141–42.
41. *Ibid.*, p. 135.
42. *Ibid.*
43. *Ibid.*, p. 158.
44. *Ibid.*, p. 159.
45. *Ibid.*
46. *Ibid.*, pp. 160–64.
47. For Pufendorf's discussion of Hobbes on this issue, see *De jure naturae*, II, 977–83, 1031–32.
48. *Ibid.*, p. 972.
49. *Ibid.*, pp. 972–73.
50. *Ibid.*, pp. 1000–1006.
51. *Ibid.*, pp. 5–6, 11.
52. *Ibid.*, pp. 1001–2.
53. *Ibid.*, p. 1004.
54. *Ibid.*, pp. 1158–60.
55. *Ibid.*, p. 1159.
56. *Ibid.*, pp. 983, 1014, 1031.
57. *Ibid.*, p. 995.
58. *Ibid.*, pp. 1084–1102.
59. *Ibid.*, pp. 1114–15.

CHAPTER 5

1. Pufendorf, *De jure naturae*, II, 980. For juristic developments in the sixteenth and early seventeenth centuries, see Julian H. Franklin, *Jean Bodin and the Sixteenth-Century Revolution in the Methodology of Law and History* (New York, 1963), pp. 18–79; Carl Joachim Friedrich, *The Philosophy of Law in Historical Perspective* (2d ed.; Chicago, 1963), pp. 51–66; R. Stintzing and Ernst Landsberg, *Geschichte der deutschen Rechtswissenschaft* (Munich, 1880–1910), I, 649–726, II, 1–11.

2. Pufendorf, *De officio*, II, 116.

3. Pufendorf, *De jure naturae*, II, 1103.

4. *Ibid.*, pp. 1010–13, 1125, 1277–87.

5. *Ibid.*, pp. 995–97, 1257–65.

6. Pufendorf, *De officio*, II, 111–12.

7. Pufendorf, *De jure naturae*, II, 1014–15, 1119–20.

8. Hermann Funke, *Die Lehre vom Fürsten bei Samuel Pufendorf* (Berlin, 1930), pp. 9–10, 49–52.

9. Pufendorf, *De jure naturae*, II, 1011, 1131.

10. *Ibid.*, p. 1164.

11. *Ibid.*, pp. 1133–40, 1183–84.

12. Cf. the simplistic argument that the end-all and be-all of Pufendorf's doctrine was his drive toward political unity through the concept of the state as a moral person, in Wolfgang Zuber, "Die Staatsperson Pufendorfs im Lichte der neuen Staatslehre," in *Archiv des öffentlichen Rechts*, N.F. XXX (1939), 33–70, but esp. p. 58.

13. Pufendorf, *De jure naturae*, II, 1104–5.

14. Pufendorf, *Elementorum*, II, 289.

15. Pufendorf, *De jure naturae*, II, 1106.

16. Samuelis Pufendorfii, "Dissertatio de obligatione erga patriam," *Dissertationes academicae selectiores* (Lund, 1675).

17. *Ibid.*, pp. 10–20.

18. *Ibid.*, pp. 21–22.

19. *Ibid.*, pp. 27, 66.

20. *Ibid.*, pp. 32–33.

21. Pufendorf, *De jure naturae*, II, 1110.

22. *Ibid.*, p. 1105.

23. *Ibid.*, pp. 1105–11, 1140–45.

24. *Ibid.*, pp. 1056–57.

25. *Ibid.*, pp. 1066–78.

26. Pufendorf, *Elementorum*, II, 288–92.

27. Pufendorf, *De jure naturae*, II, 1077.

28. Bodo Börner, "Die Lehre Pufendorfs von der beschränkten Monarchie," *Zeitschrift für die gesamte Staatswissenschaft*, CX (1954), 519.

29. Pufendorf, *De jure naturae*, II, 1074–76.

30. *Ibid.*, pp. 1063–64, 1070.

31. *Ibid.*, pp. 1072–77.

32. *Ibid.*, p. 1066.

33. *Ibid.*, p. 1074.

34. For corporate bodies, see *ibid.*, pp. 995–99; for distinctions among men, see *ibid.*, pp. 1229–73.

35. Pufendorf, *Elementorum*, II, 8–9, 61–63; *De jure naturae*, II, 1229.

36. *De jure naturae*, II, 1258–59.

37. *Ibid.*, pp. 1272–73.

38. *Ibid.*, pp. 1264–68.

39. *Ibid.*, pp. 1262–64.

40. *Ibid.*, pp. 1271–72.

41. Pufendorf, *De jure naturae* (Frankfurt, 1744), II, 412–13.

42. Pufendorf, *Elementorum*, II, 290.

43. Pufendorf to Thomasius, November 1, 1690, in Emil Gigas (ed.), *Briefe Samuel Pufendorfs an Christian Thomasius* (Munich, 1897), p. 48.

44. Pufendorf, *De officio*, II, 113. It should be noted that in his more explicit *De jure naturae* (II, 1033) he discusses the same point as a difference rather than an advantage.

45. *De jure naturae*, II, 975–76, 981–83, 1026–29, 1031–32; Pufendorf to Rechenberg, November 18, 1690, in Konrad Varentrapp (ed.), "Briefe von Pufendorf," *Historische Zeitschrift*, LXX, 196–97.

46. Pufendorf, *De jure naturae* (Frankfurt, 1744), II, 193–95.

47. *Ibid.*, pp. 191–92.

48. Besides *De statu imperii Germanici* (Geneva [*sic:* actually The Hague], 1667), "De rebus gestis Philippi Amyntae Filio," "De systematibus civitatum," "De republicae irregulari," "De forma reipublicae Romanae," all republished in the *Dissertationes academicae selectiores* (Uppsala, 1677).

49. Posthumously published by J. P. Gundling (ed.), as *Samuelis L. B. de Pufendorf, De statu imperii Germanici liber unus* (Berlin, 1706).

50. E.g., Fritz Salomon's introduction to his edition of *De statu imperii Germanici* (Weimar, 1910), pp. 1–2.

Notes to pp. 157–64

51. On the first alternative see the organization of the *De statu imperii Germanici*, where Pufendorf draws his conclusions on the "form of the German Empire" only toward the end, after his depiction of historical and contemporary conditions. *Ibid.*, pp. 116–28. On the second alternative, see J. Jastrow, *Pufendorfs Lehre von der Monstrosität der Reichsverfassung: ein Beitrag zur Geschichte der deutschen Einheit* (Berlin, 1882), pp. 4–7.

52. Pufendorf, *De jure naturae*, II, 1038–40.

53. *Ibid.*, pp. 1024, 1040.

54. The Oldfathers' translation is misleading here in its indiscriminate use of "state" for both Latin terms. For Pufendorf's usage, see *De jure naturae* (Frankfurt, 1744), II, 181–211 *passim* and "De republicae irregulari," in *Dissertationes*, pp. 302–57 *passim*.

55. Pufendorf, "De rebus gestis Philippi Amyntae," *Dissertationes*, p. 97.

56. Pufendorf, *De jure naturae*, II, 1041.

57. Fritz Salomon (ed.), *Severinus de Monzambano: De Statu Imperii Germanici*, pp. 28–32, 116–29.

58. Pufendorf, "De rebus gestis Philippi Amyntae," *Dissertationes*, pp. 93–94.

59. Salomon, *op. cit.*, pp. 116–26.

60. He also expunged the reference to "monster" and allowed full play to "irregularity" in the revised edition of the *De statu imperii Germanici*. Jastrow, *op. cit.*, p. 73.

61. Pufendorf, "De republicae irregulari," *Dissertationes*, pp. 310–11.

62. *Ibid.*, pp. 352–57.

63. Salomon, *op. cit.*, pp. 127, 140.

64. Pufendorf, "De republicae irregulari," *Dissertationes*, p. 302.

65. Salomon, *op. cit.*, p. 149.

66. *Ibid.*, pp. 140–42.

67. Pufendorf, "De systematibus civitatum," *Dissertationes*, p. 211.

68. Pufendorf, "De republicae irregulari," *ibid.*, pp. 310–11; *De jure naturae*, II, 1024, 1043–52.

69. Pufendorf, "De systematibus civitatum," *Dissertationes*, pp. 211–28.

70. *Ibid.*, pp. 243–50, 260.

71. E.g., Theodore Ruyssen, *Les sources doctrinales de l'internationalisme* (Paris, 1954) , pp. 204–6.

72. Pufendorf, *De jure naturae,* II, iv.

73. In his appraisal of Grotius, Pufendorf did refer the pacific "law of embassies" and "his other instances" to the law of nature, but he did not develop this field in his own argument. *Ibid.,* pp. 228–29.

74. *Ibid.,* pp. 226–28. For an opposing view which argues that Pufendorf's division of traditional international law into the law of nature and the free acts of sovereigns in the state of nature constituted not a disruption but a new integration of international practice into the law of nations, see Ernst Reibstein, "Pufendorfs Völkerrechtslehre," in *Österreichische Zeitschrift für öffentliches Recht,* N.F., VII (1956) , 43–72, and his *Völkerrecht: ein Geschichte seiner Ideen* in *Lehre und Praxis* (Freiburg, 1957) , I, 488–93.

75. Pufendorf, *De jure naturae,* II, 226.

76. *Ibid.,* pp. 1292–307.

77. *Ibid.,* pp. 1298, 1308.

78. *Ibid.,* pp. 1298, 1310, 1316–20.

79. Pufendorf, *De officio,* II, 140–41.

80. Pufendorf, *De jure naturae,* II, 1330.

81. *Ibid.,* p. 1329.

82. *Ibid.,* pp. 1338, 1342.

CHAPTER 6

1. On Hobbes, see F. Smith Fussner, *The Historical Revolution: English Historical Writing and Thought, 1580–1640* (London, 1962) , pp. 170–73.

2. John Bodin, *Method for the Easy Comprehension of History,* trans. by Beatrice Reynolds (New York, 1945) , p. 8. For the connections of jurisprudence with critical historical *method,* a dimension of the problem not treated here, see Julian H. Franklin, *Jean Bodin and the Sixteenth-Century Revolution in the Methodology of Law and History* (New York, 1963) , pp. 103–54.

3. Emil Clemens Scherer, *Geschichte und Kirchengeschichte an den deutschen Universitäten* (Freiburg, 1927) , pp. 139–92.

4. For the designation of humanist historiography as "pragmatic," see

Eduard Fueter, *Geschichte der neueren Historiographie* (Munich and Berlin, 1911) , pp. 67, 84, 128.

5. Heinrich Ritter von Srbik, *Geist und Geschichte vom deutschen Humanismus bis zur Gegenwart* (Munich, 1950) , I, 66–70, 77–83; Herbert Butterfield, *Man on His Past: The Study of the History of Historical Scholarship* (Boston, 1960) , pp. 36, 43.

6. Bishop Bossuet, *Discours sur l'histoire universelle* (reprint of 3d ed., 1700; New York, 1856) , pp. 3–4.

7. Walter Raleigh, *The History of the World* (new ed.; Edinburgh, 1820) , VI, 367–70; Fussner, *op. cit.*, pp. 194–202.

8. Bodin, *op. cit.*, pp. 291–302; Adalbert Klempt, *Die Säkularisierung der universalhistorischen Auffassung: zum Wandel des Geschichtsdenkens im 16. und 17. Jahrhundert* (Göttingen, 1960) , pp. 50–59.

9. Klempt, *op. cit.*, pp. 127–28; Scherer, *op. cit.*, pp. 193–94.

10. Srbik, *op. cit.*, pp. 69–70.

11. Severinus von Monzambano, *Über die Verfassung des deutschen Reiches*, trans. by H. Bresslau (Berlin, 1922) , p. 111.

12. *Ibid.*, pp. 5, 38.

13. *Ibid.*, pp. 9–21.

14. *Ibid.*, pp. 40–42.

15. *Ibid.*, p. 83.

16. J. Jastrow, *Pufendorfs Lehre von der Monstrosität der Reichsverfassung* (Berlin, 1882) , pp. 4–7; H. Bresslau's introduction to Monzambano, *op. cit.*, p. 12.

17. Monzambano, *op. cit.*, pp. 32–34.

18. Pufendorf to Thomasius, June 19, 1688, in Konrad Varentrapp (ed.) , "Briefe Pufendorfs," *Historische Zeitschrift*, LXX (1893) , 33; Pufendorf to Thomasius, April 9, 1692, in Emil Gigas (ed.) , *Briefe Samuel Pufendorfs an Christian Thomasius* (Munich, 1897) , p. 66; Monzambano, *op. cit.*, pp. 41–42.

19. Samuelis Pufendorff, *Einleitung zu der Historie de Vornehmsten Reiche und Staaten so itzigen Zeit in Europa sich befinden* (Frankfurt am-Main, 1682) , preface.

20. *Ibid.*

21. Leo Strauss, *The Political Philosophy of Hobbes, Its Basis and Genesis* (Oxford, 1936) , pp. 80–107; Raymond Polin, *Politique et philosophie chez Thomas Hobbes* (Paris, 1953) , pp. 81–107; Lewis W.

Spitz, "The Significance of Leibniz for Historiography," *Journal of the History of Ideas,* XIII (1952) , 334, 340.

22. Hobbes, *Leviathan* (reprint of 1651 ed.; Oxford, 1909) , p. 64.

23. Pufendorf, *De jure naturae,* II, 36–37. Pufendorf's position is confused here by his attribution of "not absolutely . . . , but conditionally true" to questions of fact, thereby apparently reversing Hobbes's dictum. But Pufendorf is here using the terms logically rather than epistemologically.

24. Pufendorf, *Einleitung,* pp. 5–48.

25. *Ibid.,* pp. 1–4.

26. *Ibid.,* pp. 2, 17–18.

27. *Ibid.,* preface.

28. *Ibid.,* p. 119.

29. *Ibid.,* preface.

30. Friedrich Meinecke, *Die Idee der Staatsräson in der neueren Geschichte* (Munich, 1924) , p. 288.

31. Pufendorf, *Einleitung,* preface.

32. Samuelis von Pufendorff, *Continuierte Einleitung zu der Historie der vornehmsten Reiche und Staaten von Europa, worinnen dass Königreichs Schweden Geschichte und dessen mit auswärtigen Kronen geführte Kriege insonderheit beschrieben werden* (Frankfurt am Main, 1693) , dedication (dated July 1, 1685) .

33. *Ibid.,* p. 3 and *passim.*

34. Leonard Krieger, "History and Law in the 17th Century: Pufendorf," *Journal of the History of Ideas,* XXI (1960) , 198–210.

35. Pufendorf to Pregizer, October 3, 1691, Varentrapp, *loc. cit.,* LXX, 209.

36. *Ibid.,* pp. 209–10; Samuelis de Pufendorf, *De rebus gestis Friderici Wilhelmi Magni Electoris Brandenburgici commentariorum libri xix* (Berlin, 1695) , dedication.

37. See above, chap. 1, pp. 25–29 and notes.

38. Pufendorf to Pregizer, October 3, 1691, Varentrapp, loc. cit., LXX, 210; Pufendorf to von Seilern, March 5, 1690, *ibid.,* p. 44.

39. Joh. Gust. Droysen, "Zur Kritik Pufendorfs," *Abhandiunger zur neueren Geschichte* (Leipzig, 1876) , pp. 312–16; Ernst Salzer, *Der Übertritt des grossen Kurfürsten von der schwedischen auf die polnische Seite während des ersten nordischen Krieges in Pufendorfs "Carl Gustav" und "Friedrich Wilhelm"* (Heidelberg, 1904) , pp. 2–15; Hans

Rödding, *Pufendorf als Historiker und Politiker in den "Commentarii de Rebus Gestis Friderici Tertii"* (Halle, 1912) , p. 1.

40. Pufendorf to von Hessen-Rheinfels, November 8/18, 1690, Varentrapp, *loc. cit.*, LXX, 199; Pufendorf, *De rebus gestis Friderici Wilhelmi,* dedication.

41. Salzer, *op. cit.,* pp. 84–87.

42. Pufendorf to Leibniz, March 31, 1693, Varentrapp, *loc. cit.,* LXX, 224–26.

43. For the imposition of political judgments, see especially Pufendorf's description of the revocation of the Edict of Nantes, in *Rebus gestis Friderici Wilhelmi,* pp. 1532–34; for other references, see Rödding, *op. cit.,* pp. 43–49, 71–75.

44. Droysen, *loc. cit.,* pp. 349–58.

45. *Ibid.,* pp. 375–77; Salzer, *op. cit.,* pp. 13–15; Rödding, *op. cit.,* pp. 16, 38–39; Meinecke, *op. cit.,* pp. 293–303.

46. Pufendorf to von Seilern, March 5, 1690, Varentrapp, *loc. cit.,* LXX, p. 44.

47. Pufendorf to Pregizer, October 3, 1691, *ibid.,* pp. 210–12.

48. Pufendorf to Leibniz, March 31, 1693, *ibid.,* p. 226.

49. Pufendorf to Charles XI, August 5, 1691, *ibid.,* p. 207; Pufendorf, *De rebus gestis Friderici Wilhelmi,* dedication and p. 3.

50. *Ibid.,* dedication.

51. Pufendorf to Leibniz, March 31, 1693, Varentrapp, *loc. cit.,* LXX, 224.

52. *Ibid.;* Pufendorf to von Seilern, March 5, 1690, *ibid.,* p. 44.

53. Pufendorf to Fuchs, January 19, 1688, *ibid.,* pp. 27–28; Pufendorf, *De rebus gestis Friderici Wilhelmi,* p. 445; Samuelis Pufendorfii, *Commentariorum de rebus Suecicis libri XXVI ab expeditione Gustavi Adolphi Regis in Germaniam ad abdicationem usque Christinae* (Utrecht, 1686) , preface.

54. *Ibid.;* Meinecke, *op. cit.,* pp. 293–95.

55. Pufendorf, *De rebus gestis Friderici Wilhelmi,* dedication and p. 445; Pufendorf, *Commentariorum de rebus Suecicis,* preface.

56. Pufendorf, *De rebus gestis Friderici Wilhelmi,* p. 445.

57. On Pufendorf's identification of historical objectivity with freedom of archival research, see his *Commentarioum de rebus Suecicis,* preface, and Rödding, *op. cit.,* p. 9.

58. Pufendorf, *De rebus gestis Friderici Wilhelmi,* dedication.

59. *Ibid.,* pp. 1532–34, 1611–25.

60. Pufendorf to von Seilern, March 5, 1690, Varentrapp, *loc. cit.,* LXX, 41–43.

61. Monzambano, *op. cit.,* pp. 116–28.

62. Basilius Hypereta, pseud., *Historische und politische Beschreibung der geistlichen Monarchie des Stuhls zu Rom* (Hamburg, 1679).

63. Samuelis de Pufendorf, *De rebus gestis Friderici III Electoris annos 1688–1690. Fragmentum posthumum ex autographo auctoris Brandenburgici, post primis Borussiae Regis libri III complectentes editum* (Berlin, 1784), Sections 49–67, 74–76, 78–84, 86, 88–94; Rödding, *op. cit.,* pp. 13–16.

64. Pufendorf, *De rebus gestis Friderici III,* pp. 2, 104, 107.

65. *Ibid.,* pp. 89, 100.

66. *Ibid.,* p. 104.

67. Pufendorf to Rechenberg, October 2, 1688, Varentrapp, *loc. cit.,* LXX, 34, n. 1.

68. Pufendorf to Thomasius, December 1, 1688, Gigas, *op. cit.,* pp. 32–33.

69. Pufendorf to Rechenberg, January 31, 1692, Varentrapp, *loc. cit.,* LXX, 205.

70. *Ibid.*

71. Pufendorf, *De rebus gestis Friderici III,* p. 107.

72. Pufendorf to Thomasius, November 1, 1690, Gigas, *op. cit.,* pp. 48–49.

73. Pufendorf to Thomasius, December 30, 1688, *ibid.,* pp. 35–37; Pufendorf to Rechenberg, July 20, 1692, Varentrapp, *loc. cit.,* LXX, 220–21.

74. *Ibid.;* Pufendorf to Thomasius, December 30, 1688, and November 26, 1692, Gigas, *op. cit.,* pp. 35–36, 69–70.

75. Gigas, *op. cit.,* p. 36.

CHAPTER 7

1. Charles Ernst Adam, *Vie et œuvres de Descartes* (Paris, 1910), p. 289.

2. For a discussion of the difficulties in determining Hobbes's own

religiosity, see Samuel I. Mintz, *The Hunting of Leviathan* (Cambridge, 1962), pp. 41–45.

3. *Discourse on Method,* in *Philosophical Works of Descartes,* trans. by Elizabeth S. Haldane and G. R. T. Ross (New York, 1931), I, 102–3; *Principles of Nature and Grace,* in *Leibniz: Philosophical Writings,* trans. by Mary Morris (New York, 1934), p. 26; Hobbes, *Leviathan* (reprint of 1651 ed; Oxford, 1909), pp. 274–85; *Theologico-Political Treatise,* in *Works of Spinoza,* I, 200; John Locke, *Of Civil Government* (New York, 1924), pp. 120–21.

4. *Meditations,* in *Philosophical Works of Descartes,* I, 133–34; "Reply to Objections VI," *ibid.,* II, 246; Henri Gaston Gouhier, *La pensée religieuse de Descartes* (Paris, 1924), pp. 307–9; Jean Laporte, *Le rationalisme de Descartes* (Paris, 1945), pp. 418–19, 464–68; Jeanne Russier, *La sagesse cartesienne et religion* (Paris, 1958), pp. 133–37; Norman Kemp Smith, *New Studies in the Philosophy of Descartes* (London, 1952), pp. 164–88.

5. Smith, *op. cit.,* p. 173; "Reply to Objections VI," in *Philosophical Works of Descartes,* II, 247–48.

6. *Principles of Reason and Grace,* in *Leibniz: Philosophical Works,* pp. 26–30.

7. *Essais de théodicée,* in C. J. Gerhardt (ed.), *Die philosophischen Schriften von Gottfried Wilhelm Leibniz* (Hildesheim, 1961), VI, 70.

8. *Ibid.,* VI, 49–101 *passim.*

9. *Ibid.,* p. 102.

10. Spinoza, *A Theologico-Political Treatise,* in *Works of Spinoza,* I, 9, 194.

11. Locke, "Essay concerning Human Understanding," in Sterling P. Lamprecht (ed.), *Locke: Selections* (New York, 1928), pp. 316–17.

12. *Theologico-Political Treatise,* in *Works of Spinoza,* I, 9, 119, 184.

13. Hobbes, *Leviathan,* pp. 286, 302.

14. *Theologico-Political Treatise,* in *Works of Spinoza,* I, 99–106.

15. Hobbes, *Leviathan,* pp. 314–22.

16. *On the Improvement of the Understanding,* in *Works of Spinoza,* II, 37; *Ethics, ibid.,* II, 106–9; *Theologico-Political Treatise, ibid.,* I, 10, 184–89, 202–5, 257–62.

17. "Letter concerning Toleration," Lamprecht, *op. cit.,* p. 48; *Theologico-Political Treatise,* in *Works of Spinoza,* I, 245.

18. Thus Spinoza: "Faith consists in a knowledge of God, without which obedience would be impossible, and which the mere fact of obedience to him implies. . . . Faith is not salutary in itself, but only in respect to the obedience which it implies. . . . He who is truly obedient necessarily possesses true and saving faith; for if obedience be granted, faith must be granted also." *Theologico-Political Treatise,* in *Works of Spinoza,* I, 184. Thus Locke: "The faith required was, to believe Jesus to be the Messiah, the Anointed: who had been promised by God to the world. . . . What those were to do, who believed him to be the Messiah, and received him for their king, . . . we shall best know by the laws he gives them and requires them to obey." *The Reasonableness of Christianity as Delivered in the Scriptures,* in *The Works of John Locke* (London, 1824), VI, 113–14.

19. "In order that the true doctrines of reason, that is, . . . the true Divine doctrines might obtain absolutely the force of law and right, it was necessary that each individual should cede his natural right. . . ." *Theologico-Political Treatise,* in *Works of Spinoza,* I, 246.

20. *Ibid.,* pp. 189–94.

21. *Ibid.,* p. 101.

22. "A great many things which we have been bred up in the belief of, . . . we take for unquestionable obvious truths, and easily demonstrable; without considering how long we might have been in doubt or ignorance of them, had revelation been silent." *The Reasonableness of Christianity,* in *Works of John Locke,* VI, 145.

23. Hobbes, *Leviathan,* pp. 286–87.

24. *The Reasonableness of Christianity,* in *Works of John Locke,* VI, 145.

25. *Theologico-Political Treatise,* in *Works of Spinoza,* I, 195.

26. See above, pp. 212–13. Hobbes splits the difference between Spinoza and Locke by making faith and obedience two independent and equivalent requirements of salvation. *De cive,* in Thomae Hobbes Malmesburiensis, *Opera philosophica quae Latine scripsit omnia* (London, 1839), II, 208.

27. *Ibid.,* pp. 199–200; Hobbes, *Leviathan,* p. 459. For Spinoza's similar position, see *Theologico-Political Treatise,* in *Works of Spinoza,* I, 57–68, 246–48.

28. *De cive,* in Hobbes, *Opera philosophica,* II, 198.

29. "But that Christ does require obedience, sincere obedience, is

evident from the law he himself delivers. . . ." *Reasonableness of Christianity,* in *Works of John Locke,* VI, 113.

30. *Ibid.,* p. 133.

31. *Ibid.,* pp. 139–42.

32. *Ibid.,* pp. 142, 146, 158.

33. See C. B. Macpherson, *The Political Theory of Possessive Individualism* (Oxford, 1962), p. 13, and Peter Laslett (ed.), *John Locke: Two Treatises of Government* (Cambridge, 1964), p. 87.

34. Pufendorf, *De officio,* II, v–viii.

35. Pufendorf, *Eris Scandica,* p. 173.

36. Pufendorf, *De officio,* II, 19–23.

37. *Ibid.,* p. vi.

38. *Ibid.,* p. viii; *Eris Scandica,* pp. 16–17.

39. Samuelis Pufendorfii, "De concordia verae politicae cum religione Christiana," *Dissertationes academicae selectiores* (Uppsala, 1677), p. 430. The essay was already in the first edition, published in 1675, two years after the publication of the *De officio* and only one year after the expanded edition of *De jure naturae et gentium.*

40. *Ibid.,* pp. 430–42.

41. *Ibid.,* p. 431, 435.

42. *Ibid.,* pp. 442–48.

43. *Ibid.,* pp. 447–48.

44. *Ibid.,* p. 449.

45. *Ibid.,* pp. 449–58.

46. Basilius Hypereta, pseud., *Historische und politische Beschreibung der geistlichen Monarchie des Stuhls zu Rom* (Hamburg, 1679), English trans., *The History of Popedom, containing the Rise, Progress, and Decay thereof,* by J. Chamberlayne (London, 1691), pp. 1–2.

47. *Ibid.,* pp. 9, 196, 200.

48. Samuelis Pufendorfii, *De habitu religionis Christianae ad vitam civilem* (Bremen, 1685), preface, p. 7.

49. For the puzzling blend of libertarianism and authoritarianism in Pufendorf's doctrine of church and state, see Friedrich Lezius, *Der Toleranzbegriff Lockes und Pufendorfs: ein Beitrag zur Geschichte der Gewissensfreiheit* (Leipzig, 1900), *passim* but especially pp. 101–3, and

Hans Welzel, *Die Naturrechtslehre Samuel Pufendorfs* (Berlin, 1958), p. 102.

50. Lezius, *op. cit.*, p. 69.

51. Pufendorf, *De habitu,* pp. 9–25.

52. *Ibid.*, pp. 28–29.

53. *Ibid.*, pp. 29–31.

54. *Ibid.*

55. *Ibid.*, 32–33.

56. *Ibid.*, p. 113.

57. *Ibid.*, pp. 107–17.

58. *Ibid.*, pp. 59–60.

59. *Ibid.*, pp. 57–68.

60. *Ibid.*, pp. 119–21.

61. *Ibid.*, pp. 121–91, *passim.*

62. *Ibid.*, pp. 118–31, 181–91.

63. *Ibid.*, pp. 68–72.

64. *Ibid.*, pp. 182–83.

65. Pufendorf to Thomasius, April 9, 1692, in Emil Gigas (ed.), *Briefe Samuel Pufendorfs an Christian Thomasius* (Munich, 1897), p. 67.

66. Pufendorf, *De habitu,* pp. 191–94.

67. Pufendorf, *History of Popedom,* pp. 12–13.

68. *Ibid.*, pp. 11–19.

69. Pufendorf, *De habitu,* pp. 194–97.

70. *Ibid.*, pp. 204–7, 221, 254–55.

71. *Ibid.*, pp. 220–21, 227–28, 233–37, 262–70.

72. *Ibid.*, pp. 199–204.

73. *Ibid.*, pp. 214–18, 219–20.

74. *Ibid.*, pp. 208–11.

75. *Ibid.*, pp. 211–14, 230–31.

76. *Ibid.*, pp. 231–32.

77. *Ibid.*, p. 229.

78. *Ibid.*, pp. 200, 220–23, 228, 232.

79. *Ibid.*, pp. 197–99, 212–13, 219–27.

80. *Ibid.*, pp. 231–32, 266–67.

81. For the use of the term, "freedom of conscience [*conscientiae libertas*]," see *ibid.*, p. 228.

82. *Ibid.*, pp. 232–33, 239.

83. *Ibid.*, pp. 246–52.

84. Samuelis Lib. Bar. de Pufendorf, *Jus feciale divinum, sive De consensu et dissensu protestantium, extercitatio posthuma* (Lübeck, 1695), p. 14.

85. Pufendorf, *De habitu*, pp. 212–13.

86. *Ibid.*, pp. 223–32.

87. *Ibid.*, pp. 235–36, 262–70.

88. Welzel, *op. cit.*, p. 108. For another emphasis, which questions Pufendorf's Lutheran orthodoxy and stresses the natural-law linkage between his clerical and political doctrines, see Horst Rabe, "Naturrecht und Kirchenrecht bei Samuel von Pufendorf," *Zeitschrift für evangelisches Kirchenrecht*, V (1956), 375–99.

89. Pufendorf, *History of Popedom*, pp. 202–24; Pufendorf to von Hessen-Rheinfels, July 8/18, 1890, in Konrad Varentrapp (ed.), "Briefe Pufendorfs," *Historische Zeitschrift*, LXX (1893), 194.

90. Pufendorf, *Jus feciale*, pp. 12–20.

91. *Ibid.*, pp. 30–31.

92. *Ibid.*, pp. 51–52.

93. *Ibid.*, pp. 7–10, 26–28. Pufendorf himself made the explicit comparison of this religious situation with the futility of any attempt, in a state, to persuade the ruler "by philosophy and reasoning . . . to lay aside his authority and the wealth that supports it." *Ibid.*, pp. 33–34.

94. Pufendorf to Thomasius, June 19, 1688, Varentrapp, *loc. cit.*, LXX, 33; Pufendorf to Rechenberg, November 18 and December 6, 1690, *ibid.*, pp. 197–98.

95. Pufendorf to Thomasius, December 30, 1688, Gigas, *op. cit.*, pp. 35–37; Pufendorf to Hessen-Rheinfels, July 8/18, 1690, Varentrapp, *loc. cit.*, LXX, 194–95; Pufendorf to Rechenberg, July 20, 1692, *ibid.*, pp. 220–23; Pufendorf to Thomasius, November 26, 1692, Gigas, *op. cit.*, p. 69.

96. Pufendorf to Rechenberg, December 6, 1690, Varentrapp, *loc. cit.*, LXX, 198, n. 1.

97. Pufendorf, *Jus feciale*, pp. 13–16.

98. *Ibid.*, pp. 20, 24–26.

99. *Ibid.,* pp. 21–23.

100. For the fundamental dogmas, see *ibid.,* pp. 92–98; for the Lutheran identification and the argument of the Calvinist tenets as problematical and indifferent, see *ibid.,* pp. 198–216.

101. Pufendorf to Rechenberg, January 31, 1691, Varentrapp, *loc. cit.,* LXX, 205.

102. Pufendorf, *Jus feciale,* pp. 172, 239, 244.

103. *Ibid.,* p. 274.

104. *Ibid.,* p. 83.

105. *Ibid.,* pp. 80–82.

106. Thus Pufendorf could argue not that the Calvinists had to give up predestination as a false dogma but only that they should not hold it as "a primary article," since it was not and could not be a consensual proposition. *Ibid.,* p. 238.

107. Samuel Pufendorf to his brother Esaias, February 24, 1681, in Christoph. Matthaei Pfaffii, *Introductio in historiam theologicae literariam* (Tübingen, 1724), I, 398–402.

108. Pufendorf, *Jus feciale,* pp. 92–93.

109. *Ibid.,* pp. 207–8.

110. For the exclusively individualistic basis of any covenant with God, see *ibid.,* pp. 113–14.

111. *Ibid.,* pp. 102.

112. *Ibid.,* pp. 117, 131, 185.

113. *Ibid.,* pp. 186–89.

114. *Ibid.,* pp. 180, 187, 205.

115. *Ibid.,* p. 198.

EPILOGUE

1. For the editions of the *De jure,* see introduction to Pufendorf, *De jure naturae,* II, 59a–62a. Editions of *De officio* and *Einleitung* are by my count.

2. Introduction to Monzambano, *Über die Verfassung des deutschen Reiches,* 11*–12*.

3. *Ibid.;* Emil Clemens Scherer, *Geschichte und Kirchengeschichte an den deutschen Universitäten* (Freiburg, 1927), p. 179. The *De officio,*

which was designed specifically as a textbook, was used for this purpose in France well into the nineteenth century. See Samuel Pufendorf, *Les devoirs de l'homme et du citoyen* . . . , trans, by J. Barbeyrac (Paris, 1830) .

4. Locke to Clarke, February 8–March 15, 1686, *The Correspondence of John Locke and Edward Clarke* (Cambridge, 1927) , p. 151; "Some Thoughts concerning Reading and Study for a Gentleman," *Works of John Locke* (London, 1823) , III, 296; "Some Thoughts concerning Education," *ibid.,* IX, 176.

5. "Projet pour l'education de M. de Sainte-Marie," *Œuvres complètes de J.-J. Rousseau* (Paris, 1824) , X, 50.

6. "Plan d'une université pour le gouvernement de Russie," *Œuvres complètes de Diderot* (Paris, 1875–77) , III, 492; Boucher d'Argis, "Droit des gens," *Encyclopédie, ou Dictionnaire raisonné des sciences, des arts, et des métiers* (Paris, 1755) , V, 128–29.

7. Gottlieb Hufeland, *Lehrsätze des Naturrechts und der damit verbundenen Wissenschaften* (2d ed.; Jena, 1795) , pp. 28–31; Otto von Gierke, *The Development of Political Theory,* trans. by Bernard Freyd (New York, 1939) , pp. 173–74.

8. *Principles du droit naturel et politique* (Geneva, 1763) , Vol. I, chap. 9.

9. William Blackstone, *Commentaries on the Laws of England* (11th ed.; London, 1791) , I, 40–44, 198, 243, 257, 446–50; II, 3, 390, 392, 411, 419, 490; IV, 7, 26, 31, 194. Daniel J. Boorstin, *The Mysterious Science of the Law* (new ed.; Boston, 1958) , p. 50.

10. Gaston de Montesquieu (ed.) , *Pensées et fragments inédits de Montesquieu* (Bordeaux, 1899) , I, 99–100.

11. For quotation, see Robert Derathé, *Jean-Jacques Rousseau et la science politique de son temps* (Paris, 1950) , pp. 32–33. For Pufendorf and Adam Smith, see Joseph A. Schumpeter, *History of Economic Analysis* (New York, 1954) , pp. 116–18, 122.

12. Hans Rogger, *National Consciousness in Eighteenth-Century Russia* (Cambridge, 1960) , p. 174; Valentin Gitermann, *Geschichte Russlands* (Frankfurt am Main, 1949) , II, 208.

13. Arnold Berney, *Friedrich der Grosse: Entwicklungsgeschichte eines Staatsmannes* (Tübingen, 1934) , pp. 91–92, 260; Hans von Voltelini, "Die naturrechtlichen Lehren und die Reformen des 18. Jahrhunderts,"

Historische Zeitschrift, CV (1910), 73–82. For a depreciation of the influence of natural law upon Austrian Josephinism, cf. Georgine Holzknecht, *Ursprung und Herkunft der Reformideen Kaiser Josefs II auf kirchlichem Gebiet* (Innsbruck, 1914), pp. 14–52.

14. W. von Leyden (ed.), *John Locke: Essays on the Law of Nature* (Oxford, 1954), *passim* but esp. pp. 38–39; Peter Laslett (ed.), *John Locke: Two Treatises of Government* (Cambridge, 1964), pp. 142–43.

15. Laslett's introduction in *op. cit.,* p. 74.

16. René Hubert, *Rousseau et l'Encyclopédie: Essai sur la formation des idées politiques de Rousseau (1742–1756)* (Paris, 1928), p. 103; Derathé, *op. cit.,* p. 83.

17. *Ibid.,* p. 84.

18. John Wise, *A Vindication of the Government of the New-England Churches* (Boston, 1717), p. 32 ("Scholars' Facsimiles and Reprints" [Gainesville, Fla., 1958]); Edward S. Corwin, *The "Higher Law" Background of American Constitutional Law* (Ithaca, N.Y., 1955), pp. 74–75; Hans Welzel, "Ein Kapitel aus der Geschichte der amerikanischen Erklärung der Menschenrechte," in *Rechtsprobleme in Staat und Kirche: Festgabe für Rudolf Smend* (Göttingen, 1952), pp. 387–441.

19. James Otis, *The Rights of the British Colonies Asserted and Proved* (1764) (reprint) ("The University of Missouri Studies" [Columbia, 1929], Vol. IV, No. 3), p. 64; *The Writings of Samuel Adams* (New York, 1906), ed. by H. A. Cushing, II, 437; *The Papers of Alexander Hamilton,* ed. by Harold C. Syrett (New York, 1961-), I, 86; Clinton Rossiter, *Alexander Hamilton and the Constitution* (New York, 1964), pp. 121–25; Edward Dumbauld, *The Declaration of Independence and What It Means Today* (Norman, Okla., 1950), p. 57.

20. *Papers of Hamilton,* VII, 38–39, 42; Saul K. Padover (ed.), *The Complete Jefferson* (New York, 1943), pp. 150–54, 246–48; *Letters and Other Writings of James Madison* (Congressional ed.; Philadelphia, 1867), II, 240–43, 251.

21. "Some Thoughts concerning Education," *Works of John Locke,* IX, 176; Wise, *op. cit.,* pp. 37–51; "The Farmer Refuted," *Papers of Hamilton,* I, 86; Derathe, *op. cit.,* pp. 169–71.

22. Thus the publications of the *De officio* as a French textbook in 1820, 1822, and 1830, and of German selections from it under the title *Gemeinschaftspflichten des Naturrechts* in 1943.

23. Laslett, *op. cit.,* pp. 74, 79–87, 324, 328, 331, 334, 402; Wise, *op. cit.,*

pp. 61–62. A favorite reference in American anti-imperial writings was Pufendorf's detached recognition of colonial autonomy as a legally possible political relationship. Pufendorf, *De jure naturae*, II, 1356; Otis, *op. cit.*, p. 64; *Writings of Samuel Adams*, II, 437.

24. Rousseau, *Discours sur l'inégalité*, in C. E. Vaughan (ed.), *The Political Writings of Jean Jacques Rousseau* (New York, 1962), I, 144, 187; *De l'économie politique, ibid.*, I, 259; Derathé, *op. cit.*, pp. 161, 168, 320–41, 402–10.

25. Blackstone, *op. cit.*, I, 41, 50–52.

26. *Œuvres completes de Diderot*, XV, 401.

27. Karl Stählin, *Geschichte Russlands von den Anfängen bis zur Gegenwart* (Berlin, 1930), II, 173; Rogger, *op. cit.*, p. 174; Ferdinand Maass (ed.), *Der Josephinismus: Quellen zur seiner Geschichte in Österreich, 1760–90* (Vienna, 1951–61), III, 27–28, 187–88, 205; for Frederick's contractual theory, which emphasized the duties of sovereigns while eliding the natural law and rights upon which they were presumably based, see his "Essai sur les formes de gouvernement" and "Lettres sur l'amour de la patrie," in *Œuvres philosophiques de Frederic II, Roi de Prusse* (Berlin, 1848), II, 195–201, 227–28.

28. An English edition of the *De jure naturae* was published in 1763 and a French edition in 1771; thereafter no edition was published until it appeared as one of the Carnegie Endowment's "Classics of International Law" in 1934. A Latin edition of the *De officio* was published in 1769, and none thereafter, aside from the above-mentioned resurrection during the French Restoration and Nazi regimes, until the Carnegie reprint and translation of 1927. I have found only one edition of the general history, in 1764, after our cutoff date.

29. Erik Wolf, *Grosse Rechtsdenker der deutschen Geistesgeschichte* (4th ed.; Tübingen, 1963), p. 377.

30. Note the full title of his first important work on natural law: *Institutiones jurisprudentiae divinae, in positiones succincte contractae, in quibus hypotheses Pufendorfii circa doctrinam juris naturae apodictice demonstrantur et corroborantur, praecepta vero juris divini positivi universalis primum a jure naturali distincte secernuntur et perspicue explicantur* (Frankfurt, 1688). For his later position, see his *Fundamenta juris naturae et gentium ex sensu communi deducta. . . .* (Halle, 1705).

31. *Novanglus*, in *The Works of John Adams*, ed. by Charles Francis

Adams (Boston, 1851) , IV, 82 and note. For the relevant Pufendorf section and Barbeyrac quotation, see Baron Puffendorf, *The Law of Nature and Nations,* trans. by Basil Kennet (3d ed.; London, 1717) , II, 550 and note.

32. Boucher d'Argis, "Droit des gens," and "Droit de la nature ou droit naturel," in *Encyclopédie,* V, 129, 133.

33. Wolff quoted in Otfried Nippold, introduction to Christian Wolff, *Jus gentium methodo scientifica pertractatum* (Oxford, 1934) , II, xiv; Christiani Wolfii, *Jus naturalis methodo scientifica pertractatum* (Frankfurt, 1764) , p. iii.

34. E.g., see Hufeland, *op. cit.*

35. Boucher d'Argis, "Droit des gens," in *Encyclopédie,* V, 128–29; Padover, *op. cit.,* pp. 150–54; *Papers of Alexander Hamilton,* VII, 38–39, 42; John C. Miller, *Alexander Hamilton: Portrait in Paradox* (New York, 1959) , pp. 106, 148; *Letters and Other Writings of James Madison* (Congressional ed.; Philadelphia, 1867) , II, 240–43, 251.

36. E.g., Emer de Vattel, *Le droit des gens, ou Principes de la loi naturelle* (London, 1758) , I, 4.

37. Thus the republication and new translation of all three of Pufendorf's works on natural law among the "Classics of International Law" by the Carnegie Endowment for International Peace between 1927 and 1934.

INDEX

Index

[307]

Index

Hypothesis, 64–65, 280; hypothetical natural law, 60–64; hypothetical obligations, 59, 61, 101

Induction, 2, 43, 52, 65, 66, 68
Institutions, 237–39, 254; natural, 106–17, 168; political, 106, 116–17, 130, 141–53, 180; religious, 219–20, 243, 274
International law, 19–21, 164–69, 257, 265, 289
International relations, 163–65, 168–69, 193–95, 265
Introduction to the History of the Great Empires and States of Contemporary Europe (Einleitung zur Historie der vornehmsten Reiche und Staaten so itziger Zeit in Europa sich befinden), 24–25, 181–87, 194, 196, 256; see also *History of Popedom;* Sweden, general history
Intuition, 42, 53

Jefferson, Thomas, 259
Jena University, 14–16
Joseph II, German Emperor, 2, 258, 262, 301
Jurieu, Pierre, 271
Jurisprudence, 133–69, 172, 174, 285; juristic history, 178–87; and natural law, 133–35; see also Law
Justice, 87–88

Kant, Immanuel, 33, 50
Karl Ludwig, Palatine Elector, 18–21, 273
Kenet, Basil, 259

Law, 11, 24, 35, 39, 50, 53–55, 79, 84; connotation of *jus* and *lex* in, 282; defined, 85–88; and history, 170–74; and science, 34–36; see also Civil law; Constitutional law; International law; Jurisprudence; Natural law; Roman law
Leibniz, Gottfried Wilhelm, 15, 50; on history, 171, 174, 176, 182; philosophy of, 41, 44, 46–49; on Pufendorf, 1; on religion, 204, 205, 207–8
Leipzig University, 14, 16
Leopold I, German Emperor, 32, 196
Leyden University, 18, 19
Liberty (and freedom), 126–27, 266; moral, 75–76, 83–87; natural, 84–87, 94, 101, 106–7, 112–13, 115, 120, 127, 138–40, 165, 167–69, 261; and religion, 199–200, 228, 239–40, 244, 246, 249–54
Loccenius, Johan, 170, 171
Locke, John, 2, 48, 256, 258, 260, 261, 263, 265, 266; on religion, 204–5, 208–9, 212–14, 216–18, 219, 295
Logic; see Method
Louis XIV, 10, 26, 190, 226; see also Edict of Nantes
Lund, 24, 170
Lund University, 21–24, 178, 181
Lutheranism, 2, 6, 12, 13, 18, 73, 243–44, 272, 298

Mabillon, Jean, 176
Machiavelli, Niccolò, 224
Madison, James, 259
Maimbourg, Louis, 177
Marriage, 107, 109, 116, 283–84
Marx, Karl, 33, 43
Mascovius, Gottfried, 279
Maurists, 176
Melanchthon, Philipp, 173, 177
Metaphysics, 42–47, 52, 55, 69, 73–81, 278, 281; compared with logic, 58, 65
Method, 51–68, 278
Modes, 45, 73–74, 277; relation of moral and physical, 74–77

Index

Index

Pact, 107–9, 118, 120–30, 283; covenant, 251–54; moral promise in, 100–101

Pallavicino, Sforza, 177

Papacy; see Catholicism; *History of Popedom*

Pascal, Blaise, 39, 48, 271

Patriotism, 37, 141–43, 274; *see also* "Essay on Patriotism"

Peter I, "the Great," Tsar of Russia, 2, 258, 262

Philip of Macedon; see "On the History of Philip of Macedon"

Philosophy, 39, 51–81, 278; in seventeenth century, 40–50

Pietism, 29, 246

Politics, 36, 64–66, 102, 134, 180; and history, 182–83, 184–90; and jurisprudence, 125–41; and religion, 218–44, 246–47

Politiques, 18

Polygamy, 60, 109, 284

Power, 84–87

Promise; *see* Pact

Property, 107, 112, 261, 283; and natural law, 107–8; and the state, 136

Protestantism, 197–200, 226, 241, 244–45; unity of, 244–51

Pufendorf, Esaias, 15–17, 21

Raleigh, Walter, 175

Reason, 36, 51, 53, 58, 60, 68–70; and the basis of law, 85–87, 94–95; *see also* Deduction; Revelation

Reason of state, 1, 66, 159, 165, 179, 184–86, 190–91, 193–94, 196–97, 240

Religion, 25–27, 36, 65, 276, 298; and history, 195–203; natural, 63, 95–97, 220–21, 228–29; positive, 96, 200–201, 206, 208–18, 227–28, 241–44, 247–54; *see also* Christianity; Church and state; *Divine Law of the Covenant; On the Relation of*

the Christian Religion to Civil Life; Pietism; Revelation; Theology

Representation, 144–47

Resistance (and revolution), right of, 143–44, 197–200, 261

Revolution; *see* England, Glorious Revolution in; Resistance

Revelation, 68, 206, 242–43, 247–54; and politics, 221–27, 230–34; and reason, 64, 67, 207–18, 234–35

Rights, 105, 112, 114, 116–17, 127, 137–38, 261–62; imperfect, 87, 100; *see also* Natural rights

Roman law, 19, 60, 65, 108, 133, 172–73, 179

Rousseau, Jean-Jacques, 2, 256, 258, 260, 261, 266

Sarpi, Paolo, 177

Saxony, 12–14

Scandinavian Polemics (Eris Scandica), 23–24

Scholasticism, 42, 45–47

Schwartz, Joshua, 23

Science, 34, 41, 53–55, 56, 62

Scripture; *see* Revelation

Seckendorf, Veit von, 177

Secularization, 1, 203–18

Selden, John, 271

Select Scholarly Essays (Dissertationes academicae selectiores), 24, 287, 296

Senses, 69–70, 76

Slavery, 107, 111–12, 116; based on pact, 111

Smith, Adam, 258

Sociability, 2, 93–94, 97–98, 117, 261, 264

Society; *see* Moral person

Sovereignty, 10, 30, 87, 112, 125, 128–32, 134, 261–62, 302; and government, 113–14; and international law, 167–69; limited, 144–47, 159,

Index

261, 283; powers of, 135–41; in regular and irregular forms of state, 156–63; and religion, 236–43; and social hierarchy, 148–53

Spener, Philipp, 246

Spinoza, Baruch, 39; philosophy, 41, 43–44, 46–49; religion, 203, 205, 208–16, 295

State (or political society), 65, 98; composite, 161, 163; defined, 122, 284; and family, 110–11, 115–16; forms of, 153–64; irregular, 156, 158, 160–63, 180, 288; mixed, 157–59, 261, 262, 283; monstrous, 159–60, 288; as moral person, 116, 118, 286; origin, 117–23; purpose, 116–17; regular, 135, 156, 158, 160–62; relation to natural state, 112–17; simple, 161, 163; structure, 141–53; *see also* Church and state; Politics; Sovereignty

State of nature; *see* Natural state

State-system, 163–64

Status, 77, 97, 148–49

Steenbock, Gustave, 23

Stockholm, 25, 28, 32, 33, 274

Stoicism, 18, 105, 133, 272

Suárez, Francisco, 164

Substance, 44–47, 74, 75, 277–78

Sweden, 1, 15, 17, 21–30, 32, 170, 190, 244, 275; general history of, in *Continuation of Introduction to History of the Great Empires and States of Europe, in which the History of the Swedish Monarchy and its Wars Are Especially Described (Continuierte Einleitung zu der Historie der vornehmsten Reiche und Staaten von Europa, worinnen dass Königreichs Schwe-*den *Geschichte und dessen mit auswärtigen Kronen geführte Kriege insonderheit beschrieben werden)*, 187–88; see also *Commentaries on the History of King Charles Gustavus; Commentaries on Swedish Affairs*

Synthesis, 44, 48, 55–57, 65, 91

Theology, 14, 35, 67, 73, 202–54; Christian, 206–18, 219–24, 244–54; natural, 205; and natural law, 65, 215–17, 219, 230

Thirty Years' War, 9, 13

Thomasius, Christian, 2, 257, 263

Thou, Jacques-Auguste de, 171, 173, 271

Toleration, 18, 240–46, 274

Treitschke, Heinrich von, 13

Turmair, Johannes (Aventinus), 172

Understanding (and intellect), 69–72, 76, 78, 83

Utility, 2, 35, 117–18; in history, 182, 186, 191–92; and property, 108

Vattel, Emer de, 265

Vergil, Polydore, 172

Vienna, 171

Vittoria, Francisco, 164

Voltaire, François Marie Arouet de, 2

Weigel, Erhard, 15–16, 40, 272

Wildfangstreit, 273

Will, 71–72, 76, 78, 83–84

William of Orange (and Mary), 36–37, 198–99

Wise, John, 2, 259, 260

Wolff, Christian, 2, 257, 258, 264, 265